BEYOND SUCCESS

with

KADRI KRISTELLE KARU

Also Featuring
Other Top Authors

© 2019 Success Publishing

Success Publishing, LLC
2810 Trinity Mills, #209-221
Carrollton, Texas USA 75006
questions@mattmorris.com

All rights reserved. No part of this book may be reproduced, stored in a retrieval system, or transmitted in any form or by any means - electronic or mechanical, photocopy, recording, or any other - except for brief quotations in printed reviews, without the prior permission of the publisher. Although the author(s) and publisher have made every effort to ensure the accuracy and completeness of information contained in this book, we assume no responsibility for errors, inaccuracies, omissions, or any inconsistency herein.

Table of Contents

Chapter 1
My Definition Of Success
By Kadri Kristelle Karu 7

Chapter 2
The Power Of Manifestation
By Matt Morris 23

Chapter 3
The Person You Could Have Been
By Steve Moreland 33

Chapter 4
Success Is Being Able To Live A Life Of Priorities Not Obligations
By Dr. Jim Storhok 47

Chapter 5
Key To Success Is Focus
By Jason Reid 61

Chapter 6
Roadblocks In Life Come From Our Mindset
By Robert Bucko 73

Chapter 7
How I Went Through The Lowest Of Lows To Become Successful
By Jamie Lester 87

CHAPTER 8
Fear And Self-Doubt To Feeling Good In My Own Body
By Adda Hafborg 97

CHAPTER 9
What Makes Some People More Successful Than Others?
By Maxwell Adekoje 111

CHAPTER 10
The First Time I Failed In My Life Was The Day I Was Born
By Kate Jones 127

CHAPTER 11
Redefining My Definition Of Success
By Arlene Binoya-Strugar, Psy.D. 141

CHAPTER 12
5 Steps To Becoming A Good Entrepreneur
By Jasmina Cernilogar Mihajlovic 153

CHAPTER 13
Living An Inspired, Purposeful, And Amazing Life
By Jeremy Hoort 163

CHAPTER 14
I Am Nothing. Yet, I Have Everything
By Maiko Johanson 177

CHAPTER 15
How To Work Less, Earn More And Live Free As A Lifestyle Entrepreneur
By Francis Ablola 189

CHAPTER 16
Your Partner In Crime: The Subconscious Mind
By Oliver T. Asaah 201

CHAPTER 17
The Journey Of Success
By Dr. Steven & Dr. Terresa Balestracci **217**

CHAPTER 18
Essential Success: "A Living Transformation"
By Ray Blanchard, Ph.D. **231**

CHAPTER 19
Reaching Success With Excellence
By Ellen Reid **247**

CHAPTER 20
Becoming The Man In The Arena
By Mikel Erdman **257**

CHAPTER 21
Inspiration When You Least Expect It
By Brian Mahany **275**

CHAPTER 22
What Legacy Are You Going To Leave Behind?
By Jill Nieman Picerno **287**

Chapter 1
MY DEFINITION OF SUCCESS

By Kadri Kristelle Karu

How do we define success?

Is it a lot of money? A rich lifestyle? A big house? An expensive car? Luxurious trips? Is it enough, or do we need something more to be happy?

Yes, success can be counted like this too. But success could be growing as a person, feeling happy, finding inner peace, having influence, helping others, a happy family life, good health, etc.

Often, we think of ourselves as successful or unsuccessful by comparing ourselves to others. But there is always someone who has more expensive things than we do and there are still people who have less. At times, rich people are unhappy, and financially poor people are happy. Which of them is more successful?

What is success about? Is it equal to a happy life?

When I was in my 20s, I thought I'll be successful living my dream life when I could manage my time effectively, earn good money, live in a beautiful home, have a nice car and travel a lot. During the journey of my life, I added much more of what would qualify as success for me: a happy family life, good friends, positive emotions, good health, helping other people and living a rewarding life by growing and enjoying every minute of life.

It took me years to understand what I really want and what makes me happy. People said I was successful, and I saw all these external things that proved it, but I was not happy. I was looking for my happiness in other people, money, travels, and ended up with an understanding that all we need is self-love. I think people should do whatever it takes to love themselves, live a happy life and encourage others to do the same by being an example. People who value and love themselves are an inspiration for other people.

I was not born into a wealthy family, I grew up with my grandmother, and later saw my mother's struggles with her business, depression, and difficulties. I just wanted to know if there was possibly another way to live, succeed financially, and have fun and enjoy life at the same time.

Now I know by experience that it is possible, and it's based on our own decisions. We can make decisions at every moment of our life; it does not matter where we live or how old we are.

Was it always easy to achieve it? Certainly not. Was it worth it? Absolutely!

I studied in different schools and was looking for what I really like to do. I completed my education at secondary school level, worked in a kindergarten, during studies I worked in a hospital, then trained and worked as a secretary at a bank. I liked the job, but I realized that the most important thing for me was missing – my freedom. So, I decided to study International Business and started to work as a manager and later personnel manager in a big company.

At that time someone showed me options in Network Marketing and direct selling. I was somewhat skeptical about business, but I really liked the products, so I shared my experiences naturally. People grew interested, the company paid me money, and when it was equal to my salary, I thought maybe this is an option to become the hostess of my time and be truly free. I understood by then that I had no good ideas for creating my own business and saw the difficulties in starting ordinary businesses. But I liked the freedom, the teamwork, managing my time myself and the income that Network Marketing allows you to achieve.

When I started, I had a full-time job, my son was three years old, and I just had to find extra time for my Network Marketing business. But I knew what I wanted – freedom. It's wonderful that I've enjoyed direct marketing success for 20 years now and I am really happy about it, it taught me more than what I learned in 5 years of business school. I met many wonderful people, enjoyed great self-development, fantastic travels, freedom, a good income, and these opportunities are limitless.

I am glad to share the experiences I've learned on this fantastic journey. I am still learning but also using the skills I've learned so far because they work in every area of life.

The most important thing I've learned is that you are enough, love yourself and enjoy life! All the advertisements on TV and magazines show us that if we buy this or that we will be better, more beautiful, more complete. It's not true. We are complete as we are and worthy of love. There's nothing bad in good things; it's great to enjoy life, but these fulfill us just for a moment. Very often we think other people need to give us happiness and appreciation. No, it's our job. If we love and appreciate ourselves, others will follow this.

Have a great relationship with yourself, and you will have great relationships with others.

Love yourself; then you can love others and will be loved by others.

We are used to comparing ourselves with others, but we should compare ourselves and our growth with ourselves, this is success.

People are conditioned to live in the past and regret what happened in the past, or they are looking forward to the future where their dreams or fears exist. Life is happening here and now, be present, enjoy it, be curious and open minded.

In being present and curious about life, we can see that life is full of opportunities. Often, we need some courage to catch them, but they are all around us.

People are walking on the street; there is €100 lying on the sidewalk. Many people are passing by without noticing it. Suddenly someone sees it and will pick it up — the same with opportunities around us. There are always opportunities around us. Notice them!

With every opportunity I see, I listen to my intuition; do I have a good feeling about this or not? Even when there is a good feeling, the mind is there, and the fear is pumping up.

It needs courage to deal with it.

My method for this is to figure out as much as I need about this opportunity to be sure, and when it still feels good then make a decision and start. After starting and having made a decision, the fear begins to recede. We have everything we need – the feeling and the information to convince our mind.

On the way, we encounter a lot of people, circumstances and many gifts; we have to be present and see them. The journey is the same or even more important than the destination. Sometimes during the journey, the destination will change, and this is completely okay because during this transition we will be more aware of what we want in life.

Do things that you FEEL you are attracted to, even if your mind is not supportive at this moment.

Sometimes our inner voice knows more than our mind. Figure out more about it and don't let your worries sap your energy. If you feel good, you attract positive experiences.

The opportunities are always there, but you cannot see them when you are not opening yourself to them. How do you do it? My question to myself in these situations is: What is the worst thing that can happen?

Our life is all about energy. On some level, we are the sum of the results we achieve. When we are complaining and whining that life is bad, life proves it to us, it's bad, and the opposite is also true. If we feel good, life shows us more good things. This is all about the law of attraction. What helps to raise our energy? Being thankful, doing good things, good music, walking or being in nature, etc. Find out what makes your energy level go higher.

To keep our energy at optimum levels, we need to take care of our physical body too.

Pay attention to moving, nutrition, taking care of your body, and your level of energy will be much higher — the same with our mind. If we don't use it and grow, atrophy will take place. It can be a challenge in the beginning when starting out, but as long as we feel the difference, it's not possible to stop it.

If you feel good, you will attract positive results that will make you feel even better.

When your energy level is low, you can raise it by thinking of things you are thankful for right now.

We take many things in our life for granted until they are not there anymore. So, it's worth appreciating all the time that we have, and there is lots of it. There is a saying, a person is as rich as he (or she) can be grateful for. The person can be wealthy but if he does not appreciate it, then they will always feel it's not enough. There is a secret, be grateful for what you have, and you will have more of what you are grateful for.

Visualization and affirmations.

I've been in many seminars and courses, many tutors have said, write your goals on paper, set the exact date, visualize it and say it to the mirror out loud. I always wrote this suggestion down, but I never did it. Until… One day there was a goal I really wanted. It was the next level in the Network Marketing company I worked for. This title would give me a good income, but more important at that moment, the free luxurious trip to Mauritius with my partner.

It was a huge thing for me at that time.

I was so excited about this opportunity that I would do anything to achieve it. I wrote down the goal, set a date, went to the bathroom and stood next to the mirror. Before that, I was looking around to be sure that I was home alone. I even locked my cat out, then looked to the mirror and said, "I am a Leader." The first few times it was embarrassing, then I just said it, for a while I looked straight to the mirror, and I felt that I AM A LEADER. Finally, I was feeling and acting like the owner of the title; my self-image was changing day by day.

Guess if I took this trip? Yes, I did. This kind of affirmation and visualizing yourself achieving the goal really works.

There is just one BUT... it's better not to stick to our goal if there is a feeling of pressure that the goal is slipping away from you. The great feeling, looking in the mirror, saying in present form: I AM ... and visualizing as we achieve the goal, and then going out and doing your tasks with joy and focusing on helping people, not thinking about our goal but about assisting others.

When we are stuck, we feel pressure, and our energy goes down. People who we are talking to feel it too and it causes a barrier. What should you do when you feel stuck and under pressure? Just take your attention to something else. Go and work out, walk in the natural world, do something different and take yourself off for a while from this action and result. When you feel free about it again, go and act... and have fun with it.

Enjoy every moment of the journey. We set goals, but the most important is what is happening on the way, we may even change our goals when we grow or change the direction, so enjoy.

It's important to be the biggest fan of what you are doing. People can feel it if you are sincere and excited about it, or just scared or unconfident. Action, experiences, knowledge will make you more confident day by day.

Grow, learn from the people who have already achieved what you want to achieve. Seminars, books, webinars, mentors, coaches... there are lots of options you can use for it. Learn and teach what you found out. Teaching is the best way to learn.

Be flexible. Accept that changes are great and happening anyway, whether we want them or not. So be flexible and curious about life.

Investing in self-development is never about wasting time and money. Invest in seminars, books, traveling, etc., and we also need to choose who we listen to. Did they achieve what they are talking about or not, are they experts in this field or just reiterating what they read from books or heard from others. I prefer learning from experts.

We all sometimes feel that things are not going well, but in difficult times we grow the most because we need to find other ways and solutions what we haven't used yet. So, let's play down the difficulties and say to ourselves, "thank you for this opportunity to grow."

Listen to people and add value to their lives. The more we help other people succeed, the more successful we are in turn. If we have authority with people, they listen to us in many areas including what we are doing and the products we are offering.

One thing that is holding us back in achieving success is our comfort zone. Nothing bad about having a rest, but if it lasts too long, it's better to think, didn't I fall back into my comfort zone? Sometimes, we are just thinking and doing nothing; I think we don't need to talk about the importance of actions.

Success is a habit. Make yourself do more things every day and you will get closer to your goals and dreams. If we do something consistently for 40-60 days, it will become habitual. Therefore, we need to do the new habit until we can manage it instinctively.

Look who you are hanging around with. We have, on average, five closest friends. Are they positive, motivated, and encouraging; or are they negative and pessimistic? Who do you want to be? Remember, you will become the average of these five. Choose wisely.

Leave a legacy. Your experiences will help people make better decisions.

Lots of suggestions here, but life is easy. We came here to enjoy it and grow. We can grow by choice or life makes us grow. *Growing by choice is much better.*

Eighty percent of success and happiness is about mindset. Just 20% is about our skills. So we should guard our mindset.

And last, expect miracles and miracles will happen.

Biography

Kadri Kristelle Karu believes there is enough for everyone in this world and we are limitless. If we are ready to learn and grow, we can achieve everything we desire or even something better. Her **formula works:** dream-goal-affirmation-plan-learn-act-receive.

The most important thing in life is to *enjoy the journey.*

Contact Information

Website: BeyondSuccesswithKadriKristelleKaru.com
Facebook: https://www.facebook.com/kadri.karu.5
YouTube: https://www.youtube.com/channel/UCDYbU5hYbQuvbZHYoMF798A?view_as=subscriber

Chapter 2
THE POWER OF MANIFESTATION

By Matt Morris

It had been about three days since my last bath. Not that you could even call it a bath. Every two or three days, I would find a gas station bathroom that would lock from the inside. I'd take off all my clothes, splash water up from the sink, soap up, and then splash water to rinse off. I remember always praying that no one would be waiting outside because the floor would be soaking wet.

I had completely run out of money. I had also run out of credit. I was approximately $30,000 in debt and couldn't even make the minimum payments on my credit cards. I had been forced to live out of my car because I couldn't afford rent or even $20 a night to stay in a sleazy motel. I was selling above ground swimming pools in southern Louisiana during the two hottest months of the year and didn't get paid commissions until the pool got installed six to eight weeks later. So, for two months, my Honda Civic was my home sweet home.

Sitting all alone in my car that night, I was overly aware that my life had hit rock bottom. Not only was I lonely, broke and living out of my car, but I had just showered naked in the rain in the church parking lot in which I was parked. To be specific, I had showered under the gutter runoff from the roof of the church.

The burning question in my mind that night was, "How?" How in the world had I gotten myself into this situation? I knew I wasn't there because of a lack of effort or even a lack of intelligence. (I wasn't lazy, and I actually considered myself to be a pretty smart guy.)

After experiencing both utter failure and extreme success in my life, I have become acutely aware of what exactly manifested that situation. I'm also aware of what has now allowed me to become a self-made millionaire, travel around the world to over 50 countries, become a best-selling author and speaker attracting audiences of thousands every year.

You might think what caused those results were the *actions* leading up to them because, as we know, every action does produce a result. Most people focus only on the "how to's" but never seem to achieve their full potential because the decision to take proper or improper actions is a byproduct of your original intention. If the intention is not set properly, one will almost always make the wrong decisions on what actions to take which, in turn, lead to an undesired result.

What lies at the heart of manifesting your full potential is your intention.

What is intention? The dictionary defines it as the end or objective intended or purpose. While that sounds incredibly simple, utilizing the power of intention needs a bit more clarification of how you truly manifest that purpose for yourself.

An intention is your inner belief of what is already present but has simply not manifested in physical form yet. A true intention comes with the commitment and honest belief that anything else is an absolute impossibility. You see, when you're committed to a result, it's already done. Without it already being done in your mind, it cannot be considered a true intention but simply a fleeting wish.

When it comes to achieving your result, the simplest and widely accepted model for you to follow is what we call *cause and effect*. Think of your result as your effect. Your job is to identify and create the cause that will produce your effect.

Most people naturally assume that the cause is the physical actions or the steps you need to take to get your desired effect. What I'm proposing to you here, however, is that the series of action steps is not the real cause. The actions are really part of the effect.

So, the question is then, what's the cause?

The real cause is the intention you made to create that effect in the first place. The moment you say to yourself, "let it be so," is the real cause. Without the decision or your intention, the effect will never manifest. Your intention is ultimately what causes everything in your life to manifest.

If you want to achieve a goal, the most crucial part is to *decide* to manifest it. It doesn't matter if you feel it's out of your capabilities to achieve it. It doesn't matter if you can't see *how* you're going to achieve it. The *how* is insignificant because the universe will usually never manifest the *how* until *after* you've made the decision.

If you look at the origin of the word "decide," it is actually "to cut off." Your "decision" then should be framed in your mind as cutting off any other option other than your desired result. If failure is an option in your mind, your true intention is actually failure.

So step 1 is to *decide* not to wonder if you can do it and not to think of all the reasons that are holding you back. If you want to start your own business, then decide to make it so first. If you want to get married, decide to attract a mate. Whatever it is you want out of life, make a decision and a commitment *first,* and *then* work out the *how*.

If you have doubts in your head, you will find doubts in the world. You see, my belief is that the universe can sense a lack of commitment to a goal. It's like those people who say they are going to *try* to do something and *see how it goes*. When you come from a place of uncertainty or if you're wishy-washy about your goal, then the universe is not going to help you achieve it.

When you have total certainty in declaring your intention, you attract people like a magnet. When you are energized, motivated and have declared your goal to be so, that resonates in your being, and the universe aligns itself to work with you to manifest your intention.

You must also realize that your subconscious mind is infinitely more powerful than your conscious mind and that your subconscious mind controls your outcome 100%. When you are uncertain consciously about your goal, your subconscious does everything in its power to hold you back. You see, your subconscious acts like a computer. It accepts 100% of the data your conscious mind gives it. When your conscious mind feeds it negativity, it produces negative results for you. When your conscious mind feeds it excitement, positivity, and certainty, it produces all the energy and creativity it possibly can to ensure that you accomplish your intended result.

If you want to achieve any goal, your first step is to declare it and then to clear out all words like "hopefully," "can't," "maybe" and the killer - "try." When someone tells me they're going to "try" to do something, I know that they're *not* going to do it.

Such words are all signs of a lack of commitment, that you don't believe in yourself and that you're using your own power against yourself. You see, we all have the same amount of power –

it's just deciding if we want to use our power negatively or positively. When you use your power negatively, you're saying, "let me be powerless." If you think weakness, you manifest weakness. If you project certainty, you manifest certainty.

"Energy flows where attention goes."

You get whatever you think about most often. Whatever you think about expands. Therefore, we must constantly focus on what we want!

Remember, "we" create our destiny by the committed focus of our intention.

BIOGRAPHY

Author of the International Bestselling *The Unemployed Millionaire*, Matt Morris began as a serial entrepreneur at 18. Since then, he has generated over $1.5 billion through his sales organizations totaling over one million customers worldwide. As a self-made millionaire and one of the top Internet and Network Marketing experts, he's been featured on international radio, television and spoken from platforms to audiences in over 25 countries around the world. And now, as the founder of Success Publishing, he co-authors with leading experts from every walk of life.

http://www.MattMorris.com | http://successpublishing.com/

Chapter 3
THE PERSON YOU COULD HAVE BEEN

By Steve Moreland

Hell is meeting the person you could have been.

Watching my son and daughter (then 8 and 11 years of age) wave as they left with my mother and father, tears streaming down their faces, I had no clue this was the last time I'd lay eyes on them for more than ten years.

"Maybe God is not good," I thought to myself. At that moment in 2004, I was only four years into a fifteen-year federal prison sentence. My sentence was a war to right a horrible wrong — a test with many grueling lessons ahead.

I was brought up with my dad's relentless Marine Corp code of conduct and my mom's Christian Bible, but now I doubted my every thought. I'd lost EVERYTHING. I tasted the agony of a blood-stained hurricane.

And like the Bible's Job, I blamed God for not protecting us from such horror. I prayed for an instant and easy fix. Like everyone wishes during moments like these, I just wanted everything to be like it used to be. But strength isn't forged in a cauldron of luxury and comfort.

So that we're crystal clear, this story is *not* about proving anything to a world that was not there. I can't change the past or erase what it cost my family.

My penance for failing to think better is to better our world by sharing my thoughts from my Tests and the secret Lessons of survival that carried me across a near-impossible 5,500-day march. In school, we're first taught the lesson that prepares us for the test. But in life, first we face the Test; later we learn the Lesson.

The grade is what we become through it all. In other words, that person you could have been is only Hell if he or she stands better than you chose to be!

Hell is meeting the *better* person you could have been.

Have you ever been really curious about something? Obsessed even?

Since I was a kid, I wanted to unravel this thing called thinking. If I could only understand how the few successful figures think, I might be able to make the world a little bit better. Because they are not any different than us, right? With the exception of their thought processes, that is.

Every personal development "coach" drones on about thinking. But it's not enough to know what to do, you've got to know how to do it. You can only learn how to do something by doing it, and the action of doing something creates a being. Being is about becoming someone better by doing something different.

My desire to think better in order to do and become better led me to Dr. Viktor Frankl's book *Man's Search For Meaning*. Frankl didn't just survive six years of Nazi concentration camps; he changed the world forever with his discovery of how we humans create meaning in our thinking. Better thinking creates better doing, and better doing creates a better being.

Frankl made me think. Really think. It connected to what Professor Eli Goldratt wrote in *The Goal*: "If we continue to do what we have done, which is what everybody else is doing, we will continue to get the same unsatisfactory result." Isn't that what we do - more of what everyone else has done?

So if I wanted a different life - one that honored the sacred by making the world better, I couldn't think like everyone else that I knew. Maybe you're brighter than me and already know this. But for me, this realization was like lightning had struck!

And in that instant, I knew something else. If my thinking caused my doings (my actions and habits that are known as my reality), then why couldn't I change my future by changing the way I was thinking? Eureka!

But, not so fast, I thought to myself. How was I going to *think* better - like Dr. Frankl - to *do* better, to *become* better?

Socrates (Greek philosopher 470 B.C.) taught a Secret, if you will, that was passed from his student Plato to Aristotle (Greek philosopher 384 B.C.). Aristotle planted this secret into the mind of a 13-year old prince. This secret thought changed history.

At 16 years of age, the prince led his cavalry at the Battle of Chaeronea, decimating a supposedly unbeatable army. At 20 years of age, he became king of Greece and marched his army towards Persia, solving the riddle of the Gordian Knot along the way. At 23 years of age, he defeated the Persian emperor Darius, the first time. At 24 years of age, he destroyed the supposedly unconquerable city of Tyre.

At 25 years of age, he became Pharaoh of Egypt only to return to the desert near modern-day Babylon to lead his 50,000-man army against a force of 500,000 led by the Persian emperor Darius. Charging into the front line on his legendary black stallion Bucephalus, he did the impossible and defeated the Persian emperor again, and became emperor of the known world.

By age 30, he had conquered the largest empire in history and is still studied in war colleges today for his battlefield genius, ethical governance, and unrivaled valor.

The Secret thought? "Be what you wish to seem."

The Result? One *impossible* difficulty after another - conquered!

His Name? Alexander

How is he remembered? Alexander the Great!

Hell is meeting the person you could have been.

Lessons learned after the Test lead to better actions which lead to becoming a better being, right? Remember, in life, first the tests then the lessons. Tests uncover our weaknesses so that we can learn greater lessons. What and who we became through the Tests and Lessons reflects our grade.

If we're honest, we'll admit that we often create our own deserts. And then we blame others when they must be crossed. But if we use the agony, we find something called grit. Grit is commitment bathed in love to become better than we were the day before. It's a relentless dedication to rise up and become better, stronger, and brighter. It's a refusal to quit, even when we feel we can't get up again.

The question is, will we? Will we persist after the problems that were caused by our poor thinking - and the actions that followed? Or will we just fold up and quit due to the fear of failing, never suffering the scars that come from learning our lessons? Yeah, I know. No easy answers. If it were easy, everyone would be the best possible version of themselves.

That's why I collected all my lessons into a system called Rubicon. Those that fight to be better aren't pretty. They're scarred from one battle after another because they don't know how to give up.

I give my best as a gift to anyone seeking to be better, to those that have the guts to admit they failed and the courage to keep getting up, to those that live for something so they don't die for nothing. If just a few grow stronger and survive their Tests because of the Lessons I offer, my journey will not have been in vain. http://gonerubicon.com/

In the beginning, I promised to tell you exactly *how* better thinking would help you overcome near-impossible challenges so that you do not experience Hell (meeting the *better* person you could have been). Remember, in life, you're first given the Test; later the Lesson. The grade is what we become (or fail to become) through it all.

So let's focus on *what* to do so that we can become the *better* person we *should* be, despite the Test.

The Secret of "Be what you wish to seem" comes down to *"acting as if"* you've already achieved your ultimate end. What kept me marching across the desert was my Gravestone - the ultimate end of what I could still become if I changed my thinking.

Follow me. Every gravestone can fit about ten words on it. These words express how you lived, as witnessed by those that saw the real version of you, not the fake one we wear to impress others.

Since Hell is meeting the person you could have been, how did I keep from ending up there?

It all comes down to the little videos I saw in my mind's eye. You see, I relived, feeling it over and over again, my greatest nightmare. The nightmare that they'd chiseled on my Gravestone "A quitter with excuses, like most." This propelled me to somehow find a way to keep moving forward, even when I thought I had nothing left. Even when I felt the Lord God Himself had abandoned me.

And on a good day, I'd dream of the moment when my children forgave me for my sub-par thought processes. I'd see my ultimate end, to be that someone that might deserve words like "A Better World Exists Because He Determined To Think Better."

Even when I thought I couldn't go another day, I kept going by visualizing my funeral. I actually saw the ceremony and those that I loved standing in silence. Then I zoomed in on the Gravestone to read what those that knew me longest and best etched in the granite, telling the world why I refused to take the easy way out and what I endured so that my children would never be ashamed of their father. Then I lived each day becoming more, by doing more - for others.

So try my proven exercise on for size:
- What would your family and closest friends write on your ultimate end? Why not ask them?

- What do you not want them to chisel on your Gravestone?
- What do you hope they will chisel on your Gravestone? In other words, how do you want to be remembered, or what do you want to have become?

From my exercise, you no longer need to live in fear. Instead, like Cypher Raige in the film After Earth, you can use it. "Fear is not real. The only place that fear can exist is in our thoughts of the future. It is a product of our imagination, causing us to fear things that do not exist at present and may not ever exist. That is near insanity. Do not misunderstand me, danger is very real. But fear is a choice."

You'll learn not just how to survive your worst imaginations, but exactly what to do when you find yourself tested by the great Teacher:

1. You know what you can not *do*
   a. That which will cause you to become who you do not wish to be remembered as;

  b. That which will cause you to do what you do not wish to be remembered for.
2. You also know exactly what you must *do*
  a. That which will cause you to become who you wish to be remembered as;
  b. That will cause you to do what you wish to be remembered for.

How you think sparks your actions. Your doings, added together over time, construct what and who you become. And as your thoughts manifest into your actions, you become what your mind thinks about.

Don't lose me here. Realize that your ultimate end is this expression! It's chiseled in stone, broadcasting to a future world that you bettered their possibilities!

You *thought* better, in order to *do* better, so that you could *be* better. This is the Secret that Aristotle taught Alexander, to "be what you wish to seem." This is what Frankl rediscovered in creating meaning.

Hell is meeting the person you could have been? No.

Hell is meeting the *better* person you could have been.

Biography

Steve Moreland is the Executive Director of Success Publishing, LLC; a company that helps normal people with great stories become published authors. His mission is to deliberately cause affirmative outcomes that would not have occurred otherwise. AMAT VICTORIA CURAM is his favorite Latin motto meaning "Victory Loves Preparation."

Contact Information

Facebook: https://www.facebook.com/RubiconPerforms/

LinkedIn: https://www.linkedin.com/in/steve-moreland-088730118/

YouTube: https://www.youtube.com/channel/UC3RhLSfd8W9yXH7hbnIgw6A?view_as=subscriber

CHAPTER 4
SUCCESS IS BEING ABLE TO LIVE A LIFE OF PRIORITIES NOT OBLIGATIONS

By Dr. Jim Storhok

Success is so many things to so many people. Perhaps it's a fat bank account, a large home with acreage, or a fancy sports car for you. Or, perhaps it's a loving marriage or a large family. For others, success is living a life of service through missionary work, public service, or growing a large, successful company. I feel all of these things are very worthy of being considered "a success." For me, my definition of success was to never "haveta." What I mean by that is that I despise having to do something when it's not in line with my priorities. It's not that I'm not grateful or feel blessed for my Doctoral education in the field of

Orthopedic Physical Therapy, but I hate feeling like I "haveta" go into the office and treat patients to earn a living and provide for my family.

When we have a sick child at home, or when my wife is stressed out from being up all night with a crying, fussy infant, I always feel bad about leaving her and my family because I "haveta" provide for the family by going to a traditional 9-to-5 job. Again, to be clear, I'm honored to be able to serve my clientele in our clinic. I gain great satisfaction and take pride in the fact that I'm providing a service that can change a life by providing better physical well-being and a life with better function and less pain. However, as I've always said, I love my family MORE than I love my patients.

My priorities are 1. God, 2. Family, 3. Business, 4. Fitness/Health. My ultimate definition of success, and my reason for getting into network marketing, and more recently, digital marketing, is to be able to help others live lives based upon their priorities, not their obligations. Even more specifically, my passion is to inspire other men to want to lead their families to the best of their abilities. I'm striving to inspire other men to want to create a life from which they don't need a vacation. That's what intrigued me so much about the network marketing profession. Once you put together a sales organization properly, and back it with appropriate systems to create duplication, you can create true wealth, according to Robert Kiyosaki, successful entrepreneur and author. That translates into both time and money.

A problem that I see in society today is that we have two to three categories of men. The first type is the guy who is satisfied with putting in his hours, doing the minimum to get by and live a comfortable existence. He may raise children, but it's more like a couch potato raising the next generation of tater tots. There's lots of entertainment, watching sports and T.V., video games, and not much vision, except for maybe two weeks off for vacation (when he gets paid). Now, I don't think there's anything wrong with a little TV, playing an occasional video game, or relaxing from time to time, but I do wish that more men were striving for excellence, not just exist in the home.

The second category of men I see is comprised of men who are operating at full force, out to prove something and are striving to score big time in corporate America. They are the go-getters, willing to work 80-100 hours per week to earn enough to hit the next status symbol: move into the larger home, purchase the latest sports car and have all the toys so they "look the part." The problem here is that these men may be providing financially for their family, but at what ultimate price? These guys may be present in the home physically, but often they are preoccupied with the next quota to hit or the next deadline to meet, and they aren't emotionally or even mentally available to their wives and children. Again, don't get me wrong; I don't feel that any of these desires of "success" are all that bad in and of themselves, but I don't feel that trading a healthy marriage or a relationship with your kids is worth it.

What I'd like to do is influence a third type of man –the ultimate family man. Am I personally there yet? I don't think so, but I do work tirelessly every single day to move closer to this reality. The type of man that I'd like to influence and inspire lives for his family. He isn't willing to settle for either providing for them financially by working 80-100 hours per week, or just being there physically, but having no motivation or inspiration to provide more than just getting by. My dream is to awaken in men the desire to live lives of priority, not obligation. This would be a life in which they can provide a secure financial future for their family but do so on their own terms. This would be a life in which they can build a business of their own, but do it in a way that the income is systematized.

This is what attracted me to network marketing because I met people in this industry that had those types of results. My first mentors in network marketing were living my definition of success. They have a wonderful faith life, a large home on a very private, exclusive lake, and they have a wonderful marriage as well as relationships with their friends and teammates. They lead by example and take responsibility for failures in their lives. One member of this couple has been free of his engineering job for well over a decade. To me, they were an example for me to follow and they personified my definition of success. There was just one BIG problem...they built their organization in the early 2000's in an offline fashion, and I came into the industry in 2010.

The internet and social media were changing the profession right under our noses, but I was still being taught outdated strategies, which did not help me build the same types of results that they did. The result was I got personal results early in my network marketing journey because I earned the respect of people in my market and they joined me in business. Many of them fell away over time because they weren't willing to "pay the price" and do what it took to build a business in network marketing offline: endless home and hotel meetings, one on ones, out of town seminars and national conventions. The pain of change was greater than the pain of staying the same, so they went back to the lives in which they were comfortable. Their dream wasn't big enough. I struggled for the next six years in my network marketing journey because my dream was big enough, but I was getting more and more frustrated with my lack of results due to outdated strategies and tactics. It wasn't until a cold winter day in 2016 when my business took a major turn for the better, and I found my "missing link."

My wife had run into the grocery store after church on a bright, sunny, and very crisp December Sunday. I pulled out my cell phone and started flipping through my Facebook newsfeed to pass the time. What I saw next has changed our lives and is the reason we are where we are today in business. I read a post that talked about a stay-at-home mom who built an organization of over 8,300 customers and distributors, earning a multiple six-figure income, and she did so entirely through prospecting and recruiting through Facebook from home! She was a mom to two high energy boys and wanted to be present in her home and available for her children and her husband, and she was tired of running around town doing meetings in coffee shops all the time. Long story short, I clicked on what I found out to be an advertisement for a mentorship company that specializes in teaching network marketers how to transition their business building skill sets from offline strategies and tactics to online strategies and tactics through informational products and mentorship from six, seven and eight-figure earners in the internet marketing space.

I dove head first into mentorship and haven't picked my head up for the last 16 months! In my mind, THIS was the information I was missing. This was the reason why I was stuck and struggling. I was sold a HOME business, but after working my 9-5, choking down a quick dinner, and kissing my wife and kids goodbye again to do a meeting, I was never present in the home. And if I was in the home, I was mentally and emotionally somewhere else, lost in the business frustrations as well as the financial stresses. What I saw in that Facebook ad was my chance at freedom and success, which was to be debt and financially free and have the time to spend with my wife and kids.

When I got started online, I didn't even recognize that what I was looking at was an advertisement until I got to a sales page. I was clueless to the fact that there were people out there building sales funnels, which were running largely on autopilot, and were generating leads and sales for people, including network marketers! I was also amazed and a bit angry to learn that the key to building a business that will last long after you're gone is to build a personal brand. I was never taught this! It's not about branding your company and spamming your company logo and latest incentives all over your Facebook wall, in order to "advertise." It is also not about sending copy-and-paste messages to people that you just "friended" in an attempt to get them to ask you what you do, and then prospect them for your business. It is about becoming an expert in the field who demonstrates leadership by having a vision for their lives and their teams, building influence by providing value into the marketplace consistently, building "know, like and trust" with their tribe, and developing a soft heart for people. That means loving them where they are, but at the same time having a thick skin to be able to handle the haters and the naysayers. What I've learned over the last 16 months is that it is possible to prospect and recruit largely on autopilot, leveraging social media platforms and the internet to get your marketing message out to very specific, targeted people in the world. In network marketing, not everyone is your prospect. The "3-foot rule" is garbage. The skill sets to learn, in my opinion, in 21st century network marketing are getting comfortable going live on a Facebook live video, learning copywriting skills to develop a marketing message through Facebook ads, blog posts, and emails that are captivating, influencing, and entertaining, and learning some of the technical skills that it takes to build an online sales funnel. This way, when you are talking to a prospect online using a video chat such as zoom, they are 1. targeted, 2. qualified, and 3. already interested in your product, service, or opportunity. Say goodbye to having to overcome the pyramid objection!

Since beginning to learn these skill sets, from scratch with zero online or technical experience (remember I'm a physical therapist for crying out loud), I have been able to achieve some pretty cool results. I built a Facebook fan page from zero to over 7,000 targeted fans, built an email list of over 1,100 targeted subscribers, and generated five figures of additional revenue into my business within the first six months of learning these skill sets.

I even got my website/blog set up and started generating leads and sales on nearly a daily basis! Now I don't say this to brag, but to inspire those who are reading this chapter to know that you, too, can get these results. It just takes persistence, grit, and a willingness to learn some new skill sets. These skill sets will be valuable to learn because once you master them, you can literally print money. What I mean by that is that you'll know how to generate customers and sales on autopilot with leverage in any niche or business you want in the future! How exciting is that? You just have to get a big enough dream/target, learn some stuff, and get to work! I have recently been asked to become a mentor to incoming students in the same company that I got started mentoring with 16 months ago. How cool is that? The information works and is valuable if it can propel a no-tech physical therapist from no results online to becoming a leader and expert in online network marketing in 16 months!

I'd like to conclude with this thought for you. I hesitated to write about my results because I didn't want to come off as bragging. I know I don't have it all figured out, and I'm nowhere near the results that I'm looking for in my life or my business career. However, the path is clear. I have focus, direction, mentors, and a strategy that flat out works. And the end result will provide my definition of success, which is to be able to live a life of my priorities, not my obligations. I'm never going to "haveta." And, you don't "haveta" either. If you have a target, are willing to learn some skill sets, are willing to mentor and grow into your leadership potential, you too can design your ideal life. That can be the kind of life from which you don't have to take a vacation. That can be the kind of lifestyle that was probably promoted to you when you got started in network marketing or business in general in the first place.

It's time to move into 21st-century business, and the internet and social media are already playing a massive role. Are you ready to skill up and lead your family? I hope you are. I'm in your corner, and I'm cheering you on to your victory and your personal definition of success.

Biography

Dr. Jim Storhok is a 21st Century Network Marketer who specializes in coaching and training other network marketers to utilize the internet, especially social media, to create automated leads and sales for their business. His passions include spending both quality and quantity time with his wife and children, improving the professionalism of network marketing through improved processes and systems, and inspiring other men to live lives of priority, not just obligation.

Contact Information

Facebook https://www.facebook.com/DrJimStorhok page/
LinkedIn https://www.linkedin.com/in/drjimstorhok/
Twitter https://twitter.com/DrStorhok
Instagram https://www.instagram.com/drjimstorhok/
Website http://drjimstorhok.com/

Chapter 5
KEY TO SUCCESS IS FOCUS

By Jason Reid

"Success is finding within yourself the ability to leave everyday, thing, and person better than you found them. And be happy doing it." - Jason Reid

I remember being all scrunched up over an actual non-electronic tablet, the old paper kind, with a pencil, writing the table of contents for my new "bestseller." I was probably about eleven years of age. I'm pretty sure it got thrown out a few years later, and I can't remember if I ever did get past the first chapter or not. Next was a string of businesses ranging from collecting worms in the yard to sell for bait, to making bow and arrows, to canoes, to looking for a newspaper route, to building hang gliders. None of them, including the last, ever "got off the ground." I still can't quite put my finger on exactly what it was that put such an entrepreneurial drive into me, perhaps partly being the oldest in the family, or being homeschooled, giving me a personal sense of independence.

The seed of that desire I consider a gift of "grace." It seems to me that those who have that seed know it, it might be small, but it's still there. And some of the tiniest seeds grow into the largest trees. So, for me, the question was how to cultivate that seed, so it becomes a tree of success. The answers eluded me for years, and it seemed life was against me. Everything I tried went sour. One venture to the next, from my late teens into mid-twenties, and all these great ideas (or so I thought!) would stay just out of my grasp. I, among others in my social group, was often heard saying on numerous occasions "a day late and a dollar short" of the opportunities that would seemingly slip through our fingers. "The rich get richer, and the poor get poorer" was our motto, insinuating that we were on the "poor" end of the spectrum.

In the end, I got a job, which was a good thing. I am in full agreement with Robert Kiyosaki in "Rich Dad, Poor Dad," the best reason for having a job is to gain a real-world education. There are lessons to be learned that can be best learned as an employee. First "real" job was as a carpenter building houses. From there, to a sales position at a building materials supplier. After four years, it was time to move on, and being married with two children by this time made it a serious venture, but the desire for something more won out, and we relocated. With the move came the start of yet a new business as an independent building contractor, this time, somewhat successful due to having learned a trade and determination. It wasn't easy, but we got by. Barely.

Fast forward a few years, and that brings us to the recession of 2008, a turning point in the lives of many. Work just dried up to virtually nothing, and it was a tough time in more ways than just financially. During this time, I also met a few key people who were very influential on my thinking, perhaps most importantly in helping me change my view of myself. This combined with the need to do something different to support a family, and the dream of doing more while still alive created a breakthrough for me. It wasn't a huge, radical, change-everything-in-an-instant kind, but a major deciding point that something HAD to change. And the catalyst for bringing that change about for me was FOCUS. Not in the sense of blindly seeing only one thing to the detriment of everything else, but a discipline of mind to not lose sight of the goal. In business, it can be easy to be driven, and forget the other aspects of life. Like being a husband and father, or a friend. So, the focus needs to be on the several aspects of ONE whole. My focus looks like this: Personal development, Relationships, Business. And yes, in that order. I look at this as three sides of ONE triangle.

When discussing focus, usually someone will inevitably mention the fact that you can only ride one horse at a time, a statement I fully agree with, but you do have to take care of multiple aspects of that horse to get anywhere. One must pay attention to what reins you are pulling on, watch for possible obstacles in the path, and stay on the horse all at the same time. You could concentrate only on staying on the horse and successfully do so, but you might get a surprise where you end up! And I think this way of looking at it was the key to unlocking the power of focus for me.

We all know someone who focused very well, but all they focused on was money. Focusing on that single aspect is just like staying on the horse. If that is what they truly wanted, be it far from me to state otherwise, but for most people, I think that gets them somewhere they probably didn't want to go. So as you can see, I have a definite, focused idea of what "focus" means! Though to illustrate what it has done for me, I am going to "focus" on only one side of the triangle- the business.

At the turning point, there was a decision to make. In my field of interest, there was only one way that made sense to move forward with, to make my mark. And that was the quality of craftsmanship. I focused on that product, looking for that particular, yet elusive, level of excellence I wanted. Practically speaking, this was not a pretty sight. It ended up being years of many late nights into the early hours of the morning. Thousands of dollars "wasted" in materials, listening to criticism from experts, and discovering good ideas that weren't. And yet, through it, all progress was made. Not overnight, but slowly my skill improved. I had a coach that made a tremendous difference. He couldn't do what I was doing to save his life but had the ability to help me see myself and my work from another point of view. It was a priceless experience.

Through all this was the key of focus, remaking the decision by the hour if necessary, to not take my eyes off the goal and the vision. I could see what I wanted to create in my mind, and I had to concentrate on it. Not a visualization process that brought magical results, but to not allow that image of who I wanted to be, a master in my field, fade into the background, pressured out by the noise of life. Yes, take care of what needs to be taken care of. If your mother is in the hospital, go and visit her. Maybe even if she's not. But never let the vision fade, DO something every day to bring you closer to your dream. That, to me, is focus. It's living life on purpose. Reminds me of one of Tony Robbin's great quotes,

"One reason so few of us achieve what we truly want is that we never direct our focus, we never concentrate our power. Most people dabble their way through life, never deciding to master anything in particular." - Tony Robbins.

An element of focus that was a challenge for me was to keep it positive. I remember many times, sitting there immediately after making a fatal mistake in a matter of seconds that destroyed hours of careful work. In those moments, the destiny was decided, keeping focused on the vision I wanted to achieve. And even repeating to myself over and over like a mantra, "I can do this, I can do this, I can do this." Then taking several deep breaths before starting over again. It happens by doing whatever it takes to maintain the focus like your life depends on it. Because it does. And this would be especially difficult for those whose close family members and loved ones are NOT supportive of their dream.

And it worked! People began asking for my product. The icons of my field began asking my opinions. I was offered contracts. Something was changing. I had another job to make ends meet by this time in the story. Financially, life was satisfactory. But life can be interesting sometimes, and circumstances came together to help keep me focused, pressure from behind and pull from the front you might say. It was time to make another decision and use what I had learned and move to the next level. Applying the lessons I had learned, and not stopping, has propelled me to the next level. I quit my job and went into business full-time, a daring move for anyone. The focus did not let me down, and today, I am a respected leader in my field, the business is thriving, the future looks bright, and we are just getting started.

The satisfaction of success is immense, and it would be my wish that everyone could experience it. Experiencing success is a life-changing event, once tasted, you can never live without it again. The beauty of it is that life is a journey and the opportunity to continually experience success is part of that journey, not a goal in the end. True success can actually start the first day a decision is made. I will admit it was hard to feel it then, but looking back, I can see it. I am no different than anyone else; I'm not any more special than anyone else. But the power of a decision, especially the one to live by, a different mindset than before, can separate someone from the rest of the crowd.

I am definitely not done with this success thing, and I think the ultimate success is to help other people to find it. To be the catalyst in someone's life that propels them to the next level. Now, wouldn't THAT be something satisfying to focus on?

Biography

Jason Reid is a self-made entrepreneur who has built several successful businesses. He currently owns and operates Hawkeye Falconry Supply, suppliers of *The Finest Falconry Furniture*, where all products are handcrafted to the highest specifications. He values the skills involved in his specialized field and the unique responsibilities involved in working with birds-of-prey which provides a basis for the qualities needed to be successful in any endeavor.

He has a passion for using these virtues to help others in areas of personal development, finance, and charitable work.

He has been published in American Falconry magazine and was a past columnist for "Feathers and Friends" children's magazine.

His accomplishments include a falcon breeding project that helped with the reintroduction of the once-endangered birds, and he continues to be involved in conservation projects and wild bird rehabilitation efforts.

He is a member of the North American Falconers Association, International Eagle Austringer Association, Indiana Falconers Association, and various other state and regional conservation and educational organizations. He enjoys several outdoor sports including camping and boating, as well as spending time with his family and birds. He currently resides in Fort Wayne Indiana with his wife and four children.

Contact Information

Facebook https://www.facebook.com/JasonReidHawkeye
LinkedIn https://www.linkedin.com/in/jason-reid-a054b7166

Chapter 6
ROADBLOCKS IN LIFE COME FROM OUR MINDSET

By Robert Bucko

I was born in 1984 in a small town called Snina in the eastern part of Slovakia, which is one of the poorest areas of my country. My parents worked hard to get my brother and me to University. Their mindset (and many other people's during the time) was to go to school, get the best grades, get to University, get a "stable" job (meaning they cannot fire you) to get a "secure" income. The reason my parents taught me to get a University degree and a well-paying job was because of my health conditions. My parents were always giving me all the support I needed over time. Even when I did not realize it, they were still there for me, and I am exceedingly thankful for my family. When I was a year old, doctors diagnosed me with a joint disease called "Magnus Perthes," which means my hip joints are not developed, and I will walk in pain. So when I was two years old, I was sent to a clinic for 14 months where it was forbidden for me to walk.

After the time in the clinic, I had to learn how to walk again. When I was ten years old, I had an operation where the doctors had to break my right hip joint, turn it around and fix it with a steel plate and four screws for it to heal. I remember the Head of the orthopedic department saying, "We will have to replace your joint for a titanium one by the time you are 25 years old." I lived with that statement for a long time.

I could not play any sports for my entire childhood. That is my background, and all those aspects shaped my life. I was one of the best students at school and got into University, where I studied programming and information technologies, which is one of the best-paying professions, even today.

I was also doing research in the field of applied informatics during my Ph.D. studies and also made some professional publications on the topic. I got so many great deals and job offers, but somehow, I knew that it would not fulfill my calling. I wanted to discover how I can use my skills and my expertise to serve others better. That was when I started my first company, before I even finished my university studies. It was a language school where we taught people new languages to get better jobs, positions or even start a new career abroad. Education was always the key element in my life, but very soon I realized formal education is not enough. I needed to get new skills to help more people faster, better and more efficiently.

When I was 28 years old, I was expecting to go in for the surgery to replace my hip joint for the titanium one. When I came for the last checkup, the doctor told me that I did not need the replacement, and I can come in for the next checkup only if I have some pain in my legs. I will be 34 this year, and I feel completely well. I also run and play sports on a daily basis without limitations.

You can read my story "How I was healed by God" on my blog www.robertbucko.com/blog.

After some time, I realized that all the roadblocks experienced in life come from our mindset.

I graduated from one of the most difficult Universities in my country, but that did not give me what I was expecting. The opportunity to go further with an education came with my education company. I am not saying that a University degree is not valuable, it was valuable in my case. I just want to emphasize the power of personal growth.

I have invested thousands of Euros into my own personal training. I realize that growth happens only if you are <u>constantly</u> learning. Persistence is the key to overcome any roadblocks.

People in my country still value a University education very highly. I was taught that the only way to success is to work hard for 12-16 hours a day and work for "someone" else. It all depends on who you know and if you have good connections in the right places. And because we still have such thinking, University education is still a big deal in my country.

My goal is to reprogram such thinking and teach people to reclaim responsibility from "the government, the boss, wife, husband, kids, young age, old age, etc." That is why I started an education program for young people called "Program Leader." In this program, we teach students the English language, as English opens up doors to the world, and also personal development strategies, techniques, and methods of how they can change their thinking, how to become a leader in their community, how to work on your dreams, and overcome fears that limit us.

One of my great role models taught me to build up the value of your mind. That means, no matter what the circumstances are, try to increase the value of your mind. Anything might happen to you as a person, or to your business, your career, your partnership, but no one can take away what you have learned, no one can delete your expertise, the unique perspective you have obtained from your experiences. That is the value you can bring to others, or in other words, to serve others.

My life taught me to be grateful for every minute you have in this life. I am so thankful for what God has done in my life. It is not possible to describe it in words, I am thankful for my wife, and I have just become a daddy last week of two beautiful princesses. We are full of joy, appreciation, gratefulness, and blessings. It changed the game in my life. I encourage you to stay on your track and lead yourself as the captain of the boat.

But it does not happen overnight. The single most important key to achieving success is to know crystal clear what "SUCCESS" means to YOU and then make a roadmap on how to get there. The amazing thing about that road is the never-ending process. When you get to the TOP, you will get another perspective that excites you even more.

I believe there are proven ways on how to achieve anything in your life. It requires a certain level of leadership. My first lesson on leadership was to learn how to lead myself. If you master that, you are 80% done. I would love to share my strategies and tools on how I get better every day and what keeps me on track to constantly give my better self to the world.

There are 2 KEY QUESTIONS to make your dreams come alive.

1. Knowing where I am

2. Knowing where I want to go, which includes knowing what I want to do and also knowing who I want to be (this one is the most important). Let's take a closer look at what I mean by these keys.

1. Knowing where I am. I make sure to have a good mirror. It is essential to know where I am in life, with my finances, with my relationships, with my health, and wealth as it applies to all the other areas of life. I discovered that for many people it is difficult to answer this question, "Where are you at the moment?" I do not mean physically, but where are you as a human being, as a person in terms of fulfilling your calling? Some great questions helped me understand where I was in my own life and it was a great impulse to establish new goals and

habits that helped me to reach what I wanted with less stress, less time, and fewer resources.

Try this exercise. Complete the sentences below. Write down the first thing that comes to your mind.

Life is…
Success is…
Love is…
Passion is…
Happiness is...
Joy is…
The reasons WHY I am/I am NOT/successful are…
The reasons WHY I am/I am NOT/happy are…
My biggest fears are…
The most beautiful thing about my life is…
The worst thing in my life is…

These questions give you a significant reflection, which could lead to starting a change (or a small shift) you need to do, or you are about to do. I answer them from time to time to make my vision clear. If you are honest with yourself, it is a great reflection and amazing tool to start something new or improve the way you are currently on. The great thing about this is that even if you answered these questions yesterday, today is a new day and you are not the same as you were yesterday. So much is happening in our everyday life, we learn, we reach, we love, we discover, we develop, and so on. This exercise is never the same, and it gives you the reflection of where you are at the moment.

2. Knowing/discovering:

a) where I want to go:

I always make sure to write down all of my goals. There are three stages in writing my goals list. I will not go into details on how to visualize or write down your specific goal using any well-known strategy (S.M.A.R.T. goals etc.), but I will explain the process of making such a list and how it will influence your mindset and decision making.

The First stage is: I write down all the goals which occupied my mind the most, therefore most of them are "urgent goals" such as: repair the roof, get a bigger car for my two kids where you can put a pushchair and suitcase in as well, change the flat for a bigger one, and the list continues... Interesting things happen when you do not STOP writing your goals and finish your list of urgent goals.

The second stage starts right after you will start thinking about the things you want to do, you want to achieve, you desire or dream about. Examples: go for a 2-month vacation with your family, travel around the world, see the most amazing places, buy the most amazing car, move to a better place, and so on. You will start changing things for experiences or improvements to your lifestyle! Something that will create amazing memories that you are able to collect and enjoy.

The third stage is about WHO you want to become, who you want to meet with, what significant project you want to work on, how you want to improve other people's lives, etc. One of the exercises I would recommend is to write down 101 goals. Why 101? First of all, it is more than 100. If you tell yourself to write down 100 goals, most people will end up with 60, 70 or 80; they will barely reach 90. When you tell yourself to write down 101, it is a specific number, so you will go through the process of all the stages just as described above, that is WHY 101. Writing those goals will be challenging, but make sure you enjoy the entire process, it is not a race, you have the time, and it is one of the biggest investments you could give yourself.

b) what I want to do

This question opens up the "HOW" method. How are you going to fulfill your calling? What strategy or method do you have to follow to get the results you want. There is one very simple, but useful farmer proverb in my country.

"If you want to have the same harvest as the best farmer in your village, go and ask him how he did it. Then just follow his instructions."

There are many great and proven strategies and business models in today's world to follow. There are so many great leaders in a particular industry who you can follow and use the same strategies, methods or instruction to get the results you want. That is why I want to partner with Matt

Morris. I think he is a great leader with extraordinary results. I am super excited to be a co-author with Matt and learn those strategies from the TOP leaders in the industry. As the proverb said: "Just follow the instructions."

c) Who I want to be (this one is the most important)

We have been created by the Creator in His image, that means: we are called to CREATE as well. That is why we, as human beings, are called creatures (creatures = those who create). It is that simple. How would you feel if you could create anything with no limits? Just imagine that. Make a clear picture in your mind of how exactly your life would look like if you had the power to create anything? How would you feel if you knew your specific calling, your purpose, why you have been installed into the current space and time? I can tell you there is no OTHER person exactly the same as YOU! Never was and never will be. You are UNIQUE, and this uniqueness is the way you see things in the world, in other people, your experiences, skills, and background are so valuable that someone is willing to pay a high price to get to know your view, your advice, and your point. The truth is, you have the power. Just STEP UP and BE who you are called to be! If you know who you are and the price of yourself, you become unstoppable.

These areas are essential to understanding who we are, why we are here, and what we are called to do. If you are not clear in any of those questions, it will make you go around searching and looking for new opportunities, new doors to open, from one training to another and so on. On the other hand, if you have a crystal-clear vision of those areas, you will make decisions or take actions, and it will get you to the mode of certainty, and you will be aware of the value you carry or present.

I used these exact strategies to build my companies. I made exact plans to achieve them. And you can too!

BIOGRAPHY

Robert Bucko found his passion for serving others. He helps people find their talents and strengths. He is the co-founder of the Institute of Education that provides leadership programs for people to change their mindset from fear to courage and victory.

CONTACT INFORMATION

Facebook: https://www.facebook.com/robert.bucko.9
LinkedIn: https://www.linkedin.com/in/robertbucko/
YouTube Channel: https://www.youtube.com/channel/UCaYHj1mABKAhFG4cYF9cpew?view_as=subscriber
Twitter: @BuckoRobert
Instagram: https://www.instagram.com/robertbucko/
Website: https://www.robertbucko.com/
Blog: https://www.robertbucko.com/blog

Chapter 7

HOW I WENT THROUGH THE LOWEST OF LOWS TO BECOME SUCCESSFUL

By Jamie Lester

Even though I was raised in what would be considered a white-collar family, the value and ethics of hard work were drummed into me from a young age, and my father wasted no time in teaching me the value of a dollar.

From the age of thirteen, I would spend every vacation working in my family business which was never a chore because I was always passionate about the business. We lived in Martinsville, VA and my family owned a company that produced building components for the housing industry. I always knew that after I finished college, I would join the family business.

I graduated from Virginia Tech in 1986, and a few years later my father's health started to decline. As a family, we decided that the best option would be to sell the business. I was 25 years old at the time, and for the first time in my life, I had no idea about my future.

I went back to business school at Wake Forest University, and after I graduated I took a job at a certified public accountant (CPA) firm, formerly Coopers & Lybrand; now PricewaterhouseCoopers.

During my time there, I worked with a variety of different businesses that were facing bankruptcy, which equipped me with the skill set and confidence to buy back my family business when it began to struggle financially. I originally had a partner who was an investment banker, but the partnership did not work out. We both wanted very different things. My long-term plan was to restore the business to the way it once was whereas my partner wanted to sell off the assets and then close the business down. I ended up buying him out only to discover that the business was in far worse condition than I initially thought.

I had to invest all the money I had at the time into the business, and for about ten years things were going very well; however, everything changed in 2008 when the mortgage crisis hit. We could not weather the storm this time around, and I ended up having to file for both corporate and personal bankruptcy. I lost everything except my retirement accounts. Other than losing my mother, it was the lowest point of my life. For me, having money and losing it was worse than never having it at all.

After the business went under, I moved to Charleston, South Carolina to start afresh. Things started to change when I spoke with my 72-year old cousin who had been in the real estate business for some time. He had lost everything and rebuilt it several times. He told me, "If you haven't gone broke at least once in your life, you don't have any lead in your pencil," and that I could make more money but I could not make more time. The advice he gave me made me realize that as long as time was on my side, there would always be opportunities to make more money and I took that to heart.

The one thing that I was sure of was going on someone's payroll wasn't an option. I was prepared to work as hard as I needed to, but I wanted the reward to be mine and no one else's. I founded my present business in 2011, and since then I have never looked back.

If my new business has taught me anything, it is that you will only be truly successful if you are completely passionate about what you do, and you put your heart in it. If you do not believe in yourself and the value that your business offers, then others are not going to believe in you either.

Another key to success is that you have to be a great leader. You may not think that this is something which is inside you, but I believe that it is something which is in everybody. If you do not have good leadership, then it does not matter how good the rest of your business is. Only good leadership will bring real success.

I believe that there are eight key steps to becoming a great leader.

#1 Planning

You need to focus on the things that are the most important and be decisive when it is needed most.

The true champions have a plan, commit to the plan, and then establish a routine to execute that plan. Ramon Floyd, past champion of the Masters Golf Tournament, was interviewed about his preparation for that tournament because of the uniqueness of the golf course. He said months before the tournament he would write down his strategy and the way he was going to play every shot on all 18 holes. What he found out was whenever he had a bad shot or had a bad hole, he was able to jump right back into his game plan and not waste another shot or hole. He had committed to it, so when something went wrong, he was ready. He said preparation and committing to his plan was everything.

#2 Motivation and Passion

You need motivation and desire. This is what is going to carry you through the days when things get tough.

Maintain a positive attitude and enthusiasm. Charles Swindoll said, "The longer I live, the more I realize the impact of attitude on life. Attitude to me is more important than facts, more important than the past, more important than education, money, circumstances, more important than failures, successes, what other people think or say or do. More important than giftedness or skill. It will make or break a company."

#3 Hard Work

You are always prepared to put in the hard work to get things done. I believe you can beat 50% of the competition just by showing up, another 40% by doing what's right which is looking people in the eye and being honest, and that last 10% is a dogfight, having desire, loving what you're doing, rolling out of bed with a blueprint and ready to go after it.

#4 Passion

If you're going to be effective, you have to set yourself on fire. You must do something, get uncomfortable, and work like you have never worked before for a good amount of time. You have to create a fire in your organization, and it's hard to do that if you haven't first created a passion inside yourself.

#5 Be a Good Listener

Sometimes, people on the ground know a lot more about the business than you do. It's okay to acknowledge the fact that a leader does not need to know everything. He can take the counsel of wise and able people.

#6 Hire people smarter than you

When two people agree on everything, one of them is unnecessary. Surround yourself with great people with a vision who are ready to fight for their success and do it positively; people who are tired of sitting on the sidelines and are ready to go out and make their mark.

#7 Know the ins and outs of your business

Be a student of your business. Know your subject. Leaders don't go to sleep at the wheel. They know everything that is going on in their business.

#8 Know when things are not working

Recognize when things are not working and be ready to change course.

If you know it is going to hurt when you don't meet your goals, you will work extra hard to achieve them. It is okay to take failure personally because this is what is going to spur you on to do better the next time.

Your attitude is also going to play a large part in your success. When you wake up each morning, you do not know what challenges you are going to face. However, what you do know is that you will be facing these challenges with a positive attitude and this is half the battle.

Successful people have fear just like all of us. But they do things in spite of the fear. I believe that fear should not stop you from achieving your goals.

You should take fear head on and do things that you fear the most. Tom Cruise in the movie Days of Thunder says, "I am more afraid of being nothing than I am of being hurt." That's how I've lived my life.

Closing Thoughts

To be successful in business, you must be willing to go through the dump, just don't hang out there. Losing and not accomplishing your goals must hurt and be so offensive to you that you are not going to accept it. We have a choice every day regarding the attitude we will embrace for that day. We cannot change our past; we cannot change the fact that people will act the way they want. We cannot change the inevitable. The only thing we can do is play on the one string that we have, and that's our attitude. Life is 5% of what happens to us and 95% of how we react to it. We are in charge of our attitudes. Sometimes you have to go through the absolute worst to get to the best times of your life.

Biography

Jamie Lester has a B.S. in Marketing and Finance from Virginia Tech, and an MBA from Wake Forest University. Whether he's interviewing someone to join his business or sitting with a client, he is always looking to uncover their pain and find a solution. He takes a hands-on approach to solving problems by getting down in the trenches with people rather than sitting in an ivory tower.

Contact Information

Facebook: https://www.facebook.com/The-Lester-Agency-873623722798474/
Twitter: https://twitter.com/Officelesterag1
Instagram: https://www.instagram.com/office132/
LinkedIn: https://www.linkedin.com/in/lester-agency-344105160/

Chapter 8

FEAR AND SELF-DOUBT TO FEELING GOOD IN MY OWN BODY

By Adda Hafborg

"The more we hide our feelings, the more they show. The more we deny our feelings, the more they grow." - Unknown

Here is a gift from me to you. My story can hopefully help someone in the journey from fear and self-doubt to feeling good in their own body and mind. I lived a good, safe life in Iceland with my hubby, my teenage daughter and our three dogs in a beautiful modern house with two cars. Both of us had good jobs.

But, I have always known that I am not an ordinary woman who is satisfied with living life without action and adventure. I didn't want to listen to my inner self for many years, because from the outside, everything looked good and I felt okay. But, something was missing in my life.

Deep down in my heart, I desired more freedom to travel the world, learn about other countries and get to know more people and their cultures. One cold day in November 2011, our friends came over, and they wanted us to work with them on network marketing.

For three years, people all around me had tried to recruit me into this "thing," but I had tried network marketing twice in the past, and I was never going to do it again. The strange thing is that whenever I say to myself "never again," the opposite seems to happen. I am very polite, so I said "yes" when they showed us the presentation, but after that, I said a BIG "NO, THANK YOU." When they were leaving, one of our friends said these golden words to me "Adda, it is ok to change your mind." That night, I could not sleep; my mind was on fire.

"This is good; this is something for me, I can do this." After three days, I called one of our friends and asked, "Can you guys sign me in, please?" After one year of all kinds of struggles and victories, I decided to go all in, and I quit my corporate job. People around me were skeptical and asked, "Are you really going to quit a very good job for this pyramid thing?" I said 'yes' with pride, but deep inside, I was scared. "What if this is not going to work for me?" My fear and self-doubt started to kick in, but with positive self-talk and reading books about personal development, I kept on going. My hubby and I made a contract with each other before quitting my job. If my salary in our network marketing company did not at least double in six months, I would look for another job. I was unstoppable. I did not want to look for another job. I loved the people and the freedom in network marketing.

I had made my decision... My eyes glowed with positive energy. "Let's do this," I said. My mind was full of faith; I believed in myself, the company and my team. The growth started to be unbelievably fantastic. For two and a half years, we had great MOMENTUM, and we started to build businesses in other countries as well.

The internet is a great tool to build businesses worldwide. My team was growing fast. I started to travel the world to support my team, and I loved it. I am so grateful for all the great friendships I have built with fantastic people all over the world because of network marketing. I have friends in Iceland, Holland, Michigan, Minnesota, Denmark, Norway, Sweden, Finland, Spain, Germany, Latvia, Estonia and many more.

Then during the summer of 2015, life happened to me. I had self-doubt to the point that I was making my decisions based on what other people were saying about me behind my back, not what I knew was the truth about myself. I was constantly struggling with confidence and always second-guessing myself. What I've learned from my experiences is that I need to feed my mind with positivity every single day. I need to surround myself with positive people who think of solutions like me.

All of us have good and bad days in our lives. I truly believe that if I let go of other people's opinions and listen to my own positive voice every single day, I can find a positive daily balance. I've found out a few things that help a lot with my self-doubt and confidence; these may help you too:

1. Stop comparing my accomplishments to that of my friends and colleagues.

I find that I doubt myself the most when I'm comparing what I'm doing with what other people are doing. When I compare my accomplishments to a colleague, I start feeling inadequate. My colleague's accomplishments are not a litmus test for my success. One key thing to remember when we find ourselves in this mental pattern is that everyone is on his or her own journey. I find that I am most successful in my personal and professional life when I am following what works for me and what makes me feel good, even if it is different from what the people I look up to are doing.

2. Forget about what everyone is thinking about me.

When we care about what everyone else is thinking about us, we inhibit ourselves. We often would rather do nothing and not get judged than do something and risk being criticized. Worrying about what other people think of us will continue to hold us back from doing some great things.

3. Accept that my fears and doubts are within me, and I need to give them room, and not try to escape them.

Whatever thoughts and feelings come up inside of me, I'll be ok with them. Stop resisting what I feel and think. Avoidance is not the answer. Even though fear and doubt are painful, they are not the problem; my reaction to them is. Problems arise when we try to get rid of, hide or control our self-doubt and fear. When we start accepting how we feel and think in any given moment, we start noticing that feelings and thoughts are like the clouds in the sky; they are just passing by.

Whenever I feel the urge not to take action, I remind myself to act on what I truly desire: making meaningful connections and enjoying life to the fullest.

4. I believe pure gratitude from our hearts is a powerful help in every situation in our lives.

In a study by McCraty and colleagues (1998), 45 adults were taught to "cultivate appreciation and other positive emotions." The results of this study showed that there was a mean 23% reduction in the stress hormone cortisol after the intervention period.

Moreover, during the use of the techniques, 80% of the participants exhibited an increased coherence in heart rate variability patterns, indicating reduced stress. In other words, these findings suggest that people with an "attitude of gratitude" experience lower levels of stress.

In another study by Seligman, Steen, and Peterson (2005), participants were given one week to write and then deliver a letter of thanks in person to someone who had been especially kind to them, but who had never been properly thanked.

The gratitude visit involves three basic steps:

First, think of someone who has done something important and wonderful for you, yet who you feel you have not properly thanked.

Next, reflect on the benefits you received from this person, and write a letter, expressing your gratitude for all they have done for you.

Finally, arrange to deliver the letter personally, and spend some time with this person talking about what you wrote.

The results showed that participants who engaged in the letter-writing exercise reported more happiness for one month after the intervention compared to a control group. Expressing gratitude not only helps us to appreciate what we received in life; it also helps us to feel that we've given something back to those who helped us.

5. Read positive books every day.

One of the best ways to boost my confidence is to listen to or read some of my favorite self-development books.

My favorite sources are:
- The Magic Of Thinking Big by David J. Schwartz
- The Greatest Networker In The World by John M. Fogg
- The Seasons Of Life by Jim Rohn
- Think And Grow Rich by Napoleon Hill

I put the audiobooks on my iPhone and listen to them whenever I'm walking, driving or chilling at the beach. I also spend quiet time on my balcony with a book.

6. Write in a gratitude journal at the beginning of each day.

It is so easy to focus on what we don't have rather than what we do have. Giving those feelings energy will only create more situations which I don't like to have in my life.

Instead of focusing on what I am lacking, I like to focus on what I have and what I have accomplished. Feelings of gratitude put us in a positive frame of mind. When we're feeling positive, we're feeling good. And when we're feeling good, good things happen.

7. When my decisions were made back then, I had many negative thoughts, my self-doubt took over, and I often gave up even before I started.

Mel Robbins' tips. "The 5-second rule," has changed my life. When I count 5-4-3-2-1 go... I just do the things I planned to do, and it feels good.

Okay, back to my story. All our five children had started their own lives; my husband and I were in our big house (with our dogs). That Fall of 2015, my hubby and I got divorced, and I moved out. I felt miserable. Few people knew that because I was always smiling, but in my eyes and in my heart, there was no joy. I kept on doing my network marketing business, but it was not easy. In one year, I lost about half of my team members. I was depressed and felt sorry for myself. "Poor, miserable me."

But one day, when the smell of the spring passed through my window, I decided that "Ok, Adda, now is the time for you to find your 'big girl shoes' and stop this negative nonsense." I remembered that somewhere in my notes, I had three great questions from the Dale Carnegie training that I had once used before at a difficult moment in my life.

Here are the three questions. It is very important to write down the answers honestly.

1. What is the worst thing that can happen?
2. What is the possible thing to do about it?
3. What am I going to do about it?

These questions helped me to focus on what I really want in life and to follow my dreams with a positive attitude. In July 2016, I decided to move to Spain. One of my best friends invited me to rent a room in her apartment near Torrevieja and see if I would like to build my own home in Spain one day.

It's been over two years now, and I am building up a fantastic life with my fiancé in a beautiful little town in southern Spain. I can go to Iceland to be with my grandchildren and my family, and they also come to Spain. The world is not so big after all. My network marketing business is growing again, and I am not scared of the future anymore.

It is up to me to accept my fear and self-doubt and put up a positive exception to every situation so that I can be the best version of myself on a daily basis. I believe that what we feed our brain daily is the foundation of our future. Hope you all are having a great day today, just like every other day.

Biography

Adda Hafborg is an Entrepreneur, Mentor, and Influencer. She has built her leaders' organization in 13 different countries. Her strength is her positive long-term vision. She influences others to reach their goals and find balance in life while she leads by example.

Contact Information

Facebook https://www.facebook.com/arny.halfdansdottir#!/arny.halfdansdottir
YouTube https://www.youtube.com/channel/UCeR16SV7vlekxEnbBMplwfw
Instagram https://www.instagram.com/addahafborg/

Chapter 9
WHAT MAKES SOME PEOPLE MORE SUCCESSFUL THAN OTHERS?

By Maxwell Adekoje

Why do some people do exceptionally well, and others don't? Every human being is built for success and wants to be successful, but only a few become successful. The percentage of successful people seems to be about 10 percent, about the same range, year after year.

What is success? How can you join this constant and unchanging 10% of the population?

Understanding success is the first step to attaining success. These principles took me from

$20, when I first came to the US, to becoming a proud owner and CEO of an MLM marketing company.

Success is a thought process that gives birth to a discovered purpose. The most significant gap between successful and unsuccessful people is the way they think, which reflects on their attitude, beliefs, and mindset. If the way we think is paramount to our success, why do we still have the same wrong mindset? Let me share a little story I once heard from a friend.

In 1990, a known musician built a house with N20 Million; the same year, Jim Ovia started Zenith Bank with the same amount. Zenith bank in Nigeria is one of the most reputable banks in Africa.

Today, you and I don't have a room in the musician's house, but I have an account in Jim's bank, and you probably do, too.

The house was built in Lagos, Nigeria, and remains there to this date.

Jim's bank started in a corner and now has over 500 branches in Nigeria and many international branches.

Millions upon millions transact business in Jim's bank daily.

The house is becoming dilapidated. In 2015, he SPENT more money to renovate the house and bought a Nissan Pathfinder with N10 million, an additional liability, while in the same 2015, Jim's bank MADE a profit of N105.7 billion.

Zenith bank employs hundreds of thousands of people and feeds families.

This is the difference between a successful mindset and an unsuccessful mindset. If you buy a car for N20 million today, in 20 years' time, you will be ashamed to drive it. On the other hand, if you invest that same amount in a lucrative business or an asset, it may be worth billions of nairas in 20 years. (Jim Ovia is now worth 980 million dollars, with the official dollar rate of N350. That means he is worth N313 BILLION NAIRA, all because of an investment of N20 million. Every penny in your hand is like a seed; you can decide to eat it or sow it. When you plant it, it will bear many more seeds in the future. Now, you can see why successful people think differently.

Success demands that you develop a certain type of thinking and perception about the way you see things. It doesn't matter how many degrees or talents you have; it's your thinking and attitude that keeps you small.

Attitude plays a vital ingredient in your success; it's a product of belief. You can't have an attitude beyond your belief. Your attitude comes from your platform of belief. If you associate with only poor individuals, you will think like them.

If you hang around the restaurant long enough, you will get something to eat. We become our environment unknowingly. Stay in an environment that will aid your growth.

People with a great attitude are coachable with a teachable and welcoming atmosphere. Take responsibility for your attitude; it belongs to you.

How can you alter your attitude? Here are three simple steps:

1. Fill your mind with good thinking; you can't fill your mind with bad stuff and expect to alter your mind. Be selective and guard your mind with armor.
2. Marinate and digest the good thinking you put in. Dr. Maxwell Maltz, a plastic surgeon turned psychologist, wrote: "It usually requires a minimum of about 21 days to effect any perceptible change in a mental image. Following plastic surgery, it takes about 21 days for the average patient to get used to his new face. When an arm or leg is amputated, the "phantom limb" persists for about 21 days. People must live in a new house for about three weeks before it begins to "seem like a home.""
3. Practice good things, so they get into your mind and become a part of you.

It's the thinking of a person that makes them see circumstances differently. After years of dealing with problems, I started realizing that a problem is a human definition of an opportunity to grow. If you call it a problem, it immediately takes a negative notation. If you see it as an opportunity, it becomes positive. A problem really only becomes a problem when you see it as a problem. If you want to become a person of impact, you must fill your mind correctly.

After reading the book, "Think & Grow Rich," repeatedly, I realize that human beings can alter their life by changing their attitude. Wow!

The most valuable instrument for success is the 15.24 cm between your ears. No one can live beyond the limit of their thinking; it must be altered. You're simply a presentation of your thoughts. Because of the way my mind was programmed as a child, I had to reprogram my thought process.

First, I had to discover my purpose in life, feed my mind with new beliefs. I'm possible. Marinate on the new thinking and back it up with execution.

Information does not bring transformation; conversion does.

If you don't like who you are, change it to who you think you should be. Your thinking is more powerful than any promise.

Everyone came to this earth fully loaded with purpose; discover it. You're important to the world with a purpose to do something significant. Most of our perceptions are other people's concept about us. You didn't know you were weak until someone told you. Your life is shaped and cultured by what you hear or see.

The little difference in people is their attitude; the larger version is if it is positive or negative.

A seed can be held in your wallet for 40 years and never become a tree even though the seed has a tree in it. Most people go through life carrying their greatness in their wallet rather than planting it.

Trees aren't found in the soil; they are hidden in the seed if you can get it out of your wallet and plant it.

We are like a tree serving the world our juice; plant yourself on fertile ground. Watch out for the weeds. People heading nowhere are ready to pollute your seed. Break away from people to become more. You must outgrow some people. I call it isolation. Know when to go! "Isolation to growth" is best illustrated by the story of a lobster. How do lobsters grow? A lobster is a soft animal that lives inside a rigid shell that never expands. So, how do they grow? By isolation.

A lobster isolates from predators and casts off the old shell and produces a new one; then, after a while, they repeat the process.

The lesson of the story: the lobster feels uncomfortable, then grows. Most people will never grow until they walk away from people who are continually polluting their life, solidifying the wrong beliefs in them.

Always walk away and remember to repeat this process of renewing your mind.

I can't end the chapter without talking about some key traits of success - confidence and focus.

Confidence

Confidence is a product of your belief. The way you think about yourself is the way you unknowingly behave. It's interesting how an elephant with so much power behaves like a gazelle in the presence of a lion.

Mindset

Mindset is everything; thinking is the belief system exposed. I had to alter my thinking, and my attraction instantly took a turn around.

Focus

Without focus, you will never finish. I find the Lindenberg's story to be one of the best illustrations of how focus can lead and keep you on the path of success.

Lindbergh, Charles Augustus (1902-1974), an American aviator, made the first solo nonstop flight across the Atlantic Ocean on May 20-21, 1927. Other pilots had crossed the Atlantic before him, but Lindbergh was the first person to do it alone nonstop.

From New York to Paris (nonstop) in 33 hours, 30 minutes, he made a statement to the press. He said, "At a point, I considered going back, but when I examined the fuel gauge, I realized the remaining fuel could only take me across, not back, so I maintained."

Lindbergh's feat gained him immediate international fame. The press named him "Lucky Lindy" and the "Lone Eagle."

Nothing destroys focus like options.

Nothing frustrates the success of a plan like the mindfulness of plan B.

If there is an imploring alternative to your dream, then trust me, you will soon leave the idea.

Follow your dream as if there were no choices; your life depends on it. Narrow in your focus; deal with distractions.

Keep your eyes on the eight ball. It may be tough, but it's attainable if you don't abandon it for other options.

Stay focused, burn the boats

When they arrived, he ordered his men to burn the ships. I wonder the thoughts in their minds as Cortés promptly thrust his sword. Successful people think differently; they start with the end in mind; unsuccessful people start with the beginning and never see the end.

Here's the lesson: Retreat is easy when you have the option; always see the end first.

Let that marinate in your mind for a minute.

We all cling to something that acts as our escape plan or our exit strategy. It's our safety net; "the just in case factor" is the biggest dream killer..."

Our thought tells us, "This is my safety exit, just in case *things go out of hand*." You immediately lack momentum and register a failure that was waiting to happen.

We delay action until we no longer have fear. Aside from that, our actions are narrow attempts never intended to succeed.

What are your ships? Why are you afraid to let go? Let that ruminate in your mind and write them down? What ship do you need to burn NOW? Trust me, success is in the "now" and not in the tomorrow.

The longer you ponder to act, the more likely you will never do it. What makes it hard to burn your boats is mostly the fear of the unknown called the comfort zone.

John C Maxwell, my mentor, talks about success. For success to happen, your comfort zone must be disturbed.

Nothing makes sense like burning the boats to feel good afterward.

Most of the things we call obstacles are placed there by ourselves, and we ask, "Oh why?" No one packaged it for you; it was your decision not to do the things that create change like burning the boats.

What Cortés did was to cancel the retreat option and create a NEW mindset to succeed or die, which takes us to another resounding trait of success - CHARACTER.

Character is bigger than death; that's the only reason why this story will never die. Cortés doesn't need a tombstone to be remembered.

Roosevelt described character as the decisive factor in the life of an individual that brings honor. Character speaks without words. Your character gives weight to your words; your life becomes your words. Successful leaders never get their reward in the beginning.

"Life chooses what we go through, but we decide how we sail through it." - Maxwell Adekoje

Live every day like today is your last time to impact lives.

You have greatness in you, and you have more than enough to become a person of value. The world badly needs you. Find your purpose and live a life of fulfillment.

Biography

Maxwell's life is a story about hard work, endurance, and inspiration. Originally born in Nigeria, Max first traveled to the United States at a young age, with just $20 in his pocket, seeking the American dream. Like so many who began their working life and career in a new land, the first venture in Max's career in the US was not particularly a great success. Ultimately, there were several failed attempts, but each one along the way served to grow his ambition and sense of belief in the promise of the US and what it could offer to him as a businessman and professional.

First working at a car wash, a restaurant, and numerous other entry-level jobs, Max would regularly sleep three hours daily for years at a time. He was still paying tons of bills, working long hours, and was ultimately unhappy. Despite these challenges, Max never gave up on America and the promise it offered to a young man with a dream and a readiness to realize it with hard work.

Despite this, Max encountered a moment of truth driving home from work one day. So tired in his car, he fell asleep at the wheel, crashed and nearly killed himself. It was at this moment that he knew he needed to change gears in order to change his situation and pursue a life that would deliver him the rewards he deserved.

He wanted to pursue a real American dream, the one that led him to America in the first place and not the one of him washing cars as when he first arrived.

This was when he began exploring ways to grow his own business and grow his net worth. It was around this time he found out about multilevel marketing. Having resolved to chase down a new life for himself, soon after this new career path crystalized, Max was achieving great success in his new field.

Today, he is a top sponsor with numerous awards accredited to his name. He is also the CEO of his own MLM company. Recognized as an international training coach and speaker, Max is proud to be a member of the John C Maxwell Team. While Max is delighted by his success today, he remains hungry for more and goes to work each day with the intention of doing better than ever.

Contact Information

Phone 757-235 6978

Email tmc@mytaprootmc.com

Chapter 10
THE FIRST TIME I FAILED IN MY LIFE WAS THE DAY I WAS BORN

By Kate Jones

I was born a girl, not a boy, and that was a huge disappointment to my father. As I grew up and became more self-aware, it became apparent that every time my father looked at me, there was a cloud of disappointment hanging over him. And as children do, I tried to make myself into the person that I thought he wanted me to be, believing that I would make him proud of me. So, I grew up attempting to be someone else and trying to please others. It was hard, and with each passing year, I buried my true self under layer upon layer of pretending to be someone else until the point where I began to believe the lie and lost sight of the real me.

I felt the only thing I was good at was being a failure, but deep down inside was a part of me that stubbornly refused to give up. There was a small voice deep within me that kept whispering, "I'm here. The real, true you. Let me out so I can be the person I was meant to be."

I refused to listen.

I continued to hide away and tried to be someone I wasn't.

So why am I telling you all this?

The title of this book is Success Unlimited, and here I am talking about abject failure.

Well, there comes a point in everyone's life where we draw a line in the sand, where the pain of being where we are now far outweighs the fear of any change. I reached that point. I had this toxic relationship with money. I desperately wanted more of it, but I hated the fact that no matter what I did, there was never enough. I eventually ended up in deep financial shit, stuck in an abusive relationship and in the depths of despair.

It seemed I was always destined to fail. And therein lay my problem. What I failed to understand was the Law of Attraction - like attracts like. Negativity attracts negativity. A belief in self-failure attracts failure. Limiting self-beliefs attract limiting results. When you constantly focus on the things you DON'T have right now, you will NEVER see the things you CAN have because the universe can only give you what you are focusing on RIGHT NOW.

Now, before you roll your eyes and tell me I'm going all "woo woo" on you, hear me out. Everything I am about to tell you now has its basis in quantum physics. Yep, that's right. Proven, researched, scientific fact. I am no scientist, and I won't go into a load of technical stuff about neutrons, electrons, positrons, etc. We, humans, are all, at our most basic cellular level, nothing more than pure energy. That's a scientifically proven fact. We are vibrating at various frequencies, positivity being high vibration and negativity being low vibration. That's also a scientifically proven fact. We have a measurable energy field around and within us. Guess what... that's a scientifically proven fact as well. Quantum scientists (Einstein included) have proven that all physical matter is made up of energy packets that are not bound by space and time. This energy field has no well-defined boundaries. Science has also proven that the mind has no boundaries.

So where does all this lead in terms of success? I'll take you back to the Law of Attraction. Like attracts like. What if, instead of being negative, and filling our lives with thoughts of failure, desperation and wanting things we don't have, we were to focus on the positive, look at and be grateful for the things we DO have and make the decision to love ourselves instead of allowing feelings of despair and failure?

How do you think that might change things? Surely, if the negativity in the past has brought about only more negativity, doesn't it stand to reason that positivity should bring about more positivity? Surely, if we are happy, we will attract more happiness? If we are grateful for the things we DO have, surely, we will get even more of those things? What if we put out feelings of self-love? Won't we get more love back? The answer to all of those questions is YES. The Universe only knows how to answer YES. Whatever you put out there you will get a YES back.

Negativity will return negativity. Believing you are a failure will only give you more failure. Worrying about debt will only bring more debt. Thinking you will always be alone means you WILL always be alone. Do you get the picture?

THIS WAS THE MASSIVE TURNING POINT IN MY LIFE.

I finally realized that the person solely responsible for everything negative that happened and was happening in my life was me. Boy, that was a really hard lesson to learn. Gone were all my excuses that blamed others. Gone was my justification for being angry with my father, my ex-husband and even my abusive partner.

Shit!!!!

It was ALL DOWN TO ME. Now notice, I'm not saying it was all my FAULT. I am not blaming anyone for where I ended up, not even myself. Blame is a negative vibration that only leads back to more negativity.

Instead, I've accepted that I did not make mistakes for which I could blame myself. I merely made decisions that had a different outcome to the one that I expected. And I made those decisions from a point of not knowing any better.

What this means is that success is available to every one of us. We must change our mindset, change our perspective and change who we are. We need to learn to control our natural monkey-brain that wants us to conform to what we have always experienced, to be who we have always been and to stay in our (dis)comfort zone. At this point, I am going to ask you a question. What is it you truly, deeply want? And what is it that is stopping you from achieving it? Do you want wealth, time, freedom, family time, abundance in your life, peace, contentment, fun, joy, health, to travel the world, to do whatever you want, be whoever you want, be the best possible version of yourself?

I don't think I can hear anyone saying "no" at this point. So, what is it that's stopping you from having all that? Limiting self-beliefs? Fear of failure? Disbelief? Thinking that it's only possible for other better people? Feeling you are not worthy of having all that? I can't afford to do it? I don't want to leave my comfort zone; it's too scary? What if I were to say that all those excuses were just your monkey-brain trying to protect you? What if I was to say you CAN have all of that and it's quite simple. Well, I've got news for you (and this is the MASSIVE lesson I learned that has utterly and completely changed my life).

The Universe (remember that scientifically proven stuff we talked about earlier) only knows how to say YES. So, if you ask for money, health, happiness, love, soul-mate, success, peace, fulfillment, and whatever else you want in life, what do you think you are going to get?

Now I'll put a rider in here; it's not just a case of saying "OK Universe I want blah blah blah" and expecting to get it.

Remember the Law of Attraction?

Like attracts like.

If you want someone to love you, then you must learn to love yourself first.

If you want to receive love, give it first.

If you want more money, be grateful for every penny that is currently in your bank account.

You MUST develop a different mindset.

You must learn to believe in yourself and the fact that you CAN have everything you want.

Practice deliberate thoughts and intentions (positive ones not negative ones).

Clear out all the negative junk from your mind and your life (including negative people). Surround yourself with like-minded, positive, and supportive people.

Develop a positive mindset and wealth consciousness.

Be thankful for everything you have RIGHT NOW and stop focusing on the things you don't have. Become "I am" not "I am not." Become the person you want to be NOW, don't wait.

Educate yourself on how you can achieve the level of mindfulness that brings about true joy, wealth and abundance. Read, read, and read!

Start your day being grateful for everything in your life.

Every. Single. Thing.

Every. Single. Morning.

This is NON-NEGOTIABLE.

If you want the Universe to give you everything, start by being grateful for everything you already have. Apart from being the start of getting all those things you want, it actually makes you feel positive and happy.

When you are grateful and happy, it is IMPOSSIBLE to feel fear. (Again, a scientifically proven fact. Our brain is incapable of feeling fear and gratitude/love at the same time). If you have no fear, you can achieve absolutely anything in life.

Become acutely aware of your subconscious and what it is doing. Your subconscious is responsible for all your self-sabotaging habits, from your beliefs, values, emotions, habits, imagination, and intuition. Learn to become very aware of what your subconscious is thinking and doing because most of your self-limiting beliefs, negative values, feelings, and emotions come from your subconscious and you are not even aware of it.

Learn to listen to what it is doing and correct any negativity.

Stop all negative thoughts in their tracks and replace them with positive ones.

Stop all self-sabotaging thoughts and activities.

Raise your self-awareness to a much higher level, one that you can manage and control.

Mindfulness and self-awareness are the two key things to remember and work on.

I am living proof that you CAN change your life dramatically for the better and I want to reach out to as many people as possible and show them and YOU that you don't have to remain in a poverty mindset, facing failure over and over again and feeling utterly shit about yourself.

It is ABSOLUTELY possible to change your life and have everything you ever wanted.

Success is NOT just about money. True happiness, wealth, abundance, and ultimately success comes from WITHIN YOU. It comes from aligning yourself to the one thing that connects everything and everyone – the Universe (remember it's scientifically proven and not woo woo!).

It comes from gratitude, giving and belief that you ARE worthy of having everything you want in life.

It comes from one simple decision to make a change. Don't you owe it to yourself to become the best possible version of yourself? Become the joyous, abundant, wealthy, healthy, grateful person that you have the opportunity to be.

I want you to feel the sheer joy that floods my life every moment. Even when I have moments of doubt or worry, I know how to deal with them, embrace them, analyze them, and then let them go.

I want you to have the wealth consciousness that will deliver you the financial freedom and peace you want, and deserve.

I want you to have the positive mindset that will give you courage, strength, optimism, belief, and gratitude for everything you have right now.

I want you to stop worrying about tomorrow's problems and start enjoying the peace and beauty of today, knowing that your future is secured.

I want you to understand that you CAN have everything you want and that ultimately you can have unlimited success in every single aspect of your life. And above all, I want you to learn to love yourself and know that you are loved in return.

The Universe only knows how to say YES.

What do you want it to say YES to today?

BIOGRAPHY

Kate Jones is a 55-year-old single mother and grandma who finally decided enough was enough. A lifelong self-limiting view of never being good enough in any sphere of life led to a decision to take a totally radical and different approach to life. What followed was a powerful process of personal growth and spirituality that has led to massive life changes and a mission to help others achieve the same.

CONTACT INFORMATION

Facebook https://www.facebook.com/kate.jones.55
YouTube https://www.youtube.com/channel/UCfDJBUR7J_tGR40xzVSRF4g
Instagram https://www.instagram.com/katejonesonline/
Website https://www.katejonesonline.com/

Chapter 11
REDEFINING MY DEFINITION OF SUCCESS

By Arlene Binoya-Strugar, Psy.D.

Success can be defined in a variety of ways. I define it by the ability to evolve and grow mentally and emotionally, an arduous journey I went through beginning in my early childhood. My journey forced me to reevaluate the way I operate in relationships (specifically attachment), internalizing pain, reimagining my self-worth, and ultimately redefining my definition of success.

My original idea of success caused me to chase a goal that wouldn't make me happy. My idea of success can be attributed to how I was raised and the relationship I had with my parents. Separation of parents can have an emotional and behavioral impact on children. Children can become insecure. Aided with love and encouragement from my parents despite their separation, and from other caregivers, over time, led me to develop a healthy self-image and confidence. I have learned and evolved the way I attach to people in relationships, which has allowed me to embrace a path of healing. It's not a perfect method, and by no means, a "one size fits all" process, but what I am about to share with you has afforded me knowledge and courage to know myself better and become the best version of myself.

Attachment

The foundation for our self-image, how we view and value relationships, and how we cope with stressful situations in our life can be attributed to relationships in our early childhood. Attachment is one of these factors and is the primary function in a relationship.

Psychologist Mary Ainsworth says, "Attachment is a deep and enduring emotional bond that connects one person to another across time and space." Attachment and dependableness are a child's basic needs, so they ask these questions: Are you there for me? Am I worthy of your love and attention? Will you be there for me when I need you? The way these questions are answered develops the child's attachment style, views on relationships, emotional maturity, and decision making, which ultimately formulates a person's definition of success.

Ainsworth lists four attachment styles:
1. The secure attachment style. This attachment style has a positive view of self and positive view of others.
2. The insecure avoidant style has a positive view of self and negative view of others.
3. The insecure ambivalent type has a negative view of self and positive view of others.
4. The fourth attachment style, the disorganized attachment style has a

negative view of self and negative view of others.

According to Clinton and Sibcy, "People with secure attachment styles believe that they are worthy of love, trust others and expect them to reciprocate love back to them. On the contrary, people with insecure attachment styles push people away and close themselves off emotionally to others in fear of abandonment. They're controlled by the pain in their lives and often question their self-worth."

Emotional scars are injuries, and even though they're not visible, they still take time to heal. When left unattended, like injuries, they become worse, infected, more painful, damage our lives in ways we may not even be aware of.

According to Clinton and Sibcy, "Healthy communication is a great immunizer. A healthy, open communication allows us to heal from attachment and emotional injuries by talking openly and honestly about our feelings. Internalizing and reflecting on our pain helps us distance the event from emotion and process facts. It allows us to use finite words to describe our failures, allowing us to move on and reframe the meaning of our lingering pain into a process of healing. We can reframe our feelings, or simply just let out and verbally release them. We can process a healthier way of coping with our pain, which leads us to the last process of healing - forgiveness."

Clinton and Sibcy further state "Whether it is forgiving ourselves or someone else, acceptance is the closing of the wound. Like on the body, even though remnants of the injury are still there and leave a mark, we are able to move on with our lives. Healing from attachment and emotional wounds is not about forgetting, it's about accepting, learning and moving on. It allows us to trust again and frees us from pain."

Cultural Identity and Self-Identity

Our culture shapes social norms, values, morals, and traditions which are inseparable from us. People are shaped by their culture and culture is shaped by them. I view my success on how my society preforms collectively. Harmony and interdependence are characteristics I value more. My success is determined by the success of the group to which I belong. It is a group effort, and each member is given the same value and recognition. A very eastern view, yes, but I was able to merge it with a very individualistic idea of success as well.

On the contrary, self-reliance and independence are greatly valued in an individualistic culture. Western cultures prioritize the success of the individual, despite the effort of the group. Both have their pros and cons, but while still heavily having a collective view of success, I am able to incorporate individualistic aspects of success which help me overcome aspects of my leadership style and mindset that could be interpreted as limiting.

Behavioral Change: Brain, Mind, Body

Daniel Amen, a renowned neuropsychiatrist, says "When your brain works right, you work right. When your brain is in trouble, you have troubles in life." Amen has conducted thousands of single-photon emission computed tomography (SPECT) brain scans and has discovered formulas that are harmful and helpful to our brains.

The Amen Clinic has listed many things that can hurt our brain:
- Brain injuries
- Drugs and alcohol
- Obesity
- Sleep apnea
- Smoking/caffeine
- Diabetes
- Hypertension
- Toxins
- Low Vitamin D, thyroid, testosterone, blood sugar
- Poor diets/sugar
- Stress/depression
- Lack of exercise
- Poor decisions
- Unhealthy peer groups
- Not knowing your own brain.

Brain habits that can help heal our brain are:
- Good decisions
- Conscientiousness
- Positive peer groups
- Protecting the brain
- Clean environment
- Physical health/exercise/healthy diet
- Healthy weight
- Eight hours of sleep a night
- New learning
- Killing automatic negative thoughts
- Omega 3s
- Gratitude
- Stress management.

Although I've listed the good and bad things for your brain, it's not that simple. Changing habits and behaviors is hard work, and it's even harder to break habits we aren't even aware of. Many of us associate failures with the lack of willpower, not enough motivation, weakness of character, or personality flaws to make changes in our lives; however, it's not because we don't know the negative effects of our bad habits, but because we don't know how to change.

James and Janice Prochaska constructed six stages to guide us to change our bad habits.

1. Precontemplation - I am not ready; not intending to take action in the next six months
2. Contemplation - I am getting ready; intending to take action in the next six months
3. Preparation - I am ready; ready to take action in the next 30 days
4. Action - I have made the behavior change but for less than six months
5. Maintenance - I am doing the new healthy behavior for more than six months
6. Termination - I am confident with the change, not tempted to relapse

By implanting all of these schools of thoughts, I have been able to change my outlook on life and relationships, heal from old emotional wounds, and reframe my mindset to succeed. I now understand my ways of thinking in groups and as an individual. My leadership style is connected to how I see myself in relation to other members of the group and how I value them. Overall, I am able to see the synergistic relationships between our habits, and how it affects our health (brain, mind, and body) and the quality of our lives.

Biography

From her humble beginnings, Arlene Binoya-Strugar, Psy.D. never quit. As a social scientist, she not only has a deeper understanding of human behavior but also has applied these teachings into her life. She used her personal experiences, educational and cultural background to increase her emotional and social intelligence in leading groups and to understand human aspirations. She is a social scientist with a passion for understanding human pain and experiences to improve human lives and existence.

Contact Information

Facebook: https://www.facebook.com/braingysticsintegrative
LinkedIn: https://www.linkedin.com/in/arlene-strugar-psy-d-a635602/
Website: www.braingystics.com

Chapter 12
5 STEPS TO BECOMING A GOOD ENTREPRENEUR

By Jasmina Cernilogar Mihajlovic

Have you ever asked someone what he or she thinks about you? How does he see you?

Do you want to know why people treat you like they do?

What if you asked people what they think about your work?

Maybe you are scared to hear the truth, and it seems easier to hide and be invisible.

If you have asked, then you know how it feels and if you haven't you should try.

It's worth the try. I am always surprised and honored because people around me see me like the person I always wanted to be. They see my dreams and my fears. It's nice to hear from people that I live my dreams.

People often tell me, it's so easy for you, you are so confident, you know what you are doing, or you are so determined and always find a way.

Who, me? Are they really talking about me? It's like I don't know that person. I am a little girl who doesn't know how to react and then when no one does anything I try to find a way. I am not confident. I am just determined to succeed; I want to make a better day, a better year and a better world for everybody.

I can share my knowledge and help people. I can share my experience and my common sense to help people from stress so that they don't go through the tough times I did. Maybe, I can help them think differently and open their mind to positive and beautiful things in life and business. It's bigger and stronger than me.

Many times, I want to quit, and I hide from everybody, but it's always just for a short time. I am here to tell what I must tell. I want to change the world.

My mission is to teach common people how to be an entrepreneur and how to organize their administrative activities, books, taxes, money, and finances. I enjoy every moment of it.

From idea to business success is a long journey. Nobody can do it for you. You'll have to do it yourself.

Everything starts with your first few steps. I've done things differently for more than 15 years. I've had to figure out a lot of things through trial and error.

You must learn new things constantly, be focused, determined, and not fear failure. If you fail, try again till you succeed.

If you have an idea, project, or a dream; and want to become an entrepreneur, you have to go through these five steps and learn the fundamentals of entrepreneurship.

1. How to open a company
2. How to do business
3. Costs
4. Business report
5. Marketing

Let's discuss the five steps in more detail.

Step #1: How to open a company

The laws are different depending on your country. You may need to get familiar with the rules in your country, the costs, the benefits, and your applicable taxes.

It's important to understand the taxes you need to pay, your obligations on book-keeping, invoicing, employment, etc.

Understand as much as you can before you start your business. It's important to do your due diligence, understand the laws in your country, and ask as many questions as possible before you even start.

Step #2: How to do business

This step involves taking care of administrative activities, organizing work processes, making sure that you have enough finances, opening a bank account, calculating profit margins, doing your bookkeeping, handling taxes, dealing with clients, suppliers, and employees.

It might be hard to think about all the activities in your business before you even start. You might want to figure things out along the way, but the process will be less painful if you prepare yourself. Preparation will help you stay more focused on your business without losing time and energy figuring out processes while you are on the run.

Step #3: Costs

An entrepreneur needs to know his costs. He should find legal ways to reduce taxes. He should know the difference between costs, expenses, outflows, revenues, and inflows.

Distinguishing between these terms is important. Not knowing these terms can land you in trouble. It's like driving a car blindfolded.

Imagine your business is doing great, you have several orders, you are selling good, but if you are not going to track your expenses and revenues, you will never know about the financial health of your business. So, learn about economics, read stories about other entrepreneurs, imitate them until you are ready to innovate and experiment with new things on your own.

Step #4: Understand business reports

As an entrepreneur, you will need to deal with banks, clients, and suppliers. It's important to understand the language of business and know the rules of the game.

It's important to know the difference between a balance sheet, income statement, cash flow statement, capital gains report, and how you could optimize these for your business.

You may not be an expert in economics, and you need not become one. But you must know at least the basics of running your business.

It's your business, and the responsibility of its success depends entirely on you. A startup is like a newborn baby, and you'll have to nurture it through the delicate initial stages where the business can be vulnerable. You can't learn everything, but you can gain just enough knowledge necessary to understand the fundamentals of business and economics.

You may think that you can do without it. But I suggest that you learn as much as you can before you start. A few mistakes can set you back by several years. I believe knowledge is everything and a person without knowledge is at a significant disadvantage.

Step #5: Marketing

You might have a great product, but what if no one knows about it? Marketing is one of the most important cornerstones of a successful business.

All you do, write and say about you and your company is marketing.

You have to find the most appropriate way to inform people about your business. Your customers must like you and your product. My coach Lenja says "You must first tattoo yourself in your client's hearts and then their wallets."

You need to know some things about internet sites and how you can spread the word about your business. You have to learn a lot about social networks and how to use it for your business.

Advertising is the key to success today. How can you use it for your business to attract more clients?

You have to think about your marketing plan, and maybe you don't even know what it is.

It's not enough to just have a business idea, but you should also have a strategy on how to do it. And to do it you need the knowledge that makes you better and more prepared than your competitors.

These are just a few things you should know about entrepreneurship before you start. I have to admit I didn't even know half of it when I began. If I did, my entrepreneurial life would've been much easier, and I would've reached my goals much faster.

My sincere suggestion to all of you is to chase your dreams, don't stop if you come across obstacles because there will always be something that seems difficult to overcome. Everything can be done. Things that seem impossible are not always impossible. Things will come to you if you truly desire them, work on it, and don't let other people discourage you.

Fortune favors the brave. That's the entrepreneur in me talking.

Biography

Jasmina Cernilogar Mihajlovic is an entrepreneur with a heart. She's been running a tax consulting and accounting business for the last 15 years. Her mission is to teach people to become good entrepreneurs. She has her own way of giving knowledge that comes from her experience of helping several entrepreneurs.

Contact Information

LinkedIn: https://www.linkedin.com/in/jasmina-%C4%8Dernilogar-m-a5941552/
Twitter: https://twitter.com/jasminacermih
Instagram: https://www.instagram.com/jasminacernilogarmihajlovic/

Chapter 13

LIVING AN INSPIRED, PURPOSEFUL, AND AMAZING LIFE

By Jeremy Hoort

My family was as far from normal as it gets, with my two Fathers both working as drug dealers until I was 13 years old, but still, I grew up surrounded by love, faith, and discipline.

After I turned 13, my biological Father went to Federal Prison, while my other Father chose to follow a different path, one that I consider being much harder. He gave it all up, the drugs and the crime, and instead focused his efforts on his faith. For a while, we lived relatively happily, albeit modestly, until the divorce of my father and mother.

After the divorce, my mother took care of three children all by herself. Neither of my Fathers supported us financially. And so, from a young age, I started to learn about the corruption of people, governments, police, and I began to see what money does to people and society. It's destructive.

My life was like something most people only see in the movies – we would hide silver and gold bars in our laundry baskets and wait until we could launder it through a business. We were constantly playing cat and mouse with the police and the federal government.

In a way though, I was lucky, because despite the illegal activity, my siblings and I were always loved. We were always disciplined and taught right from wrong. And I was also lucky that my fathers weren't tied to any organized crime, so they were able to walk away.

My biological Father served five years in a federal prison for possession of 200 pounds of marijuana. He was set up by his own friends in a federal sting operation. While he could have shortened his sentence, he served full time, because he refused to snitch on others, and for this, I was proud of him. He did the crime, without tattling on others to get a lighter sentence.

My Step-Father raised me while my biological Father was in prison, and I consider him just as much a Father as my real Dad. He made the hard decision to give up the illegal life for good and left the drug trade after finding his faith in the bible.

I plan on writing a detailed book about my Fathers and my childhood, where I'll divulge all the dirty details, but here I wanted you to see that our lives are about choices and our thoughts. I chose to be the direct opposite of my Fathers when it came to my schooling, career life and my time in the military. I never allowed myself a failure or even sub-par performance, ever. I could have followed in my Father's footsteps and lived a life of crime, chasing cash, but instead, I decided to focus on High School and afterward, on my military career.

I learned that regardless of our history, we choose who we will become. Living in the past, and holding grudges will lead to becoming consumed by negative thoughts. Everyone has one main choice: to be a victim of their circumstances or to take control and be a lion of their own lives. I chose to be a lion and so far, I've reached my goals, and been successful in most aspects of my life.

My life after childhood and high school was one of many tough choices, but by age 18, I was out on my own, and I chose to join the United States Air Force. I only signed a four-year contract, but I made the mistake of not having a lawyer look over that contract, which made be obligated to serve for eight years, if the government needed me. It was a lesson learned that you must be careful what you sign.

I completed four successful years working on the fighter aircraft of an E&E specialist but went to complete a total of 10 years' service, working with and around fighter jets like the F-111 Aardvark fighter-bomber (whispering death), F-16 Fighting Falcon, and F-15 eagle. I also completed five years of extra duty in the Air Force Base Honor Guard.

With commanding officers talking highly of me, and several awards and medals under my belt, I could have returned to the military as a commissioned officer, and that was my initial plan. However, my first son was born just after 9/11, and then my plans changed. Instead of returning to the military, I finished my business degree at the University of South Florida in 2015.

I can honestly say that I think all of my current success is due to me being the best father and husband I could be for my family. I now have three beautiful boys: Bryce, Grayson, and Vander who are all the light of my life. I also have my wife, Meagan, who is the rock of the family and is the most beautiful and intelligent woman I have ever met. I'm so happy to have her in my life – it looks like my prayers were answered, because I now have my lioness, and I love her more every day.

I think it's important to create our world in our own minds first, and then it's up to us to decide what's important to us as individuals, and what we're going to do in this life. I think we create our futures long before they happen through what we think and how we act, so keep those negative and limiting thoughts away from your creativity.

Now that I have achieved my success, and created my perfect family, I now try to make a difference on a local level. I started Dash Health Consulting so that I could make a difference by helping one family or business at a time.

We all only have one life to live, a life that's ended with a (-) dash. None of us know when that dash is going to come, which is why it's so important to live every important moment.

I was inspired by many family members, mentors, and my faith to create a lasting legacy and make the world a better place so that by the time my dash comes, I've done my bit to help others achieve success and happiness. I want to help the whole person, from health to wealth while allowing individuals to leave a legacy that will last for many future generations. Legacy in this sense isn't just about wealth, in fact, wealth has little to do with it. My legacy will be the life I lead, Legacy may seem like wealth, but that isn't the case at all. My personal legacy will be the life I lead, my family, and the book I leave for my family and sons along with my charity, CHILD Charity USA (www.childcharityusa.com).

CHILD Charity USA stands for:

Children
Health
Investment
Learning
Development

The goal is to educate children about finance and health. We work with schools for a better tomorrow and help deliver education that will help our children to be successful. Denzel Washington once said: "Don't aspire to make a living, aspire to make a difference" and that's what CHILD Charity USA is all about.

Wealth isn't guaranteed, not for me, not for anyone, but I believe that I've already achieved success and that this is just the tip of the iceberg.

I've always been good at numbers, and so I tried to base my corporate career around them, but I struggled to find a career I agreed with. Every role I tried seemed to be based around selling clients services or products that weren't always right for them.

I became fed up with businesses only promoting the products they were able to sell, rather than genuinely helping clients with a dilemma or pointing them in the right direction. So I created Dash Health Consulting so that I could help people succeed, from Health to Wealth. It's a unique business, the first of its kind.

We focus on what the client needs, bringing businesses together to work for and with clients, rather than just promoting one type of product or service. I hope that Dash Health Consulting will disrupt the market and help millions of people succeed. I created a company that has a huge amount of products and services at its fingertips, for those that want to build their own business.

As well as putting entrepreneurs and businesses in touch with the right services, we're also delivering business and finance education through our website. This is something I haven't seen any other financial advisor, company or business do! I am so excited to share my one-of-a-kind company with the nation.

I'm writing my book to inspire others to focus not on instant rewards, but on the journey towards success. Everywhere you look, you'll see people trying to sell 'get rich quick' schemes that don't necessarily work, but I expect more. I believe that by helping each other as well as ourselves, we'll solve a lot of nationwide issues, and we can all benefit and find our success together. If all you want is a way to make quick money, so you can live the life of a millionaire, I suggest buying a lotto ticket and a prayer.

We need to make new services and products that don't just help one person or business. There's some amazing technology out there that can be used to make this world a better place; it's only our own creativity that's limiting us.

Is success based on a paper currency and the ability to hoard as much as we can as quickly as we can, not caring what it might do to others? Sure, pursuing money might work short term but what kind of damage will we be cleaning up? I believe we'll find ourselves back where we were in 2008, with more bubbles in the economy.

My book and my business aren't about get-rich-quick plans; they're about the truth and a different way of looking at things. I've built a business that offers a number of solutions to a huge number of people.

The business world today is a house of cards, and if you don't just want to take my word for it, there are many other experts much smarter than myself warning us that it's unstable. The trouble is that no one wants to admit it, because admitting it would make the economy even more delicate. But it is bad, and we need to admit this to ourselves so that we can move on to a more controlled economy.

I was once good at poker. I could have pursued it further, but I chose to help others first. I might play poker again one day, but I fully understand that it's gambling. What I don't understand is how people can think the stock market is any different. Rather than putting money into gambling, I believe people should be looking to create products that protect the economy and earn money as well. There are so many different ways to do this, so many different ways to protect people first, and genuinely help them, rather than just selling regardless.

We all have greatness inside us, and we can all excel in life, we just have to access our talents, develop them, and put them to use. Your job doesn't define who you are, it's just a means to an end, a tool.

I challenge you to live an inspired, purposeful, and amazing life. Your life is a ship that only you can captain. Remember not to view failures as a bad thing, think of them as clues. Each failure is a clue that you're heading in the wrong direction, and in its own way, it will steer you in the right direction.

Listen to the strangest secret by Earl Nightingale.

"Do not go where the path may lead, go instead where there is no path and leave a trail." - Ralph Waldo Emerson

Biography

With over 20 years of experience in customer service, ten years of USAF Honor Guard structure, Jeremy Hoort brings amazing talent, taking care of the client from health to wealth to a whole new level. The one of a kind platform of experts in one location at https://www.dashhealthconsulting.com/– is truly unique and inspiring. It changes lives forever while giving back through their charity CHILDcharityUSA.com.

Contact Information

Facebook https://www.facebook.com/jeremy.hoort
LinkedIn https://www.linkedin.com/in/live4life/
Twitter https://twitter.com/ReachDashDCH
YouTube https://www.youtube.com/channel/UCM9A0b9JTL41tTEWYD7OGVQ
Instagram https://www.instagram.com/reachdashdhc/
Website https://www.dashhealthconsulting.com/
Blog https://jeremyhoort.wixsite.com/website

Pinterest https://www.pinterest.com/craighoort/
Charity https://www.childcharityusa.com

Chapter 14
I AM NOTHING. YET, I HAVE EVERYTHING

By Maiko Johanson

I am so deeply honored to share my humble thoughts in this chapter. In this eye-opening journey, let these wonderful people be your guides on the way to your unlimited success.

As we enter this life, naked and unaware of what lies beyond, we have already decided to be successful because we won the first race to be born.

As we grow, we are full of wonder and excitement about learning something new every day.

Our self-image is, "I am enough," "I am successful in everything I do," "I am awesome," "life is wonderful."

What we don't know is the fact that we observe the environment we are in, and it will form our way of thinking and acting. This first part of our personality, until the age of six or so, will remain with us. The most significant part of our belief system is developed by the example of our parents, siblings, attitudes, thought patterns and the immediate environment in which we live.

Then, as we develop an acceptable way of independent thinking, we are sent to an educational system where everything changes. It is the beginning of a careful molding of our minds and a new belief system about how life should go and should be lived. We dream, and we want to be somebody else; we choose role models, and we start acting like them, thinking it's cool and that is our identity, that might be a part of our essence, and we get lucky to become who we were meant to be. But, that's not the way it actually works out for the majority of people.

We start to lose the mindset that "I am more than enough." We grow, learn, get a job, etc.

We seek; we dream; we experience the magic and the ugliness of life.

First, all is well. We work hard for a better future; we hear stories about success, fancy things, different possibilities and lifestyles we want for our lives as well, but nothing changes. We don't feel content; we start to question things; we try to make ourselves feel better by consuming alcohol, drugs and junk food to give us little relief or to numb us down. Years go by, and we are stuck in the system that sold us an idea that there is freedom in entrepreneurship and that is possible for us, but most of us are blind to see that we are now modern-day slaves.

We have developed negative self-talk in our heads about us, and we are troubled in our heads how others see us. Questions like "Am I enough to do this" and "Am I capable for this and that," will take over, and we find ourselves lost in our own lives. We still have dreams about a better future, but we don't realize the negative ball of energy that is now growing bigger.

We start to be a victim and blame others; we start to talk about people behind their backs. Life sucks, and we need to escape.

We don't realize the power of thought and feeling because nobody teaches us that in school.

We don't know the laws of the universe and the power behind them. We are at a breaking point in our lives where usually something happens. This point in our lives can make us or break us. If we are shaken up properly, we might gain some new energy for the understanding that we need to change our lives, our selves, and that we have the power to do so.

I broke my back six times before I needed to go to surgery. It changed my view of life. I had to go to Peru into the Amazon jungle and take part in a one-week Ayahuasca retreat to lose the pain I had been carrying with me since my childhood. I learned a lot, and it made another change in my personality. I felt free, but I still lacked the confidence to step up another level in my actions. I got malaria and almost died before I woke up, to realize that I needed to love more deeply the family and closest friends I have.

I now understand deeply that I have only one life, and I need to be true to my calling. We don't have to go through so many painful and scary experiences to realize we are the architect of our life. Maybe we accidentally stumble on some motivational video or a book that changes our view of life, and we take action to change our lives because the old ways are simply not getting us anywhere. From this realization of an awakened mind, we pray for a better future and, because we had a rough path, we feel hope, and that changes us to feel better and attract better thoughts.

Like attracts like is a combination of words we grow up with, but we do not give it any real attention until we are pushed towards it. Here I, talk to the people who understand my thoughts or who want to understand. I talk to you, someone who is looking for a change, and that very reason is why you are reading this book. You want and need changes in your life, and you are developing your thinking to the point where you know that you don't know about things, but you need to know more for the change to come. This place in one's thoughts is magical, because you have changed your vibration just by realizing something, and that something gives you power.

A person creates their life just by thought. Whether or not you believe it does not matter because it is the truth, and if you just take the time to think deeply about it, you will realize that. Like attracts like, so your thoughts will attract like-minded thoughts, and that process will grow.

You should take time to think about your childhood and the dreams you had in the past, to realize that a big part of them have come to manifest already in your life. You just have been blind to see it; you have been like a zombie just staggering through life. We as human beings are all sensitive to the energies around us. We all say things like, "I feel this way," or "I sense that something is going to happen." Think more deeply about what you feel or sense. This is something we cannot see in the physical world, but we can feel it and sense it.

These thoughts will open up a new world, and that world is full of wonder and magic just like when you were a child. It is hard to comprehend at first, but I promise you that your life will change as you let yourself go into the world of thought.

We all have the power to feel, sense and think. If we think about what it means, it all comes back down to energy, vibration or high frequency. They are the same thing. Choose a word that resonates with you and go from there. Feeling and sensing is something we all know but we cannot see, so we call it energy. Thoughts are in our heads. We can hear them but cannot see, so they are energy?

Earl Nightingale said, "We become what we think about most of the time." Think about that; reflect on that; let it sink in. The people that sing think about it most of their time. People who do sports think about it most of the time. The person who thinks about writing becomes a writer. The person who wants to be an artist becomes one.

The person who is crazy enough to think that he wants to change the world thinks about that most of the time and eventually is the person who does it. Nobody comes to make them who they want to be or what they want in their life; there is no savior. You are your own savior; you are the change; you have the power to change things in your life, and it all starts by thinking.

It is something so simple, and that is why it's hard to grasp at first, but as you start to play with that idea, you will notice the changes in your thoughts. You don't have to know how to do the change - you just have to think about it and feel good about it; this is all you need to do. As you think, you will attract more like-minded thoughts. Like-minded thoughts will attract like-minded people. We all have experienced and heard, "I felt so drawn towards that person," and "We had such good chemistry."

Like attracts like; it is energy! Like-minded people together form a mastermind as it is taught by Napoleon Hill, and from that, things start to change. I truly believe that, because I have known it in me, I have sensed it in me. I did not have the intellectual skills to explain it, but I knew this was something to learn about. I started reading all the self-development books I could get my hands on, and I started to look into the science by going through books to explain all of that to me in a little bit more detail.

The science behind everything does not matter; what matters is what you want. Think about your thoughts; start to be the observer of your mind; start to write things down to get clarity about your thoughts. You become self-aware; that will grant you a gift of patience and understanding of how unaware you have been before. You start to see the negative thought patterns, and you start to know you can reprogram your thoughts into positive ones.

This book is filled with golden nuggets of wisdom that will help you to make the change in your life if you truly want it! The fact that you are reading this book is a powerful step toward your future, and I salute you for that. It does not matter how far you have gone in your personal life or how successful you are in your business. We all have self-doubt at some level; we all are afraid of something. I am here to tell you that you will be alright; everything will be alright; you just have to believe in yourself! I believe in you! You are enough! You are a beautiful human being! We all have things we are not happy with about ourselves, but that is what makes us humans, that makes us unique, that makes us perfect as we are!

The best advice I can give you is to "develop self-awareness." You can do this by turning off the tv and just go for a walk, or simply sit in silence and marinate in your thoughts within yourself and listen. Be mindful about what is going on. Just observe and learn. It is quite hard to do at first, but you will get better at it! Develop your intellect by reading books; it will open up understanding about your own psychology. Eat good organic food; take care of your body. Meditate, and the biggest gifts you can offer yourself are compassion, patience, forgiveness, and self-love. It will make your inner self feel better and, from that, your whole perspective of life will reflect back to you in your reality.

If you want to change things in your life, change things in your life! You have that power!

If I could do it, then I am more than certain that you can do it, too.

I wish and pray for self-awareness, self-love, compassion, forgiveness, and patience to all the people in the world.

Biography

Maiko Johanson believes that everything in life will fall into place without labels.

He is a seeker, writer, son, brother, uncle, a friend, a man, and a world traveler. He believes that he is nothing, yet he has everything.

Contact Information

Facebook: https://www.facebook.com/Maiko.Johanson
YouTube: https://www.youtube.com/channel/UCTO5_OJ_64m2X6_ZYfiHilA?view_as=subscriber

Chapter 15
HOW TO WORK LESS, EARN MORE AND LIVE FREE AS A LIFESTYLE ENTREPRENEUR

By Francis Ablola

If you spotted me at Starbucks grabbing my morning double espresso or white mocha, you wouldn't think much.

My normal work attire consists of a t-shirt, basketball shorts and a pair of old flip-flops. Chances are I haven't shaved in a week, and my backwards cap is hiding the fact that I desperately need a haircut.

You'd probably never guess I just wrapped up a marketing campaign for one of my clients that brought in an additional 7-figures in revenue, or that

I'm masterminding a project that will bring in thousands of new potential customers in just a few weeks.

I operate under the radar, and that's the way I like it.

I call it being a "Lifestyle Entrepreneur."

I work only when I feel like it, with the people I like investing my time with and do it by my own rules from my Floridian beachfront office overlooking the Atlantic Ocean.

The rest of the time you'll find me at home with my beautiful wife and my bouncing baby girl, traveling the country meeting with fellow "Lifestyle Entrepreneurs," and learning new skills that create massive results for my clients and me.

I love what I do, and it's exactly how I designed it.

I don't say this to brag or boost.

I wasn't born with any special talents or advantages.

I tell you this because it's possible for anyone to design a business that supports YOU and your desired lifestyle.

And if you truly want to earn more, work less and enjoy life, then read this special message below.

I'd like to share with you how I went from a 20-something college dropout to corporate burn out, to living a life of AWESOMENESS by design… and how you can do it, too.

<u>Why I Never Want To Grow Up!</u>

It's easy to get lost in what the universe throws at you. Long hours, stressful days, increasing frustration, lost time with family and friends – when you're not in "control of your world," you accept this as status quo.

So many people get caught up in the day-to-day, working for a living and forgetting to create a life.

I know this from personal experience.

Starting out in my professional life, I thought I was doing everything the right way.

I had a good job, at a big Fortune 1000 company, with an impressive title, and an office with a window. Check.

I'm all set, and life couldn't be better, or so I thought.

And all of that's fine if that's what you want. But, if you've got the entrepreneurial bug in your DNA, you'll get antsy quickly.

(My guess is if you're reading this right now, then you know what I mean.)

To me, all the hype about the "grown-up life" was a lie.

You do a good job, work longer and longer hours, sit in more and more meetings, and end up spending more than you make.

I got a plaque and certificate of appreciation.

I wanted more than a plaque, a warm place to sit for eight to nine hours a day, 401K and the cost of living raise every year.

I consider myself fortunate that I found out early in my career that I wanted more, and was willing to go get it.

<u>Early Warning Signs</u>

Ever since I was a kid, I've had the "be my own boss" itch. Remember the kid in your neighborhood carrying around a bucket wanting to wash your car, or going door-to-door offering to cut your grass for a few bucks over the summer and on the weekends? Yup, that was me.

And it didn't stop there. At 12 years of age, I had a crew of neighborhood kids going door to door selling our services. We were a growing enterprise. During the week, I hustled selling pixie sticks and bubble gum in the lunch room, a venture not looked upon too kindly by the teachers.

There's a saying that the grade C and D students own businesses, and the A and B students end up working for them.

I'm living proof that this statement is valid. I'm not ashamed to say that I barely made it out of high school and left the university before they could kick me out.

Meanwhile, I was working, learning about business on my own, trying new things, taking risks, taking action and getting results.

Over the years, I've had other ventures... You name it, selling advertising to local shops, web design services, multi-level marketing companies selling everything from gas rebates to groceries online. Some were good; some were bad, some were profitable, some not, but All Learning Experiences.

One of the keys to being an entrepreneur is to be willing to fail forward and do it fast.

I'll admit my first major business attempt after leaving college was a major flop.

I'm thankful for it because I discovered a lot about myself and the people around me, which were both positive.

I was in my early 20's and thought I was unstoppable. I knew it all, and I could do it all.

I had a steady job working for a web development company that I helped build from the ground up, but I got bored and wanted more. (You'll see this is a pattern for entrepreneurs.)

So, I quit with nothing lined up.

To add to the urgency, I had planned in two weeks' time to propose to my high school sweetheart and girlfriend of six years. (She said yes, by the way!)

The next year was filled with uncertainty and total confusion on what I should do next. I filled my days getting my hands on every course, book, and CD and attending every seminar I could to learn how to make my business work.

I took on odd projects; we lived off my new fiancé's first-year teacher salary and racked up thousands on credit cards using advances to pay the rent. I even traded my services for gift certificates to a restaurant.

Yes, I worked for food, literally.

I often tell people the worst thing that can happen if you go out on your own and it doesn't work is you have to get a job.

Well, that's what I did. And because I spent a year developing skills and growing my ability to add value to the marketplace, I made myself more valuable in the workforce which landed me in a prime position using the new skill sets to open career options that a college dropout like me would otherwise not have available.

But by now, you know how I feel about working for someone else. So, as soon as I could, I ventured out on my own again and this time with <u>A New-Found Confidence And Solid Game Plan.</u>

Through my experience, I created a game plan of exactly what I would want my business to look like, and what it would take in time and resources.

My new goal was to create a business that supports my life, and not the other way around. I can, fortunately, say I've thrown out the conventions of traditional business and am operating quietly under the radar and still able to create a fantastic lifestyle for my family.

Here are a few key lessons I've discovered that have allowed me to fulfill my personal and business goals:

Attitude: There's a thin line between success and failure. Winners push beyond past failures; they learn from every experience and use the past to fuel the fire to succeed.

Communication: Your ability to communicate and influence applies in every area of business – working with vendors, team members, clients and, of course, making sales.

Creating a network: Your network equals your net worth. It's often said that your income is a direct result of the five people with whom you spend the most time. I'm a natural introvert, but I've ignored my natural tendencies to build a strong network of top-level players.

<u>Support system:</u> Stop listening to negative people in your life. They won't serve you or help you reach your goals. I've been blessed with a wonderful partner; my wife has been supportive every step of the way. Also, the people I've attracted in my network all share similar goals, and that only serves to push us forward.

<u>Find a mentor:</u> I've been fortunate to have worked with many people who I consider mentors. This is the ultimate shortcut to success – finding someone who has what you want, who's done what you're doing, and who has a proven path to reach your goals.

<u>A business vehicle:</u> What many don't realize is there is so much opportunity just waiting for the armed and ready entrepreneur. You can take your skills and fill a need, or plug into a ready-built system. If the system works, do it.

Risk: Willingness to take calculated risks. Fear stops many people from achieving their goals, but the best way to overcome fear is to face it.

Leverage: Here's the key to freeing yourself from work. Outsource, leverage time and other people's resources. If you don't like doing a repetitive task, don't do it. If you can easily train someone else to take work off your hands, then do it. You'll have more time to work ON your business.

Know your reason why: It's the driver behind everything you do, especially if your goal is to create a lifestyle-driven business.

My *why* is to spend time with my family and enjoy our time together without having to worry about financial restraints. I've been fortunate to be a part of almost every second of my brand-new baby girl's life and watch her grow every day.

This is the lifestyle I've created, by design. And, now that you know it's possible, I hope you will take time to figure out what matters most to you and live your dreams.

BIOGRAPHY

Francis Ablola is a marketing strategist and award-winning business writer. His unique ability to effectively communicate with and influence wide audiences has generated millions in revenue and created tens of thousands of new opportunities for his clients. From Fortune 1000 to garage start-ups, he has been helping companies succeed using highly effective yet unusual advertising.

Chapter 16
Your Partner in Crime: The Subconscious Mind

By Oliver T. Asaah

What is the subconscious mind?

The subconscious is the guardian angel of the conscious mind and the queen motivator of our actions.

The subconscious influences every second of our lives in everything we do or fail to do; it is dictated by programs that have been systematically installed in our subconscious starting from birth. It is our partner in crime that micromanages the roles we play: actors, participants, or spectators in the theatre of life, as the case may be.

Some of these thoughts are empowering while others are disempowering. Disempowering ideas are those that hold us back from exploring, exploiting, and manifesting our passion and unleashing our full potential. Empowering ones help us get closer to our destiny. Many minds focus on disempowering thoughts.

How is the subconscious programmed?

The subconscious is the invisible master pilot of our actions. It *tele*-guides our thinking; our thinking dictates our actions, and our actions show who we are.

What can we do to shape our subconscious to work for us?

In the Nweh and some other cultures in the Cameroons, twins are believed to possess some magical powers: they can bring good and bad luck to their family. Twins can inadvertently hurt family members by inflicting severe pain mysteriously. Upon satisfying their demand, they mysteriously fix their fetish deeds.

Once upon a time, at the age of six, one of my step twin-sisters was upset with me, and she promised to sprain my leg. She kept staring at my right leg. Consequently, after a while when I stood up, I realized I couldn't walk. My right leg was hurting, so I submitted to her magical powers, coaxing her to forgive me and return my leg to normal. Instantaneously, my leg came back to normal.

This belief, like many others, have existed from time immemorial; it is held to be true and inextricably interwoven with the lifestyle of believers. Some beliefs might not be true, but extreme belief and faith make them seem real to us. The subconscious is programmed similarly.

The subconscious is programmed in three ways: persons (family, teachers, mentors, peers, friends, associates), place (environment) and things (experiences, media, books, films). These three dimensions encode the subconscious at varying degrees. They determine who, how, where, when, why we acquire our programs. These questions will facilitate the process of reprogramming our subconscious.

The programming of our subconscious starts from conception. According to Joseph Susedik, "Talking to children in the womb has a tremendous impact on their development." He recommends a calm, serene environment for a pregnant mother. A solemn atmosphere ensures the birth of a child with utter trust in the parent. The Dallas *Times Herald article, May 15, 1982,* wrote that Joseph and Jitsuko Susedik believed any parent can raise brilliant children; they just need phonics, environment, and curiosity; the earlier, the better. (Ziglar 1985).

"Only if the child has complete trust, can he or she be taught. You must teach your children with love, gentleness, and only at a time they are willing to learn," Susedik says.

Also cited by Ziglar 1985, Dr. Carole Taylor, Ph.D., head of the Tolatr Academy in Pittsburgh, Pa., believes once children master phonics, they can read anything, even college texts. Dr. Taylor has daughters, ages 10 and 14, enrolled part-time in pre-med courses in a community college. She applies the person, place and things factors responsible for programming in empowering her daughters.

How can we access programs in the subconscious?

This is a journey into the realm of our being to enjoy human endowments: self-awareness, imagination, conscience and independent will; that differentiates us from animals. Just 'deep' it: (Dig, Employ, Expect, Profit) and the salt and the sweat will yield the malt.

Unlike consulting a doctor when we are sick for diagnostics and prescriptions, we have to DOCTOR ourselves in reprogramming the subconscious; that has been my experience. To me, DOCTOR means: Diagnose, Operate, Cure, Treat, Oxygenate and Respect. The exercise is very personal, serene and engaging.

"Faith is a state of mind which can be induced through repeated affirmations or instructions to the

SUBCONSCIOUS MIND through the principle of autosuggestion," said Napoleon Hill.

I started with an insight and ended up with sight; I have seen tangible results in my life such as an impeccable positive mindset, which is the reason I am writing this chapter. My baseline of positive attitude is fantastic, then super fantastic and finally super duper fantastic.

My contagious, positive attitude has given me beatitude at my job site, earning me the nickname FANTASTIC! I have seen colleagues who were less enthusiastic, and other employees who were moody brighten up and raise their level of happiness at least when we meet and communicate. This is the mirror neuron effect as described in positive psychology.

Begin with the outcome in mind. You have to see the project from start to finish by visualizing how the successful result will impact your life. Believe in the magic of believing before the process and see it manifest itself. Take a leap of faith forward into the unknown and see your undertaking bear fruit. If you believe it, it will work for you and vice versa.

Physicians have testified that patients who believe in their prescriptions see the best results.

You can use the following outline to try for yourself:
- Look for a serene place. For instance, take a notepad, flashlight, and pen into a closet.
- Jot down all thoughts that come to mind, both empowering and disempowering.
- Exhaust all thoughts until they begin to repeat themselves.
- Separate programs into group (A) – empowering; group (B) - disempowering.
- Transcribe into positive heading (A): rich, happy, healthy, lucky, generous, successful, likeable, intelligent, confident, strong proactive, good-humored, smiley, blessed, hardworking, attractive ... and negative (B): poor, unhappy, sickly, wicket, bewitch, dishonest, stupid, weak, unlucky, quarrelsome, hated, moody,

greedy, unattractive, procrastinating, lazy, self-doubt.

Group B will dumbfound and daze you, but it is a crystal ball if harnessed. It will take you to the crest. It demands tremendous personal effort. When the daze is overwhelming, take a break but do not freak; resume after regaining sanity.

Negative programs also come from errors we committed in the past: unrealized dreams and aspirations, unforgiving and retributive attitude learned from unforgiving and avenging people around us, hatred of self/others, liking/love of self/others. The entire process is an ORDEAL: (Open, Right, Developmental, Enforcement, and Action (for) Life). It is the right action. Just be open and enforce it for your personal development. Eventually, your energy will lead to unstoppable synergy.

"You are the way you are because that's the way you want to be. If you wanted to be any different, you would be in the process of changing." said Fred Smith.

We are 100% in control of the process of decoding/re-encoding our subconscious and unleashing potential, just like we are in control of our attitude. The difference is that our negative programs might be influencing our attitude. Let's program our subconscious to work for us.

"The greatest discovery of my generation is that a human being can alter his life by altering his attitude." Said William James.

How can we reprogram the subconscious?

To be blind is bad, but worse is to have eyes and not see." said Helen Keller.

Synchronize the final process; fill the vacuum left by decoded negative programs with positive ones. It is the most difficult but groovy part of the process. Our burning desire to succeed will hone our power to alter the status quo, release our potential and unshackle us.

Unlike our minds, the subconscious works round the clock over our lifetime.

I came up with this formula to clear my path: Steadfast; Proactive; Assertive; Discipline and Emphatic (SPADE). I decided to pick up my SPADE and dig my goldmine. This metaphor propelled me to un-clutter my mind and get rid of the noise that held me back from moving forward. I apply SPADE in my daily activities.

SPADE forms the north arc; Action forms the south arc, meeting in the middle to form the circle of life. Diameter states: do it now; there is no tomorrow.

The Decoding and Reprogramming Process detailed here is systematic and has worked well for me:
- Understand the original cause of negative programs.
- What fuels programs?
- Negative programs are decoding support systems. (Is it the person, place, or thing?)
- Positive programs: supportive energy. (Is it the person, place or thing?)

- Use answers to handle corresponding situations promptly and assuredly.
- Note positive programs against negative ones.
- Example: rich > poor.
- Replace disempowering programs with corresponding empowering ones.
- Declare, affirm, meditate.
- Celebrate success and progress.
- Repeat process until corresponding positive programs replace negative ones.

I used the mirror technique created by Dr. Laura De Giorgio, a clinical hypnotherapist, in the decoding and encoding procedure. I look at myself squarely in the eyes in the mirror, build trust and bond with myself first. I encourage you to use this technique as well. Look in the mirror, ask self: am I poised for change? And be honest. The mirror reflects our image back to us, facilitates introspection, reaching into the subconscious to install our new software respecting our probing inquisitorial response/drive.

The mirror technique also helps translate our daily mantras, pep ourselves and prime our limitless possibilities. We have to Be, Do & Have respectively. Never try to Have, Be and then Do. Are we taking full advantage of our positive programs? Release their full potential. In the ORDEAL we will face obstacles, objections, mesmerisms, dilemmas… but our faith alone will resuscitate us.

I experienced a rollercoaster in some programs, and momentary crest falls in some. SPADE, daily meditations, declarations, and affirmations helped me get over most of them. Listen and watch motivational and inspirational tapes. Adjust or quit the relational illness environment that is holding you back and develop a nourishing mindset. READ (Rise Every day Above Death) & STUDY (Seek TuneUp Drive Yourself) consistently. Reading is the first step. Studying what you just read tunes you up, so you can apply yourself correctly through acquired knowledge; that is power!

You must take a conscious, meticulous approach to master your new positive programs through practice and exercise and unlearn the negative ones. The more engraved disempowering software was in your subconscious, the harder you have to work to reprogram it. For me, I revisited the reprogramming process several times, and I still do for the hard ones. I believe that the earlier in life one gets this awareness and uses this technique; the more reversible the situation. Once positive ones take root, you must practice and accentuate their benefits to prevent negative programs from resurfacing. The procedure is simple but not easy. Everyone can learn the art, apply the tact, earn the act, tell the facts and sell their story.

My first name is OLIVER (Open Life Invitation Earn Riches). I am inviting you to open up your life by giving reprogramming a chance because I am living proof that it works; this is not pontification. While in the process, I realized that I needed help, an accountability partner. Incidentally, my last name is ASAAH (Asking Seasoned Assistance Always Helps). That's how I decided to make my names acronyms and then put them in full to empower me in all my ventures.

We always need help from a loved supportive one who can hold us accountable and measure our progress, and reprimand us accordingly. It must be someone we trust and respect enough to bestow our life's purpose.

"Were it not for Tenzing the native guide, Edmund Hilary would not have made the historic climb of Mt. Everest." (John Maxwell 1984).

Do not frustrate yourself by expecting exquisite performance initially. Donald Trump's Apprentice became the number one reality show on NBC after several failures, but he chose to follow his instincts and not expert advice; hone your partner in crime for invincible results.

Everyone has empowering and disempowering programs. Just make sure the ratio greatly favors positive programs.

The reality is that 97 percent of the population works for three percent because our programming influences our choices. We can alter that equation by reprogramming our subconscious mind.

Biography

Being one of 24 siblings and having a Bachelor's in Law, Oliver Asaah has a powerful mélange of human relationships. He has several years of experience in network marketing in multiple companies. Oliver is a wellness entrepreneur building one of the biggest organizations in Genewize, a DNA customizing health, wellness & skincare solutions company. He is a speaker and mentor/coach who has a passion for motivating and inspiring people. Oliver has vested and harnessed the power of the subconscious through reprogramming and using his SPADE formula to maximize intuitive energy and synergy for personal and organizational achievement.

Contact Information

Oliver T. Asaah
Wealth Pool Industries
P O Box 1261
Greenbelt MD 20768
Phone: 301 537 2068
oliverasaah@yahoo.com

Chapter 17
THE JOURNEY OF SUCCESS

By Dr. Steven & Dr. Terresa Balestracci

Success is like a recipe; there are many ingredients. So, if there were a recipe for success, what would it be?

Well, perhaps the first step would be to have a dream, a reason, a why. Without this, it would be like going on a vacation without knowing where you are going.

Next, you need to have a plan or a vision. It would be the procedures to get to your destination. Some call it your roadmap.

After that, you would need the desire and passion to get you to your destination. We agree this would be your "fuel" to get you from point A to point B. This is vital to driving you toward your goal. Next, you need a support team or an accountability partner. This is very important so that you have people to encourage you along the way. This will assist you in overcoming the challenges that you will undoubtedly face.

You may not always have control over some of the challenges that you will face along your journey, but two things you can control are your thoughts and with whom you surround yourself. Achieving success is not easy, but surrounding yourself with people who believe in you, and support and encourage you will accelerate the speed at which you can reach success. This would also include reading books that inspire you to succeed and grow as a person.

Finally, the last step would be to celebrate! When you achieve your goals and dreams and every win along the way, you should rejoice and be thankful for the many blessings that you have.

We believe that a key ingredient to achieving success at any level is having faith, not only in ourselves but most of all, having faith in God. We believe that God puts dreams in our minds and hope in our hearts for a reason. He truly wants us to have the many blessings that he has to offer. We are truly thankful for the dreams and desires that the Lord has placed in our hearts and minds, and the daily courage He graces us with to live them out.

Placed in my heart and the daily courage He graces me with to live them out!

Our favorite quote on success is by George Sheehan which states, "Success means having the courage, the determination and the will to become the person you believe you were meant to be."

We love this quote because it is also the true meaning of success. Nowhere in the quote does it talk about how much money you make or how many material objects you possess. This quote can truly be applied to any person and any situation.

Without courage, you allow fear to prevent you from taking the next step that is vital to achieving success. Without determination, you allow challenges to prevent you from continuing on your path to achieving success.

One of the major challenges that we believe holds people back from achieving success is fear. Overcoming fear is one the most difficult things to do, but if a person does not overcome a fear that is a roadblock to achieving their goals, they will never achieve success associated with that goal or dream.

We believe that any super-successful person has had to overcome many fears and obstacles on their journey to success. And, by pushing through, you will grow as a person and be another step closer to achieving success.

An analogy that we can apply is that of a small child who is trying to walk. First, the child has to have the courage to take the first step and even after they try and try and fall many times, which represents the challenges, they must keep going, or they will never succeed in walking. If this child were to allow their fear of falling to get in the way, they would never even try again.

This is why we believe that it is an innate instinct for us to want to achieve. It is up to us whether we are going to allow the challenges that we face on our journey of success to strengthen us or weaken us. This is simply a decision that we must make that will allow us to turn our challenges into strengths.

To us, success is pursuing your dreams and goals despite the challenges that may occur during the process. We have had many challenges in our businesses and personal lives.

Whether it is a two-month delay in the build-out of our office space, an employee that has stolen from us, one of our kids getting sick, or losing a loved one, we have faced these challenges and never lost sight of our dreams and goals. What we have realized as we have grown over the years through our experiences and education is that the challenges never stop coming, but how we react to them has changed. For example, a situation that five years ago would have distracted us and taken us off the path to our goals for weeks or months, now only lasts for hours or days.

A mindset that we have learned to draw upon is to improvise, adapt and overcome which has allowed us to open our minds and understand that our minds are extremely powerful, so powerful that it brings to mind other quotes we continue to draw upon and try to impress upon others to do the same.

Just a few of these are:

"Whatever the mind can conceive, it can achieve!" and as Henry Ford has said "Whether you think you can or you think you can't…You're right." Something that Yoda said in the Star Wars series, "There is no try, there is only do or not do." Lastly, an important concept that we teach our kids, "Never let anyone's opinion of you become your reality unless it is a Positive opinion!"

We believe the greatest tip we have learned in life and business is forgiveness and being able to leave the past in the past. Not only is it vital to forgive others when they have wronged you, but it is just as important, to forgive yourself.

Not forgiving yourself can destroy your self-worth. And, it can send you down a path of self-destruction and mediocrity. It has happened to us many times in our lives where we were presented with challenges, things that hurt us financially and emotionally, and we dwelled on them and allowed them to steal happiness from our lives and enthusiasm from our spirits.

We have personally seen people in our personal and professional lives who carry baggage from the past and allow it to destroy their lives. They wind up getting ill, mentally and physically and prevent any chance of happiness and success they ever had.

Because of the personal growth and development training that we have experienced, we realized how much they held us back, and delayed and distracted us from our goals and dreams in the pursuit of our success.

We believe that some of the most important keys to achieving success are having desire and passion. We both grew up in Italian-American households where there was a great deal of influence from family members.

Food was always present no matter what the occasion or lack of occasion. The main thing about this combination of family, food, and conversation was passion and desire. These people were very passionate and expressive, to say the least, about what seemed like everything they spoke of, regardless of whether it was a sporting event, last night's dinner or a day at "work."

The majority of them desired to be more successful than the last generation, as was the last generation's desire for them. This love of life and people was a driving force in their pursuit of happiness and success, and has influenced us and helped to define who we are today.

Other major influences that have impacted our lives are our role models and mentors. While we learned from many authors, speakers, and educators, we do have a few favorites.

Two of our favorite role models are B.J. Palmer, developer of chiropractic and world-renowned educator and entrepreneur, and Warren Buffet, world-renowned entrepreneur, and business mogul. They represent success achieved through passion, desire, and vision.

Two of our favorite mentors are Marc Accetta, world-renowned trainer, speaker, and entrepreneur, and Matt Morris, world-renowned best-selling author, speaker, and entrepreneur. Marc and Matt are both incredibly successful people who have taught us so much about life and helped us achieve our current level of success through their guidance, incredible leadership and training. They are passionate about teaching people to achieve the success that they have, which is a quality that we greatly admire.

The thing that we are most passionate about is helping people. This is why we pursued our careers in chiropractic. We feel that chiropractic can positively impact people's lives more profoundly since we, as doctors/teachers, empower people to take a more active role in their health and well-being rather than being victims and passively existing through the symptom-based system that the current healthcare model offers.

We also have passion and desire to help people through our other business in the industry of network marketing and travel. It is with this business that we have learned personal growth and development skills, as well as the skills to create additional streams of income and be able to assist others to achieve the same. As we experience wins in our businesses by helping people, we achieve spiritual and emotional wins for ourselves. This is the satisfaction that continues to motivate us to keep going in our pursuit of success.

Another desire we have as we continue to pursue our dreams is that we make our children proud of us. We believe that the best way we can do this is to live with passion, have the courage to finish what we start and lead by example.

We try to be as mindful of this as possible as we raise our three children. We want them to have their own dreams, and we do not want to live vicariously through them and prevent them from reaching their full potential. Also, we remind them that even when they have a class or subject that they do not have much interest in that they should put forth the effort, because they might just be surprised at the outcome, especially about the growth of self-confidence and self-worth.

When we were growing up, we always had the desire for our parents to be proud of us; however, now that we have kids, they are who we most want to make proud. We feel that achieving this would be one of the greatest successes in our lives.

As parents and successful business owners, we believe that you have to lead by example. Whether you see yourself as a leader or not, many of us are viewed that way because of the actions that we take and the way that we inspire the people around us. Leadership is a combination of many qualities that an individual must possess.

A true leader is someone who can motivate people to take action through communication and representation as well as having the ability to overcome resistance to challenges to attain a common goal for the betterment of both the individual and the team. A great leader, Zig Ziglar, once said, "If you help enough other people get what they want, you get what you want."

Finally, for us, we have realized that success in a culmination of many components with some of the main ones being faith, vision, passion, desire, belief, courage, resilience, attitude, humbleness, integrity, honor, purpose, leadership, knowledge and the application of knowledge.

We are truly blessed and humbled to have the opportunity to share some of our thoughts on success to positively impact the lives of others with the hopes that this will assist them on their journey of success.

Biography

Dr. Steven & Dr. Terresa Balestracci met in Davenport, Iowa, while attending Palmer College of Chiropractic where they both graduated with Doctor of Chiropractic degrees. They have owned a successful chiropractic office in Bridgewater, New Jersey, for over 15 years. They have been involved in network marketing with a company called WorldVentures where they rank in the top 1% of the company's independent representatives. Michael, Gianna, and Cristian, their three children, inspire them to strive to achieve higher levels of success and for whom they desire to leave a legacy.

Contact Information

Dr. Steven & Dr. Terresa Balestracci
Phone: 484-375-5380 / 484-375-5385
Address: 2385 Silvano Dr., Macungie, PA 18062

Chapter 18
ESSENTIAL SUCCESS: "A LIVING TRANSFORMATION"

By Ray Blanchard, Ph.D.

If you knew you only had a short time to live, and then it's going to be over, what would you do with the rest of your life?

This message is for individuals who desire to succeed beyond measure and who are urgent to live their true potential. That means living with purpose and passion. That means having the courage to dream big and to go after what you want like the present is all you have. In this crash course on self-transformation, several basic understandings and distinctions are shared so you can flip the switch to your success. It will be the reader's challenge to live such wisdom and to keep those distinctions alive.

My story may be like yours, a typical "zero to hero" scenario. It reveals lessons for a clear path to change lives for the better. It is amazing how these humble beginnings built such a solid foundation for the achievements that followed.

I am one of 12 children, born to a strong-willed Mississippi farmer. I am the youngest of six sons. My mother always stressed learning from your hardships and moving on without complaining and giving something to your neighbors along the way. Life was a struggle for my parents, always barely making ends meet. Finally, when I was about 12 years old, the ravages of a tornado tearing through the little shotgun house we lived in forced us to pick up and leave the farm my father worked since he was born some 66 years earlier. I had been a "smart" little kid in the country school where my aunt was the principal, and most of the grades were in the same room.

But, moving to the big city in St. Louis, I was quite unprepared to compete with my classmates initially. Not liking that, I worked hard to prove myself, to help the family out and make my parents proud. I got a job in a grocery store and ran a newspaper route. I paid for my clothes and school supplies. By the second year in high school, I was able to start sports, where I learned to strive even harder and always aim to win. By taking a new job in the morning before school at the local hospital and running two miles through the park to make it to morning classes, I became a good athlete and student. My counselors took notice of my efforts and decided to help me get into college since my parents would not have been able to help me at all. Forging ahead with encouragement from my advisor, I finally got a break. I went to night school at Washington University in St. Louis until I earned the opportunity to go full time. One professor took a special interest in me, after noticing my love for classical philosophy, and helped me to get two degrees and a fellowship to a doctoral program where I excelled.

Two key mentors pushed and goaded me to keep moving until I graduated to become a Doctor of Philosophy in Psychology after a little more than three years. My proudest moment was when my mom was able to come 2,000 miles on her first airplane flight to see the first of her brood get an advanced college degree. Since then, other mentors at significant stages of my life helped me go to the next level of success, through the wisdom they had gained and imparted to me. The unbelievable support from these life coaches has taken me around the world in more ways than one and has stewarded me to extraordinary accomplishments and joy. I feel blessed and grateful, and I live with the passion for giving back.

The greatest success lesson in all my experiences is to *"always believe,"* especially when the light is dim, and there doesn't seem to be a way out. Keep your belief strong and determined to outlast the challenges. Don't ever give up on what matters. You often gain the victory in the darkest hour, by that one extra heave or burst of effort like your life depended on it. In the race for life, it's that last act that gives you victory or marks the final arrival of a long journey.

The completion of a heartfelt commitment is the ultimate arrival. But, it is the process of getting there with joy and passion that is the best and most meaningful. If you can live your life with joy and ease while attaining satisfaction in personal, professional and spiritual affairs, you are a success.

On your way to the top, it is important to give back and help someone else. *"Reach back and pull someone else up."* Pay it forward. This is both satisfaction for you, and it makes a difference in the social consciousness of the world. These are the yin and yang of a principled life, and the most important character traits in achieving complete success – getting results and being a giver.

Four key factors are always present in my successes and are most often in those giants we revere as well: (1) hard work, (2) knowledge, (3) attitude and (4) love of God or the Almighty.

Hard Work

Let's face it - life can be tough. Not many successes have been authentically achieved without hard work. That does not mean that life has to be hard. It just means be prepared and go the extra mile. Make it a practice.

For instance, if you are exercising, do a few more minutes or add a few extra repetitions. It is well established that the greatest consistent results come from the extra efforts rather than the easy actions with which you start.

In relationships, you should stretch yourself and have a few more authentic conversations with loved ones and colleagues each week. You will quickly realize that you have super-powered your network of support. Support is vital to being the best you can be and to giving peak performances. Plus, you tend to open up a lot more opportunities and possibilities, personally and professionally, because you reached out.

Refrain from having to be "right" in every conversation. "Being Right" is a social disease and an addiction that destroys relationships on all levels. At least two or three times a week, be conscious of your impulse to dig in your heels to argue your point. Then "let it go." Create win-win interactions and experiences that will uplift your friendships and open more space for everyone to grow. All will be happier and healthier for it, and it is widely believed to add a few more years to your life as well.

These acts may take more focused awareness of your relationships, but the rewards are worth it in terms of your experience of success. You shape the consciousness landscape that surrounds you and enhance your social capital among your peers.

Also, invest a few hours a week in personal growth and inner development activities. The value you gain accumulates and even compounds. By the end of a month, you will notice a big difference. By the end of a year, you will have put in almost a week's investment into yourself. Remember that, after your maker, YOU are the ANSWER and the key to your success.

I strongly suggest pursuing effective empowerment seminars as well. You can learn more about yourself sometimes from such outside sources than you can ever learn from your already existing views of life. I had a true "enlightenment experience" in a seminar in the early years of my professional life, which was life-altering. I treasure it to this day. It could be like that for you, too.

Knowledge

Knowledge is the key to power. And, power is the ability to turn possibility into reality. The first principle of knowledge is to "know thyself." To accomplish that, one needs to examine his life and see what makes himself tick thoroughly. Sorting through your past experiences and beliefs can tell you why you feel, think and do what you do, and why you get the results you get. Realizing this gives you access to your life script and behavior patterns at the root level, thereby allowing you to create a new map or blueprint for success.

You should practice going into deep thought a few minutes a day to specifically examine the genesis of various beliefs you have, and make corrections that would lead to more expertise, free choice and precise actions that create the results you want. Learn to use the "stop-look-listen" process for self-reflection and life improvement. Stop being on auto-pilot and reactive behavior. Look at life from a new angle or perspective. Listen to your heartfelt commitment rather than negative self-talk. This will help you to make strides toward your higher goals steadily.

Also, take time to reflect on the material you read each day, and examine it from different angles and understandings. Don't be a "yes" machine. Challenge ideas. This is a practice in discipline and critical analysis, which enriches your creativity and ability to invent new possibilities.

You should dedicate an extra two hours a week focusing on a hobby. It will keep you fresh and will likely play a part in the rest of your career, by adding richness and a new dimension to whatever you do. The added time per year that you put into your deeper interests and career will put you heads and shoulders above your peers and will give you the competitive edge to increase your chances for greatness.

Attitude

All reality is dictated by the context that supports it. Positive thoughts lead to positive attitude and actions, and negative ones lead to negative outcomes. In effect, thoughts are things. It would be prudent to deliberately train your attitude and thought processes to generate your desire. This is the key to flipping the switch to success.

Several years ago, one of my good friends who had a less-than-pleasant attitude came to this realization and did something about it, and it significantly shifted his business. He made a paradigm shift to accentuate the positive and eliminate the negative. He started a slogan for his company and followed it: *"I shall not complain."*

He made it a point to eliminate at least a few complaints a day, noting each time he interrupted his negative thoughts. The impact of eliminating several hundred negative imprints a year altered his outlook and ultimately created more customers.

Consider doing the same exercise for a year. Include thoughts about your job, family, neighbor, the weather, love life, bank account, the economy, friends, etc. *"You reap what you sow."* Change your mind and change your life.

Love of God or the Almighty

The human condition is the continuous search for meaning and fulfillment. This usually brings up our spiritual reality, what sustains us and supports our reason for being.

Truth and meaning are a matter of interpretation. We are continuously interpreting and assessing our spiritual reality, making meaning out of it, and using our interpretations and meanings to act in ways we think would fulfill our lives.

Regardless of how one arrives at their conclusion, the majority of well-known great achievers indicate that material success alone is meaningless, and success without having a sense of fulfilling a higher purpose is emptiness.

Some people, for instance, interpret that there is a greater source of life and meaning outside of our own interpretation, and it is our pleasure to serve It. Some do not. We get to choose for ourselves, which is true for us. Our happiness and motivation often depend on it. For me, the Almighty source of life and meaning is God.

The pursuit of meaning or truth is a very personal and private matter. The sooner you begin the quest, it is to your advantage. Regardless of what you discover, the act of giving and making a difference through service seems to be on the right path to finding out. It provides the most empowering sense of purpose and deep satisfaction that propels us to achieve.

Contributing to world transformation and peace are popular undertakings. Healing the environment, ending hunger on the planet or providing health needs to the sick are also possibilities. Serving your community, church or charity are other ways to quell the thirst. Contributing a few hours of service a week will culminate in several weeks a year of giving to others and making a difference. It makes you feel good about yourself. It is life-redeeming, and it powerfully affects your sense of value.

Success is determined by how well you live your life. Wealth, character or a combination thereof, are the measures. The defining factors include: the risks you take, the courage you demonstrate, the ease in letting go of disappointment and pain, the ability to shift your points of view and come off "autopilot," the ability to think and create possibility in the face of the impossible, how you include people and bring them forward, the patience and love expressed and received, and the difference you make in the lives of others.

Leaders possess these qualities in abundance, and in sharing them, they make the difference between potential and reality. *"Having what it takes and not using it is a waste, but living such qualities can transform the world."*

Success is self-realization. Being real and being oneself is the most one can be. Our challenge is to strive for such completeness so that we reach the pinnacle of human achievement and excellence. My favorite quote, *"To thine own self, be true,"* captures it succinctly.

The way of the Buddha is an exquisite example. It is the way of ease, where effort and effortlessness are balanced in perfect harmony. It demonstrates integrity, which is *Essential Success.* The life of Jesus is a perfect model of success in action, handling challenges and relating to others. He is an example of acceptance and inclusion, never giving up, purpose and passion, and overcoming while still loving - *A Living Transformation.* Together they represent our ultimate goal, which is to be whole, perfect and complete. And that is *Essential Success: A Living Transformation.*

Biography

Dr. Ray Blanchard, the founder of Blanchard Consulting Group, is a seasoned entrepreneur, consultant, and media producer. He earned his Ph.D. from the University of Oregon and garnered praise for his films *THE ANSWER To Absolutely Everything* and the *FIRESIDE FORUM.* With more than 100,000 client-graduates worldwide, he was elected to the esteemed *Transformational Leadership Council.*

Contact Information

Dr. Ray Blanchard
youcountnow@gmail.com
541-912-8571
www.rayblanchard.com

Chapter 19
REACHING SUCCESS WITH EXCELLENCE

By Ellen Reid

It seems like every day I wake up, and there's something new and different about my industry. And I don't mean some little change; I'm talking about something earthshaking, life-changing, revolutionary.

Okay, maybe it's not every day. However, it started a few years ago, and the momentum is most definitely building. I work in the publishing industry, specifically the self-publishing end of it. I've been involved in this exciting field since 1998, and I have seen what feels like a century's worth of changes take place in just over a decade. These include things like digital printing, print on demand, and, most recently, e-books and readers.

However, one thing I have observed to be constant is that those authors and books that have been successful – and in fact, people who are successful in any area of endeavor, whether business or personal life – are those that demonstrate excellence. I have made excellence the cornerstone of my success.

"Excellence" has become my mantra, my branding, and my way of life. I'm not saying that excellence will guarantee success. However, I can't imagine real success without excellence being a part of it.

I wouldn't say excellence has always been a part of my life. However, it is something that was tempered in the fires of my life's adventures. My father was of the narcissistic persuasion, so no matter what I accomplished it somehow became about him. I soon learned that he demanded perfection, which, even to this day, I don't believe is possible. However, I was continually striving to do better and better. I may have missed perfection, but I guarantee you, I developed a real track record of excellence.

As I grew and matured, pursuing studies in personal growth, I came to learn how to transform my feelings of frustration with my father's unattainable demands into positive motivation to excel. Whether it was in my first career in sales and marketing, where I rose up the ranks to international buyer, frequently being sent to Asia to develop products, or my current consulting/book shepherding career, in which I have been acknowledged Beverly Hills' Premier Book Consultant, I found myself compelled to both produce excellence and encourage others to it.

Excellence is an interesting concept. People know it when they see it, but they may not know *why* they recognize something as excellent.

In my work, there are certain definite guidelines for what excellence is not. For example, typos in a book are a sure sign of less than excellent work – and this erodes the value of the message. So, for me, one major element of excellence is attention to detail.

That can be reflected by a well-proofread galley, which is pretty evident to everyone. But, it can also be reflected in subtle things like the amount of space between lines on a page (called leading – which is a term taken for the days of hand-setting type with individual letters cast from metal, like lead, and adding a line of lead in between the lines) or the amount of space between letters, called kerning. (I have no idea why they call it that.)

Another thing – one of those changes I was talking about – is that computers instill a false sense of ability. Anyone with a computer and Microsoft Word can create what may look like an actual book. But it's not, which you can tell when you compare a page done in Word with a page done by a professional with a page layout program. This leads me to another big tip: Know when you can handle something yourself and know when it will serve you to bring in a professional.

When it comes to excellence, professionals are worth their weight in platinum. What I have observed is that some people are great at some aspects of their work, mediocre at other aspects and downright poor at others. So, one key I've found for myself and that I share with clients is to evaluate what's necessary for any task and determine which you can legitimately do yourself and which you need help to do.

I counsel people to be ruthless with themselves and not be afraid to admit there are just some things they're not great at doing. While there may be some subtle message in our culture that says we're supposed to be able to do everything ourselves, in my experience, it's the very rare person who can do it all with excellence.

With writers, the things they need to look at include the actual writing of their book. Even the biggest names in the business, authors who have made millions and published lots of books, will tell you that one of their greatest assets and allies is their editor. While you may not be an author, you most likely do write letters for your business. Make sure they are well proofed, if possible by someone other than you. Catch all the typos, make sure it looks good on the page, neither too high or too low on your letterhead. Make sure your point is stated and what you are asking the recipient to do is specific.

Okay, I know you may not send a lot of letters, but I'll bet you send several emails each day. While some of the ideas above may not apply, do proofread your emails for typos and grammar. And make sure what you're saying is clear.

Back to my writing clients. Not only do they need to start by making sure their manuscript is in excellent shape, but they also need to have a powerful cover. This means they need to get a book cover designer, not the daughter of a friend of theirs who did very well in her college design class. Book design is a specialized field and not every good graphic designer knows the ins & outs of book cover design. Ditto interior design. You would be amazed at the difference in readability when a good interior book designer gets hold of a manuscript.

Presumably, you can translate what I'm saying here to your own life and business. If you are putting something out that represents you or your business – and I mean anything from a wedding invitation to a printed brochure – make sure it's done right, by a professional if necessary, if you want it to reflect excellence. And do your homework; if you're looking for a professional, don't just pick the first name that comes up when you google graphic designer. Part of excellence is following up with samples of work and references from others who have used the person's services.

Another area that comes up for my clients is promotional writing. On books, that's everything from the title and subtitle, to the back cover and the short author's bio. What I often have to communicate with my clients is that just because they can write an excellent book does not mean they can write the text that is needed to sell their masterpiece. Again, it's a matter of finding a professional who can articulate what you're offering in a way that potential customers will recognize it as having value to <u>them</u>. My experience is that many – maybe most – people are so close to their message, product, or service, that they want to tell everyone about all of it. A good promotional copywriter will be able to advise on how much needs to be said to generate interest, and how much is so much information that you lose interest.

Bottom line, what I preach and what I practice is that the right resource people – those who demonstrate excellence – will contribute to my excellence. And that contributes to my success.

Which brings me to the question, what is success?. When I was younger, I thought success was easy to measure. It had to do with how much money you made. Then, after I had made a fair amount of money, I discovered that I didn't feel particularly successful.

So, I began exploring success from the inside out, which involved things like spirituality and personal growth. Those explorations revealed many avenues that I am still considering and dealing with myself. This is a lot like peeling away layers of an onion in that there's always another layer to work through. I expect these pursuits to be ongoing pretty much as long as I've got a body and am here on this earth.

In the end, it was probably this inner questing that brought my awareness to excellence. I find that to have genuine satisfaction in my life, I not only need to have balance in my life but I also need to make sure that I am feeling fulfilled by what I am doing. I am driven to do excellent work and to have my work reflect the excellence of who I am– and, in a very real sense the excellence of who we all are. I find great satisfaction in encouraging my clients to be more of who they can be.

I can't tell you how great it feels to hear how thrilled a client is when they receive their book from the printer and hold it in their hands for the first time. In virtually every case, they tell me that it's far beyond what they had ever envisioned. They feel great, and I feel good because I know they have achieved something they can be very proud of – because it reflects excellence.

Biography

Ellen Reid is a Book Shepherd extraordinaire. Since 1998 she has been assisting authors in exceeding their dreams for an outstanding book they can be proud of, and that stands up to any competition. Acknowledged as Beverly Hills' Premier Book Consultant, Ellen has built her career on excellence. She is the author of the award-winning *Putting Your Best Book Forward; A book shepherd's secrets for creating award-winning books that sell.*

Contact Information

Ellen Reid
Book Shephard
(310) 862-2573
ellen@bookshep.com

Chapter 20
BECOMING THE MAN IN THE ARENA

By Mikel Erdman

I grew up on a farm in southwestern Oregon, in a very small town named Bandon. It's famous now because a rich guy from Chicago came and built some of the top-rated golf courses in the world there. When I was growing up, it was nothing like that. It was a sleepy coastal town surviving on the final feast of the logging and fishing industries and very little else.

My dad was in the meat business just like his father before him, and his grandfather before him. In the summers, we fished our commercial salmon troller for Chinook and Coho salmon and occasionally took off after albacore tuna if they came close enough to the shore. Working these businesses meant long hours and sore muscles and a lot of ingenuity and resourcefulness to stay afloat.

I was surrounded by hard work while growing up, the kind of work that they would feature on the television show "Dirty Jobs." In fact, these were the type of jobs that you had to have a whole different set of clothes for work than you'd ever wear for anything else. It was next to impossible to get the smells out once you've worn them around the feedlot or in the back end of the boat with diesel fumes, fish innards, and cow manure.

From as early as I can remember, I was doing chores and participating in the family businesses. Believe it or not, just growing up in that small business, the do-it-yourself atmosphere had a lot to do with me achieving a high level of success in my life. I learned a whole lot of lessons about dealing with adversity and rising to the challenge.

I saw the magic of new ideas formulated in my mind and then brought to reality by the power of vision, dedication, and persistence. And I learned one of the most important lessons about success right there in the middle of those hard, dirty jobs — that not all good ideas work out and true success comes to those who are willing to face their failures and step out once again to achieve their dreams.

In fact, if you look at some of the most successful people in the world, their careers never shoot to the top without any challenges or setbacks along the way. Some of the most respected and revered leaders in our land seemed to be just a long string of failures accentuated by moments of greatness and characterized by the unwillingness to give up or give in.

Take this person for example:

He was born into poverty and early in his life, his family was broke and were forced out of their home. He had to work as a child to support them. His mother passed away when he was only nine years old. By 22, he had started and failed in his own business. Shortly after that, he ran for public office and lost, then started a second business which failed within two years, on borrowed money. A few years later, his fiancée died unexpectedly, and he suffered a complete nervous breakdown. Throughout his life, he lost eight separate elections, but in 1860, he was finally elected President of the United States of America. Who was he? Mr. Abraham Lincoln.

There is no question that Abraham Lincoln is one of the most revered leaders in all of American history. When you look at the record of his life, however, you'd be hard-pressed to believe in his greatness, up until the point that he successfully led his country through one of the most critical periods of its existence. What if he had given up? What if he had quit after his first business failed?

It's clear that Mr. Lincoln's failures did not define the altitude of his achievement. And this point is true for you too! It's one of the hardest lessons to learn and is critical to your success in life. You have the power to change. You have the power to make course corrections throughout your life and learn from the challenges that you encounter along your journey. You and only you can permit yourself to use that wisdom to move forward and make your mark on the world.

Growing up in an entrepreneurial environment and seeing this cycle of success and failure play out has led me to understand that it isn't a single defeat that can cause you to lose the game of life. Your success is based on your willingness to get up off the ground, dust yourself off and get yourself back in the game. You must understand that it's just part of the process and isn't unique to you.

In my own life, I've had to overcome a few colossal failures. I once started a real estate advertising technology firm that took off like a rocket ship. We had developed a novel new technology product that made a lot of sense in the marketplace and added a lot of value to the businesses of real estate agents, mortgage lenders and other real estate professionals who used our systems. We grew the company from zero, with no outside investment, to over 1 million dollars in sales and from 2 to 35 employees within 18 months. I thought we'd hit the big one, and I was only 33 years old at the time.

It felt like that entrepreneurial dream had come true. There were a lot of expenses, but the cash-flow was great, and it looked like we had made it! In fact, this was the first time in my life that I knew what it meant to have no money troubles at all. We were completely debt-free outside of the home and had plenty of reserves stashed away. We had more money than we knew what to do with it.

I wish I could tell you that the fairy tale lasted, the business continued to grow, and we rode off into the sunset with our bags of riches. It didn't. In the second winter, the business changed fast. The technology that our business was based on completely revolutionized within the two years we were in business and made a large part of what we delivered irrelevant. And the employees and overhead didn't slow down at the same rate as the revenue coming in.

They say that the larger a ship is, the longer it takes to slow it down or change its course. That is true in business. All of the sales revenue that we made in the run-up of the company had been reinvested, and the overhead started to eat us alive. We ended up closing the company at the three-year mark with hundreds of thousands of dollars of our personal investment lost.

Let me tell you something that hurt. I mean it physically hurt. I was crushed. I had poured three years of my life working up to 16 hours a day to make this dream come true. I had a serious case of self-doubt that I could ever make anything successful again. I mean, if you had something so powerful that took off so fast and made so much money while doing an incredible amount of good in the world and you lost it all, wouldn't you question your ability to make it happen again?

It took a couple of months to start feeling better after that failure, but the resilience that I learned back on the farm showed up, and I set my sights on the next chapter of my life. I got busy and came up with a new plan. I set out to reinvent myself. I had to pull myself and my family out of this financial wasteland. I went on over the next three years to have the highest personal income years in my entire career.

What would have happened if I'd just given up? Sure, I had a lot of reasons to lie on the couch and throw a big pity party. A lot of people would have understood why I wasn't achieving anything after seeing that huge "swing-and-a-miss." In fact, I had a few of them telling me that maybe I should just lie low, you know, get a safe and secure job and give up on those big dreams. But I knew, deep down in my heart, that the failure of that one business couldn't define who I was in the world and the value that I could continue to bring people in so many ways.

It's the same way for you too! No matter what trials and tribulations you've faced on your journey thus far, you can decide right here and now that you're going on to bigger and better things. You can set your sights on the pinnacle of your achievement and with commitment, hard work, and persistence, you can make those dreams turn into reality.

Most importantly, I want every one of you to know that you have everything it takes to achieve your goals. You have been given the most powerful computer, a sound operating system, and the most incredible architecture ever known on the face of the Earth since the day you were created. It's up to you to harness that power and make a decision to accomplish your goals.

Recently, as we were celebrating the New Year and looking forward to the great events and successes to come in the year ahead, I had a startling and somewhat chilling revelation. This was not just a new year; this was a new decade. A new decade! I realized that at the end of this decade, I would be nearing 50 years old, my children would be most of the way through their school years and off to college, and I would have come upon the time in my life that I had always dreamed of, being retired early and traveling the world. I gulped hard and felt my hands get a little clammy.

I got just a little bit anxious about what I would accomplish, starting off into this new era of my life. There have been many times in my life that I was in this same position. It seems like the nervousness never quite goes away. That familiar dark, burning feeling in the pit of my stomach that begs the question "Mikel, are you up to the challenge?"

I made a decision right then that this decade would be the most productive era of my life and I would dedicate myself to plan and execute better than ever before. You see, that has been one of the most critical secrets to my success, and it's the same with every other successful person that I've ever met, listened to, or read about. The willingness to take the uneasiness and uncertainty of challenging circumstances and face them head-on is a hallmark of a true leader.

Napoleon Hill, one of the greatest thought leaders who ever lived, said it best "Whatever the mind can conceive and believe, the mind can achieve."

James Nesmith had a dream of improving his golf game – and he developed a unique method of achieving his goal. Until he devised this method, he was just your average weekend golfer, shooting in mid- to low-nineties. Then, for seven years, he completely quit the game. He never touched a club. He never set foot on a fairway.

Ironically, it was during this seven-year break from the game that he came up with his amazingly effective technique for improving his game – a technique we can all learn from. In fact, the first time he set foot on a golf course after his hiatus from the game, he shot an astonishing 74! He cut 20 strokes off his average without having swung a golf club in seven years! Unbelievable! Not only that, but his physical condition had deteriorated during those seven years.

What was his secret? Visualization. You see, Major Nesmith had spent those seven years as a prisoner of war in North Vietnam. During those seven years, he was imprisoned in a cage that was approximately four and one-half feet high and five feet long.

During almost the entire time, he was imprisoned, he saw no one, talked to no one and experienced no physical activity. During the first few months, he did virtually nothing but hope and prayed for his release. Then he realized he had to find some way to occupy his mind or he would lose his sanity and probably his life. That's when he learned the power of building his future in his mind's eye.

In his mind, he selected his favorite golf course and started playing golf. Every day, he played a full 18 holes at the legendary country club of his dreams. He experienced everything to the last detail. He saw himself dressed in his golfing clothes. He smelled the fragrance of the trees and the freshly trimmed grass. He experienced different weather conditions – windy spring days, overcast winter days, and sunny summer mornings.

In his imagination, every detail, the individual blades of grass, the trees, the singing birds, the scampering squirrels and the lay of the course became real.

He felt the grip of the club in his hands. He instructed himself as he practiced smoothing out his down-swing and the follow-through on his shot. Then he watched the ball arc down the exact center of the fairway, bounce a couple of times and roll to the exact spot he had selected, all in his mind.

In the real world, he was in no hurry. He had no place to go. So, in his mind, he took every step on his way to the ball, just as if he was physically on the course. It took him just as long as the imaginary time to play 18 holes as it would have taken in reality. Not a detail was omitted. Not once did he ever miss a shot, never a hook or a slice, never a missed putt.

Eighteen holes of golf every day, seven days a week for seven years. Twenty strokes off his score for a lifetime best score of 74.

Here is the question for all of us as we start our new decade:

What are you visualizing?

What do you have your mind focused on and where is that focus taking you?

Without a clear vision of where you are going, you're likely to get lost along the way. You may end up looking back at the beginning of 2020 wondering which road you took and how you arrived where you are.

It's your choice. It all comes down to a few simple planning steps and committed action on a daily basis in the direction of your dreams.

1. Fix in your mind the exact goal or desire in your life.
2. Determine exactly what you intend to give in return for the achievement of your goal.
3. Establish a definite date for the achievement of the goal.
4. Create a definite plan for carrying out your desire and begin at once, whether you are ready or not, to put this plan into action
5. Write a clear and concise statement including the exact goal, what you intend to give in return, the time limit for its achievement and the plan through which you intend to succeed.
6. Read your written statement aloud for a minimum of twice daily, once

immediately after arising in the morning, and once again immediately before retiring at night.

In closing, I'd like to leave you with two comments. The first of these is that your failures don't define you and can't defeat you unless you let them. Failure is simply a reflection point on your way to your ultimate destination. Failures are an opportunity to learn what to do better next time and to develop the wisdom that you'll need to impact the lives of many in a positive way.

Lastly, I want you to know that taking a step into the unknown on faith is purely courageous. If you have a desire to become more in the world, if you have a song in your heart that has not been released to the wind, if you have a blessing inside of you waiting to burst out showing your greatness to the world, then get moving. Don't waste a single moment worrying about what might happen if you fail. Do everything in your power to avoid failure but accept setbacks as part of the process of achieving your dreams.

And finally, a favorite quote from one of our cherished American leaders, Teddy Roosevelt, who reminds us that the person of action and determination is to be admired:

"It is not the critic who counts; not the man who points out how the strong man stumbles, or where the doer of deeds could have done them better. The credit belongs to the man who is actually in the arena, whose face is marred by dust and sweat and blood; who strives valiantly; who errs, who comes short again and again, because there is no effort without error and shortcoming; but who does actually strive to do the deeds; who knows great enthusiasms, the great devotions; who spends himself in a worthy cause; who at the best knows in the end the triumph of high achievement, and who at the worst, if he fails, at least fails while daring greatly, so that his place shall never be with those cold and timid souls who neither know victory nor defeat."

Biography

Mikel Erdman has been engaging and inspiring sales and marketing professionals for more than 15 years. A product of the success principles he teaches, Mikel started his entrepreneurial career immediately after graduating from college. He became a self-made millionaire at the age of 30. He has successfully started and grown multiple companies in the mortgage, technology, and advertising arenas.

Contact Information

Mikel Erdman
Goodyear, Arizona
(360) 450-3551
http://www.mikelerdman.com

Chapter 21
INSPIRATION WHEN YOU LEAST EXPECT IT

By Brian Mahany

There is a picture on my refrigerator, a picture of a little boy. He is a little boy that I have never met, a boy with a bright smile even though he is suffering from an extremely rare and deadly cancer. Why is this picture on my refrigerator? Hopefully, by the end of this story, you will know the answer.

Although I have a large and beautiful home office, I frequently set up my laptop in the kitchen and work there. For many people, the kitchen is the "center" of their home. Across from the kitchen table stands the refrigerator. Like most other homes, our refrigerator does more than just keep food cold; it also serves as a message center and a place to display pictures, artwork, and magnets from trips taken long ago.

There are four pictures on my refrigerator. A Christmas family photo sent by a friend, one of my long-ago deceased family pet mastiff named Bear, a picture of my late father taken during World War II, and one of the little boy whose name I do not know.

Our world is filled with many people who struggle through life. They are everywhere. People living paycheck to paycheck. People struggling in dead-end jobs or failing relationships. You don't have to look far to find these people. Some only have to look in the mirror.

The sad reality is that a few will never find happiness or take advantage of a second chance in life. They will never see or seize the opportunities around them. From my days as a police officer and later as a prosecutor, I saw many failed lives. People who made the same mistakes repeatedly, who abandoned God or their higher power, who simply gave up hope or who turned to drugs, crime or alcohol as their sole salvation.

Thankfully, there are many people around us who make us smile, who motivate us to do better, who offer hope in uncertain times.

Fortunately for me, I have many successes in life. Career successes, financial freedom, travel, and a great family and friends. With all those successes, I should have no complaints. But few of us lead fairy tale lives. Misfortune happens to everyone at some point in his or her life. Disease strikes, businesses fail, relationships often hit rough spots.

Last year, my streak of good luck hit a rough patch. The firm I worked for fell on financially hard times and suddenly had to let some folks go. As the last hired, I was also the first fired. Ever the optimist, I looked at my sudden loss of work as an opportunity, a chance to start my own law firm.

Eagerly, I began ordering stationary, developing a website and scouting for new clients. What I did not anticipate were the thousands of other great lawyers that were also losing their jobs and a large number of recent law school grads that could not find any work in the field.

One very bright young lawyer I know found himself working as a part-time assistant zookeeper in charge of "cleaning up" after elephants and other large animals. Although happy to have a job, this certainly was not the career he signed up for when enrolling in law school three years earlier.

Just as these lawyers were struggling so was our new business. We happened to pick the worst economy in decades to hang out our shingle and start a business.

My earlier enthusiasm soon turned to fear. Without any money for advertising, how could we let clients know of our business and bring them to our door? How would we pay office rent? Our lack of income was beginning to weigh me down.

The legal profession was also changing. New lawyers facing tens of thousands of dollars of unpaid student loans were suddenly advertising rates so ridiculously low that we wondered if clients would even consider paying for our experience and hiring us.

Each day, the fear became worse. How much longer could I keep up with the mortgage? If suddenly finding myself unemployed at age 50 and struggling to start a new practice in the worst economy of my generation was not enough stress in my life, my beloved mother passed away.

With each passing day, the fear became worse; it turned into depression.

In November of 2010, one of my best friends called to ask for a favor. Would I accompany him to a fundraiser? I certainly was not thrilled with the idea, particularly with little money to contribute.

I attended more out of a sense of duty and did not know anything about the event other than the fact that one of our mutual friends organized it. Once there, I learned that the event was not simply a fundraiser. It was an event to celebrate the life of a young child suffering from a rare and virulent type of cancer. It was a way for the parents to give back to the community and say thanks. It was also an event to raise money for a charity that helps other families of children facing serious illness.

Not until I arrived did I learn how selfless the family was that threw this party. More importantly, not until I arrived did I realize that the little boy was the son of a mutual friend.

On my way to the event, I called my friend and pledged to stay for a few minutes of pleasantries then politely bow out. It was a Friday night after all, and I had plans to share a few cocktails with other friends at a sports bar and watch a game.

Throughout the cocktail hour, the little boy was running around the party. He ran from table to table surrounded by adults in jackets and dresses, this little boy. He was beaming, taking pictures and laughing. Surely, this could not be the boy who has cancer. He was probably the kid of some parents who couldn't find a babysitter that night.

As the dinner began, the lights were dimmed, and a media presentation began about the boy and his family. His doctors talked about the months of hospitalization, the pain, and the need for future care; his mother and father (both police officers) talked about their efforts to keep the family both solvent; and the family thanked the hundreds of caregivers, friends, and neighbors that rallied behind this little boy.

Fellow police officers and neighbors built a jungle gym in the backyard so the boy could play (he missed months of school and playgrounds). Local businesses helped grant the boy's wish to attend a Milwaukee Bucks basketball game (from the pictures, it looks like the team came through with front row seats).

This little boy who spent much of his life in the hospital and who faces a very uncertain future is the same little boy who was running around the hotel ballroom smiling and laughing.

Suddenly, my plans to "politely bow out" so I can have a beer with my friends seemed so unimportant. There would be many opportunities to go out on other nights. I had a great time that night and took home a photo of that little boy and placed it on my refrigerator.

The next morning while eating cereal, I began looking at the other pictures on my refrigerator. In particular, the one of my father, Lieutenant Howard Mahany of the U.S. Army Air Corps, proudly kneeling on the wing of his P-51 Mustang fighter plane. The plane displaying seven flags representing seven enemy aircraft destroyed.

That morning while looking at the photos on my refrigerator I learned two important lessons and returned to work on Monday with a renewed sense of energy and a much different perspective on life and work. Happily, I can say that since that morning, my fear is in check, my practice is doing very well, and again, I remember all those blessings that make me thankful for each day.

What are those two lessons learned that morning?

First, that life is precious. We need to embrace each day and the opportunities each day brings. Life is always going to throw curve balls now and then. Unfortunately, in these new economic times, people lose their jobs and homes every day. And despite many recent medical miracles, we all will die someday. The impossible odds faced by that young man suddenly put things in their proper perspective.

If we focus too much on our problems, we lose sight of the opportunities. That boy and his family could choose to focus on the pain, the bills, the lost childhood. Instead, they threw a party to thank everyone who helped them and to provide opportunities for other kids facing life-threatening illness. Don't ever try to tell that child he doesn't have the same opportunities as other kids. In some ways, he has more.

Without energy, inspiration, and motivation, life becomes more difficult. It's not enough to simply love your work. Success is inspired and sometimes that inspiration can be found in the strangest of places.

Obviously, inspiration is more than just a picture on the refrigerator. It's the realization that opportunity is everywhere if you look. I went to work on Monday that week and suddenly found all sorts of opportunities. I find my inspiration from great writers like Matt Morris, Timothy Ferriss, and their books. I find inspiration in church. And most of all, I find it through the stories of others, like the little boy on my refrigerator.

I said there were two lessons that next morning and wanted to address the other. They are equally important. The other photo on the fridge that provided me with renewed inspiration was that of my father. Dad was a fighter pilot and ace in World War II. In aerial combat, you survive by killing the enemy before he kills you. It's brutal but that simple.

Fortunately, life for most of us doesn't involve killing, but it does involve action. Anyone can spend his or her life planning, plotting and studying. The successful ones among us, however, are those that are also "doing."

Just like in combat, at some point, the planning has to stop and be replaced by action. Reading marketing books, hiring advertising consultants and developing detailed action plans have their place in any new business. No one should march into battle without a plan.

For many of us, however, we get so wrapped up in the planning that life passes us by before we take the opportunity to act.

As I said before, there are opportunities all around us. To enjoy them, however, we have to take chances and act. Our men and women in Iraq and Afghanistan take huge risks every day. Some pay the ultimate price in defense of our freedom and give their lives. The risks we take are usually not as deadly but to have any chance of success, we have to face our fears and take those risks.

What did I learn that day and the next morning? That life offers us inspiration in the most unusual places and that to succeed, we must not only be inspired but must also act decisively when opportunity knocks.

By the time this book is published, there will likely be new additions and changes to the outside of our refrigerator, but two photos will remain forever.

Biography

Brian Mahany is a lawyer with a national practice helping victims of fraud get back their hard-earned money. He also helps people and businesses with tax problems and those accused of white-collar crimes. A lawyer for 27 years, Brian previously served as Maine's revenue commissioner, as an assistant attorney general, and a criminal investigator. In 2008, he was part of the Wesley Snipes defense team. He lives in Milwaukee, Wisconsin.

Contact Information

Brian Mahany
(262) 970-8500
P.O. Box 511328, Milwaukee WI 53202
www.mahanyertl.com

Chapter 22
WHAT LEGACY ARE YOU GOING TO LEAVE BEHIND?

By Jill Nieman Picerno

When people think of what kind of legacy they would like to leave behind, they usually think financially. However, when I was a child, I knew that my legacy would be my children. I thought that the most important thing I could do for the world was to raise my children into becoming amazing adults. I always wanted to have two girls, sisters, as I never had a sister and always thought that would be so great. My wish did come true. I am blessed with two incredible girls. My first daughter, Jacquelyn, was born when I was 28 years old. Then two years and ten months later, Caitlyn was born. I was fortunate enough to become a Stay-At-Home Mom the day Jacquelyn was born, but this didn't just happen. My husband, at the time, and I worked very hard to pay off debts and make sure that his income would be able to provide for our family to live comfortably once I became a Stay-At-Home Mom.

I am also a CPA, and I started up my practice a little while after Jacquelyn was born. I ran my small practice from our home, which allowed me to continue being a Stay-At-Home Mom. I chose this career, while in college, specifically with this in mind. Parenting, not my CPA practice, would always be my number one job. I have read so many books about children and child raising, talked about my children and their various stages of development with my friends and family and even asked strangers their opinions about parenting. Once I began the parenting role, I set off towards creating my legacy. I knew that having an honest and completely open relationship with my girls when they were teenagers would be crucial to creating the legacy I wanted to leave behind.

Parenting is a tough job. It requires a ton of energy, and you need to realize how a parent shapes a child's future. We all want the best for our children, but sometimes, that gets lost in the day to day activities. We need to write down our goals for parenting. Look at how you were parented. What did you like about your parents' parenting styles and what is it that you don't like about their styles?

Many of us rarely take the time to sit down and think this through. Sit down right now and take out a sheet of paper. Let your mind go back in time and remember how your parents raised you. Write down everything that comes to your mind, without stopping, letting your mind flow. Keep writing until you believe you have captured your parents' parenting styles on paper. Now the fun begins. We are all creatures of habit, so many of us just parent as we were parented. That doesn't need to be the case. What type of parenting style do you want your children to experience? How do you want your children to feel about you and them? Remember to start creating your legacy with the end in mind.

Parents often ask me how I created such an honest and completely open relationship with my girls. Many things helped create our incredible relationships along the way, but there is one rule that I have had from the beginning of my parenting role. This rule, I believe, was the foundation of my relationships with my girls. My rule from the beginning was "No Lying."

Lying is always wrong. My girls learned at a very early age to speak the truth which was not a very easy task to accomplish. Children will lie to their parents. They lie to their parents to avoid being punished for something they did wrong in their parent's eyes. My girls did not like to be punished, like all children, but they did lie to me to avoid being punished. They soon figured out though that when they lied to me to avoid being punished, their punishment became ten times worse than if they had just told me the truth from the beginning.

They also learned that if they did tell me the truth right away about what they had done wrong, they wouldn't get in as much trouble as if I had caught them in the act. This was a little bit of a reward for telling the truth right away. Both my girls learned this rule and realized that telling the truth had its benefits.

Honesty is something their mother values. If my girls were not honest with me and lied, I would be very disappointed in them. Children do not want to disappoint their parents. Children just want to avoid getting punished. Parents should try to catch their children lying at an early age and instill in them the value of honesty.

Become a great detective. Learn the body signals that occur when someone is lying to you. Children will usually delay answering your initial questions. When they finally do answer your questions, their voice will have a slightly higher pitch to it. Their hands may cover their mouth or rub their nose often. Facial expressions will change. Their face may look paler and stiffer, their nostrils may flare, and their lips may look thinner and tighter. Avoiding direct eye contact, squinting or closing their eyes may also give them away. Their body may become stiffer, shoulders may be pulled up, and their elbows may be held close to their body. These are just a few of the body signals that parents may want to be on the lookout for.

Once you do know your child is lying, take action. Do not explain to them how you know they are lying. All they need to know is that you know they lied. Then tell them this is unacceptable. Explain to them the first punishment they were going to receive for having the inappropriate behavior. Then let them know that since they lied to you about what did happen, the punishment will be ten times the initial punishment they would have received.

Remember to have the punishment fit the inappropriate behavior, but make sure it is something you can and will follow through with. Your child also needs to realize that you were upset about their inappropriate behavior, but you are so much more disappointed in the fact that they felt the need to lie to you. Children lie to avoid punishment, but they do not want to disappoint you and lying creates disappointment.

When children start to reach the teenage years, this lying rule needs to be set in stone. You still need to be able to detect the body signals your child exposes to you when he/she is lying.

We must also realize that this age is a very difficult stage in your child's development. Try to remember how you felt or acted like as a teenager. Yes, that does scare some of us, and we don't want our children to make some of the same mistakes we did.

They do need to make some of their own mistakes, as they don't always learn from being told what to do and what not do. Being overly strict parents is not the course of action that seems to produce the best results related to some of their teenager's actions. I do believe this, as I know things about my female friends that their parents would not believe about their teenagers if I told them. Parents need to not parent with blinders on. The information I know about their friends becomes handy when trying to steer them towards a better path in life.

Teenagers are influenced by their friends more than their parents. You have to be one of their friends too. Always be the parent first and their friend second. Teenagers will not tell you that they like you being their parent and setting rules, but this honestly does make them feel loved. They know you care about what happens to them.

My girls think some of my rules are a little over the top, but they understand my reasoning behind my rules. They know they are loved. It's a fine line between having too many rules or too few rules or too strict rules or not strict enough rules. Hopefully, with this point, you have built that honest and completely open relationship with your children, as this will help guide you in setting your own rules for your teenagers.

This brings me to a question that has come up with my girls. Should I treat my girls the same related to the rules I have; yes and no. Yes, some rules should be the same, but every teenager is different. I remember having dinner with my girls one night, and Caitlyn began talking about one of her friends drinking her parent's alcohol. I asked

Caitlyn, "Which friend is that?" Caitlyn proceeded to tell me, in so many words, that it was none of my business and she didn't want me to tell her parents. I then explained to her that she did not need to tell me which friend of hers was doing this, but then she would suffer the consequences of my parenting rules being differently related to her than her sister.

Of course, life is not fair. I continued explaining to Caitlyn that Jacquelyn has told me many things about her friends and I haven't mentioned it to her friend's parents. My trust with Jacquelyn will be higher, and she will have more privileges related to hanging out with her friends than Caitlyn would. Needless to say, Caitlyn decided to tell me which friend of hers was drinking her parent's alcohol and we moved on from there. I have always kept my girl's secrets about their friends safe with me, except for one time. The only time I believe that I should tell another parent something about their teenager that my girls have shared with me in confidence is if it can be life-threatening. I got my daughter's permission to talk to the teenager's parents, as she was worried about her friend's life as well. Everything, fortunately, turned out great.

The teenage years are always interesting. I love that my girls feel so comfortable coming to me with any questions that they may have, but when the teenage years rolled around, their questions became life path altering.

Their questions became more about sex, drugs, boys, girls and so many other important topics about life in general.

Sometimes when one of my girls would come to ask me a question, inside, I am freaking out, but on the outside, I act as they asked me "What are we doing for dinner?" I was so proud of my girls being able to ask me any question they felt they wanted an answer about.

My girls realize that I don't know everything, but I told them we could always find out the answer together.

One question I remember one of my girls asking me was "Will you die if you have sex before you are 19 years old?" My daughter was just entering her teenage years, and one of her friend's moms had told her friend that. So began the talk about sex. I did tell her that "You do not die if you have sex before you are 19 years old." I think that the mother was trying to protect her daughter but didn't have an open relationship with her daughter to talk things out. This then led us into a conversation about AIDs, STDs, etc. The questions my girls came to ask were always a time to have discussions, and for me to steer them in the right direction. I realized that no one person can control another person. So I have tried to give my girls as much information as I thought necessary for them to make the correct choices in life. My girls and I are so glad we have this honest and completely open relationship. It hasn't always been easy, but it's always been worth it.

My life path continues today on creating a legacy for my incredible girls. This is how I measure success.

Biography

Jill Nieman Picerno is a very proud mother and entrepreneur. She is a student of parenting, finance, real estate and network marketing. She has thrust for knowledge, loves to meet new people, and visit new places around the world. She is a Certified Public Accountant, owns several real estate properties and has her own travel business, www.travelgirls.biz. She is also in the process of creating her very own parenting book.

Contact Information

Jill Nieman Picerno
10940 S Parker Rd, Ste 472
Parker, CO 80134
303-400-5100
jill@travelgirls.biz

ISLAND SOLITAIRE

A Year on Korea's Not-so-secret Paradise

By John Burgman

Island Solitaire
©2018 by John Burgman
All rights reserved.

This book recounts the author's experiences and research while living on mainland South Korea and on Jeju. It contains the author's memories of people, conversations and various happenings. Although great effort has been made to present the past in an accurate manner, the reader should keep in mind that memories and recollections are always personal and fallible. As a courtesy and in an attempt to grant privacy, some names and identifying details about individuals in the text have been changed. Additionally, when referencing South Korea in a contemporary sense, the author refers to it as such—South Korea. In cases where the country's distant past is being referenced, the author refers to the region simply as Korea.

Cover photo by Eric Hevesy. All rights reserved.

Printed in the United States by Piscataqua Press
32 Daniel St., Portsmouth NH 03801
www.piscataquapress.com

ISBN: 978-1-944393-71-7

Contents

Prologue	i
Chapter 1: Enter the island	1
Chapter 2: Separation of fact and fiction	10
Chapter 3: What is it about islands?	19
Chapter 4: Mountain lives	32
Chapter 5: The East-West connection	38
Chapter 6: Food in flux	46
Chapter 7: Tangerine dreams	52
Chapter 8: The long and winding tale	60
Chapter 9: A multitude of rebirths	66
Chapter 10: Ruin and reconciliation	72
Chapter 11: Portrait of the monk as a young man	80
Chapter 12: One-day mother	89
Chapter 13: Southbound	99
Chapter 14: Local motion	109

Chapter 15: 1,000 previous meetings	114
Chapter 16: The surrounding waters	121
Chapter 17: Ghost night	129
Chapter 18: A receding tide	136
Chapter 19: A day at the races	144
Chapter 20: Day and night	153
Chapter 21: In a fog	160
Chapter 22: The newness	166
Sources	177
Acknowledgements	182
About the Author	184

Prologue

Here is a legend that I would like to share. Centuries ago, a mighty dragon resided on a beautiful island in the middle of the ocean. The dragon was revered by the spirits of the world because the dragon lived off the lush island forests and drank the pure seawater surrounding the land. However, the human ruler of the region felt threatened by the dragon's size and power; the ruler knew that without nutrients from the earth, the dragon would surely grow weak and lose all its authority.

The human ruler proclaimed that the mighty dragon should be killed, and dispatched an army of warriors to destroy the rivers and rocks on the island that satiated the mighty dragon. Always attentive, the dragon observed the destruction of its home and decided to flee the island by slinking into the surrounding waters. As it did so, the warriors spotted it and began to viciously cut its throat. The warriors used their swords to pierce the dragon's tough scales and their knives to slice through its strong neck muscles. The water around the island turned red from the dragon's blood, and eventually the mighty dragon expired on the shore—hunched halfway into the ocean, stuck forever in between the island and the water. The other spirits of the world mourned the dragon's death, and the land and sea that had witnessed the dragon's brutal murder continuously wept. The sound of their crying would compel people in future generations to visit the island and pay respects to the valiant dragon spirit.

The legend might be fictional, but it contains elements that are very real—the island was the South Korean island of Jeju. The human ruler was supposedly Qin Shi Huang, emperor during China's Qin Dynasty about 2,200 years ago. The emperors of that dynasty were known to go to extreme lengths to protect their positions of power, in the form of book-burning and purging scholars and academics. While ordering the slaughter of a huge dragon is not part of the factual historical record, tourists can still visit rocky cliffs on Jeju known as Yongmeori, said to represent the figure of the dragon retreating into the violet-colored water.

I like the story of Yongmeori because while it is uniquely a part of Jeju, it also hints at a collective desire we all share. People don't haphazardly go to islands; they often seek them out and are enticed by a certain element—whether it is the loud, mythic crying of the sea or their own yearning for exploration—that cannot be ignored. Other islands of the world have comparable legends that explain why people are enticed to visit their shores too.

I have an informal theory about islands, based on casual observation of the adventurous spirit in travelers over the years. I think people are naturally drawn to islands. Call it an inclination that we have, or call it a filament of our survival instinct that attracts us to the security of land. No matter what label is given, there seems to reside in humankind now and throughout history an instant captivation with those small patches of land surrounded by vast bodies of water. It is why there have been countless songs and poems written about islands over the centuries, why entire magazines and book series have been devoted to them, and in part why people have been exploring them practically since the beginning of time.

Island musing is not bound by nationality or culture. It is not exclusive to the tropics and is not a gimmicky creation of tourism advertising firms. Motivations for seeking out islands have evolved over time, but traveling to them has always been an endpoint for our species. In other words, there seems to be something timeless and universal about gazing out to sea, suddenly spotting a green speck in the blue monochrome, and wanting to check it out.

This book was composed in that vein. It is about my time on an island that happens to be part of South Korea, but the book is by no means a scholarly work about Korean culture. I have read plenty of those types of texts, and they have their place in research. I have tried to fill this book with details and observations about Korea, but it has always been with the goal of better comprehending my personal experiences.

Living on a modest island in any part of the world entails a degree of exhilaration from the isolation, but also some sense of separation, of distance. There is also almost always a blended way of life because outsiders have influenced every inlet, atoll and archipelago, for better or worse. Islands across the world often have something of a large-scale multiple personality condition. Given the natural spatial limitations, island locals nudge up against tourists, homegrown businesses compete with external corporate development, the young generation wants to get off the island while the older generation often finds contentment in staying, the wild trees edge up to the golf course, and, of course, the stable land that holds it all meets the temperamental sea that could wipe everything away in an instant.

I wanted to know what it was like to stand in the crossfire of such relationships, to see what place ancient island legends have in a modern context. Mostly, as a long-time resident of landlocked American towns, I wanted to give into my desire to live on a remote chunk of land in the middle of water. My initial plan was simple: go to a faraway island and see how things progress from there.

Whenever I'm back in the United States, I make a point to take a canoeing or kayaking trip through the watery passages of Northern Minnesota's Boundary Waters. This region has some of the most pristine, untrammeled wilderness in all of the North American continent, with a

Island Solitaire

million acres of forest and innumerable freshwater lakes latticed along the Canadian border. In the 18th and 19th centuries, French workmen known as voyageurs paddled canoes on the same lakes in search of animal pelts that were used in the construction of fashionable hats back in Europe. The many islands along the way provided morale-boosting rest stops where the voyageurs would light a pipe of tobacco, snack on pemmican, or sing a song. The voyageurs' progress through the wilderness was measured largely by how many of these stops they took in a given day, traveling from break to break, island to island.

Once, on one of my own canoe trips, I was guiding a group of younger paddlers down a slender lake, and we pulled up to a grassy strip of shoreline for lunch. It was an agonizingly hot day, made worse by the fact that our canoes were aluminum. Paddling beneath the blazing summer sun, we might as well have been wrapped in cooking foil.

Seeking relief, we all scarfed down peanut butter-slathered bagels and plunged into the cool lake water for a swim. It felt revitalizing to dive into the darker depths and let the cold liquid soothe all of my sunburned skin and tired muscles. When I could no longer hold my breath underwater, I would shoot up to the surface, feel the brief warmth of the sun and claw down to the chilled lake bottom again. At some point in this swimming loop, I noticed that some of the younger boys of the group were treading water and gesturing towards the horizon. I turned and saw what they were referencing: a lone island, no bigger than a Volkswagen, in the distance on the lake.

John Burgman

The island's rocky surface was shining in the midday sun.

"Can we swim to it?" one of the boys asked enthusiastically. Out of habit from being the authoritative figure in the group, I promptly asked the boys why they wanted to swim to such a tiny, non-descript bit of land. From my position, it looked like nothing but lichen-covered boulders, moss and a ring of beige reeds. Without even having to think on my question, the same boy responded, "We just want to see the island up-close." The rest of the boys hollered in agreement, and I didn't want to be the one to stand in the way of such an honest objective.

I sometimes recalled that moment when I began living on Jeju. Wanting to see an island up-close was an adequate, simplified description of my own motivation. I had known that my interests would likely change from time to time, as is typical with long-term travel, but I was sure that an intrinsic island-ambition would be constant. In the crosswinds, both literally and metaphorically, I would be open to following leads as they came. And to the best of my ability, I did just that, jaunting from destination to destination, making a point to understand the island place and my position on it as much as I could.

Without further ado, perhaps that is a perfect image with which to begin now—standing alone on Jeju, looking around in a daze, bracing for whatever was about to hit me.

1. Enter the island

The question popped into my mind one day, "Where am I?" Immediately after that, a second question hit me like a fist: just how had I gotten there?

Considering the sheer size and wonder of the world, it is remarkable for a single, small patch of land in the immensity of the ocean to make it onto anyone's radar. In fact, prior to 2002, when nearly half of the small Asian island of Jeju was christened a biosphere reserve by the United Nations Educational, Scientific and Cultural Organization (UNESCO), relatively few people outside of the immediate vicinity had ever visited the island, much less lived there permanently or considered its wealth of natural features. Flanked by the Korean mainland to the north, China to the west and Japan a few hundred miles to the east, Jeju had maintained something of an undiscovered quality while its neighboring land masses vaulted into the global economic and tourism conversation. At 714 square miles, Jeju is a little larger than the more famous sun-baked islands of the world like Martinique and San Lucia, but much smaller than the collective Bahamas or Cuba. In the past, Jeju rarely made the covers of glossy travel magazines or getaway lists, nor was it ever exhaustively profiled in major Western publications—unlike, say, Thailand's Koh Chang string of islands, Vietnam's Halong Bay and other Far East locales that cashed in on the idea that paradise could exist on their sandy shores if the paying Western customers were willing to make the long flight.

That's the point—for decades, if travelers from Europe or the United States wanted to see Asia for the first time, they generally headed to Tokyo, Beijing, Bangkok, Hong Kong, or Seoul. If those same people wanted a tropical fix, perhaps they booked plane tickets to Jamaica, Aruba, or Fiji. Jeju was a little further off everyone's radar, a little less traveled by the hordes of globetrotting vagabonds. And places like that have always intrigued me.

Growing up in the farmland of the Midwest, my dream was to move to Hawaii, where I could climb volcanoes and lie about on the beaches in perpetuity. As I grew older and an academic interest in South Korea blossomed, Jeju was framed to me as South Korea's version of Hawaii, so I instantly wanted to move to the mysterious island that resided like a freckle on the oceanic face of the globe. When I eventually had the opportunity to make my home on Jeju many years later, however, the circumstances of my life had aligned not in the neat choreography that I had long dreamed. Rather, I found myself struggling to stave off several depressing factors—and a collective negativity that necessitated action.

For starters, I had staked all of my hopes on writing a novel that, along with snuffing out any social life, had taken a lot of time to complete. I received contradictory suggestions from two book publishers who had expressed initial interest in the novel's premise: One editor said that I should turn the fiction manuscript into a travel guidebook, which was a long-winded way of telling me that the actual story was worthless; the other editor urged me to delete most of the novel's details to give the story "more universal marketability." Needless to say, I was irritated and finally crestfallen when both publishers eventually passed on the novel altogether.

I was also trying to keep alive a relationship with a woman who lived nearly 300 miles away—the distance feeling elongated with every lengthy phone conversation and every lonely night I spent on Jeju. Added to this were the supplementary facts that I had essentially run out of money and discovered my apartment on Jeju to be overcome with mold.

My lifelong island dream—to live and work on Jeju—was feeling more like grimy, sub-tropical exile.

The last straw was a bus accident one morning. I had awakened at sunrise, hoping to get in a couple hours of rock climbing before a large, low-pressure system rolled in and unleashed a bombardment of turbulent weather. Unbeknownst to me was that the hulking thunderheads had been preceded by a patch of smaller clouds, and those clouds had dropped light sleet onto Jeju's roads at dawn. I had been on the city bus for about two minutes when it slid on the road's slick glaze of ice, angled awkwardly through an intersection and barreled into a lamppost. I was thrown from my bus seat and landed on shattered windshield glass. Worse, at some point in my airborne trajectory, my ribs had thumped against the sturdy plastic armrests, and I had bounced down the bus aisle like a human pinball.

I spent the next two days tweezing bits of glass from my scabbed knees, but my throbbing ribs and my aching sternum were the real problems, as they deemed me immobile. Every action was painful—inhaling hurt, sitting in a chair hurt and raising my arms hurt. One of the few productive activities I could do was to help my neighbor, a wiry medical school student named Hyojun, study for his upcoming exams—but such rote delivery of assorted endocrine system quiz questions grew old quickly.

Busted up and laid out, I felt worthless, lonelier than ever, and I started to wonder what the heck I was doing on this small, peculiar island so far from my birthplace.

I would have stayed in such a mental funk for a long time had I not been approached by a complete stranger in a coffee shop one morning. The stranger, a young Korean woman dressed in bright hiking attire, asked why my posture was so wonky as she filled her tumbler with a latte.

I explained the bus accident to the woman and pointed to the bandages on my knees. She cocked her head to one side and then smiled, as if something had suddenly come to mind. Leaning in closer, she extolled the virtues of an annual Jeju festival during which an entire small mountain, known as an *oreum*, is lit on fire.

When I pressed the woman for more details, she said that the fire mountain festival is a ceremonial burning of the old farmland to spur the growth of fresh grass, but the fire mountain festival also serves as a way of dispelling all the bad luck, lingering sadness and nagging negativity of a previous year.

I didn't know how to take her comments at first. The pain in my ribs was entirely real, yet this woman—a complete stranger—was pushing on me a flaming mountain that would metaphorically burn away my life's bad vibes. I thought about slinking towards the coffee shop's exit, but I was also too intrigued to leave.

As our conversation continued, it became clear to me that the woman was being sincere in her assertion that I could benefit from the festival, that I would find something intangible there that might be, as she said, "healing."

"Medically healing?" I asked.

"Well," she said, pausing, "more like refreshed."

The woman sipped the foamy brim of her tumbler and added an intriguing caveat: "Your wishes for newness will come true at the fire mountain festival."

I tried in the moment to politely entertain her optimism, but the whole time, I was wondering if other people on Jeju actually believed all of this. How could a burning mountain grant wishes, and why would anyone perceive such a thing to be true?

"If you truly knew the island's way," she said with a

smile, "I think you'd understand."

I mulled over her words for the rest of the day. Part of the challenge in deciphering where genuine belief and willful imagination diverge is the fact that even Korean culture is largely nebulous on the separation. Take, for example, South Korea's official website for Jeju, where tourism activities and factual history are presented on a digital palette of colorful beach photos alongside hyperbole. The site states quite frankly: Jeju is inhabited by 18,000 gods and goddesses, and is full of myths about them. Such a statement is breezily included with numerous other, more conventional facts, such as Jeju having a mild oceanic climate throughout the year.

An examination of any traditional, communal gathering on the island such as the fire mountain festival, therefore, inevitably becomes a gaze at the island's entire heritage.

At one time, Jeju's governor even stated, "You might say that Jeju is 'the last island on the earth where gods and goddesses still live.'"

Deciding where the truth ends and the fiction begins is a tricky process. So again, I was left to wonder how much of all this the locals believe.

In his book, *Confucius Lives Next Door*, T.R. Reid goes into great detail about Asia's social miracle, which is the fact that so many Asian countries—South Korea among them—have become major players in world affairs while maintaining remarkably low statistics when it comes to the ills that plague the other key powers of the world—crime, drug use, domestic problems and so forth. But it could be said that a place can maintain such an adherence to its ancient and often fantastical habitudes, not simply out of custom and tradition, but out of beliefs that are still very perceptible in the social architecture. As I would come to discover, nowhere exemplifies this more than Jeju, with its paradisiacal aura, its rapid economic growth, its ancient mythos, its dialect that is so different from the parlance of mainland South Korea that some linguists consider Jeju's vernacular to be its own language. And of course, the island has its mysterious fire mountain festival.

Jeju's dialect is appropriate to note precisely because it provided me with insight into the island's modern-day social configuration. Certain words and expressions that I encountered resembled their equivalent Korean mainland form. For example, the Korean food kimchi is sometimes spoken as jimchi on Jeju. However, other expressions bear no resemblance to their linguistic counterpart. In standard Korean, the casual expression for "Oh, really," is "Chincha," but on Jeju, I repeatedly heard it expressed as a totally different, lone syllable, "Gi." The prevailing explanation for such variation and truncation was the island's weather: generations upon generations of locals having had conversations amid harsh winds blowing in from the ocean had trimmed words and syllables down to the minimalistic sounds and enunciations that best cut through the moving air. Jeju's dialect is slowly dying now, however, as many young island locals have chosen to adhere exclusively to "Seoul style" speaking and, therefore, grow up practically unable to understand the dialogues of their dialect-speaking grandparents. Most fascinating to me was how some islanders would switch back and forth from standard Korean to Jeju's dialect, often within the same conversation. Hearing it was like beholding a verbal microcosm of the island's current status—unique and traditional one minute, congruently Korean, even cosmopolitan, the next.

All of this is to say, there were large cultural complexities at play when I decided to examine the island deeply and meticulously, and finding out how a burning mountain could actually—supposedly—set my life back on track would take time.

But I had time, thanks to my busted ribs. I also had a nearby library, a university, local neighbors and an entire landscape on which to seek answers.

Best of all, I had no expectations.

Back in the 1960s, consumers in the West were warned that the very media they were using could significantly influence their perception of the world. Travelers nowadays are no different. A modern vagabond undertakes a trip with a plethora of assumptions, conjectures and preconceived notions about a destination thanks to the Internet, social media and more traditional resources like guidebooks, magazines and word-of-mouth recommendations. It has become a rare enterprise to explore anything without prior knowledge and gradations of familiarity, so when I first learned about this mysterious fire mountain festival, of which I knew absolutely nothing, my spirit was lifted and my interest was piqued. I had no consumptive base other than that chance meeting with a random woman in a cozy coffee shop.

So, I set out to find the meaning behind the fire mountain festival, and to explore Jeju's past and present until I could understand why a festival like that existed. And if I wanted to whittle down those objectives to smaller, more manageable pieces, learning a little history seemed like a logical place to start.

2. Separation of fact and fiction

Feeling a bit loopy from pain pills for my ribs, I rode a bus through the humid dawn in Jeju City and sensed the island waking up. Stoplights blinked above increasingly busy intersections, restaurant owners dumped fresh eel and fish into sloshing water bowls, and a lone traffic guard waved cars steadily past a quaint elementary school. It was hot outside, and the hefty morning swelter was thankfully dampened every so often by a breeze sliding off the ocean. Palm trees swayed on the sides of the road. It was the type of morning that lifts one out of bed by itself, loneliness and nagging depression be damned.

Jeju City is the largest urban expanse on the island of Jeju, spread like a puddle along the north-central coast. Divided into multiple smaller regions, it is the island's formal and artistic capital. Thus, it was a fitting place for me to start looking for answers about any cultural practice or nuance. Specifically, the Jeju Folklore and Natural

Island Solitaire

History Museum was sprawling and pleasantly devoid of the usual museum starkness and sterility—and perfect for providing a lens into the past.

The museum was larger than I expected, and perhaps this had to do with the fact that it was surrounded by urban establishments that seemed more suited for a city—a bank, a food mart, a hotel and a garish structure called the Paradise Wedding Hall. One had to walk past these places on the main thoroughfare of the city to reach the museum, which emerged seemingly out of nowhere around a bend for me, preambled by a massive parking lot. At a quick tally, I counted 12 parked tour buses—not bad business for a weekday morning.

The museum grounds were an impressive display of huge decorative boulders, bushy trees and stone walkways. With an admission price of just 500 won—the equivalent of 50 cents—for island residents like myself, the museum struck me as a budget-friendly site that would probably host a lot of high school field trips. Almost on cue, this thought was followed by a tumble of voices behind me, and a large group of groggy teenage students unloaded from a school bus to begin a tour of the exhibits.

The first thing I noticed when I entered the main museum structure was not anything having to do directly with Jeju's history, but two enormous, eel-like oarfish—common in the waters surrounding the island—preserved in a glass tank of water and looking quite dead, shedding their gelatinous skin in formaldehyde for eternity. From the aquarium, I wandered through a mock cave lined with plaques, lava sculptures and faux fungus. The island of

Jeju was created during the Cenozoic Era, and it is essentially a massive piece of basalt rock from one large volcano that is steadily receding into the ocean. So, these phony caves represented the *Geomunoreum* lava tubes that originally slunk beneath the surface of the island and left behind contorted lava drips and bubble-like shapes that still exist.

Moving to the next room in the museum hall, animals of the island were showcased as stuffed trophies—egrets, ducks, cranes, the striking black-capped kingfisher, snakes, frogs and deer. A nearby sign informed museum attendees that Jeju is also home to 350 species of citrus.

I couldn't help but stop, perplexed, in front of a display with odd signage: PHALLIC STONE. Behind the display glass were several cylindrical sculptures that looked exactly as one would imagine large rock designated as phallic stones to look. Jeju mothers in the long-ago past preferred male offspring to females, as boys would be higher on the Confucianist hierarchy in Korean society of previous centuries. And rather than simply leaving the gender of their unborn children up to chance, the mothers would pray for male children—and use the stones as part of the rites. Particularly, Jeju locals of the past would direct their prayers to a fertility goddess named *Samsin Hallmang*, whose main job was to deliver children to the families that had worshipped her dutifully.

Ironically, opposite to the requests inherent in those prayers was the historical fact that Jeju had been known for its women, not its men. A plaque in the museum explained this in detail. In the long-ago past, the

Island Solitaire

patriarchs and the young boys of Jeju households ventured out to sea or farmed the fields and served in the Korean military, but women also played roles in fishing and gathering seafood for their respective families. Fishing was a dangerous job that also carried with it a stigma; the revealing nature of the women's divewear, even decades ago, was controversial in the very conservative Korean society. Yet, despite any social condemnation, the bounties gathered by the Jeju women were often as integral to a family's income as those of the husband. In fact, the women of Jeju, and the customary sea diving associated with them, has now become so entrenched in Jeju's cultural identity that entire wings of the Folkore and Natural History Museum are devoted to diving equipment and artifacts. Books have also been written extolling the virtues of Jeju women, almost to the point of excess. The women of the island have been described as being strong-willed, hearty, self-motivated, bold, courageous, resilient and warm-hearted, among other praiseful adjectives. One book on Jeju history that I came across had an entire chapter titled, simply, "Women."

Perhaps the most substantial measure of the prevalence of this thinking—giving the women of Jeju a degree of exclusivity not found in the rest of Korean culture of the past—is that a saying has developed over the years stating that Jeju is known specifically for the merits of three components: its powerful wind (which is the reason why Jeju's vernacular typically truncates words), its abundance of large rocks and, naturally, its women.

John Burgman

My museum tour continued with a stop at an ice cream bar, and then concluded with a stroll through a marine hall bedecked with skeletons and life-sized models of porpoises, whales and sharks. I watched a short video about the *goung-dung-gut* ritual, an elaborate shamanistic ceremony performed by island locals that entails tossing food out to sea to please the ocean gods. The narrator of the video stated over images of food floating atop the ocean waves, "The sea people hope to have a better life tomorrow than today," which struck me as a pleasant outlook for anyone embarking on any endeavor.

In the end, the museum tour didn't turn out to be the wealth of insight about myths and the fire mountain festival that I had hoped, but it had offered some insight into the formation of the island and the culture that would eventually construct so many legends.

I crossed the street, bought a soda at the food mart and watched additional tour buses pull into the museum parking lot. Several of the buses were from local schools, but others were sightseeing companies giving tours to Chinese vacationers. Museum subculture, if there exists such a concept, has flourished on Jeju in recent years. Consider this: along with several history-themed museums, the small island has a botanic garden, a folk village, a stone park, an art museum, a computer museum, multiple glass museums, a chocolate museum, a sex museum, a lightning museum and a trick art museum.

There's also a Leonardo da Vinci museum, despite the fact that da Vinci never had any recognized connection to Jeju. In fact, so many of the museums on Jeju lack any direct connection to Jeju's historic culture that a new identity is taking shape on the island, beyond basic tourism. It's a wholly unique brand of globalism, enticing and inviting wide-eyed travelers to the island to learn not only about folklore, geology and heritage, but also about the nuances of completely disjoined subgroups. Jeju is becoming, in other words, a sort of cultural melting pot that eschews the minor detail of actually possessing a vast array of cultures. With a population of roughly 600,000 people, Jeju is increasingly crowded, yet it remains homogenously Korean in its ethnic composition. Although the foreign population increased more than 20 percent in a single recent year, it's still impressive that an island of locals maintains, additionally, originalities such as a teddy bear museum, a sex-themed sculpture park and a car museum, to name a few more popular tourist destinations.

Most impressive is that all of this is working—that is, it is working if the ultimate goal is to bring tourists to Jeju. It was reported in 2012 that the busiest air travel route in the entire world was the path in the sky from Seoul to Jeju, with more than 10 million passengers traversing the air space in a single year. To entice people to take up residency on the island, rather than just tour it, the Korean government even offered citizenship contingent on the purchase of island property. To be clear, this was Jeju's effort as much as it was that of mainland Korea's governmental bureaucracy. In 2005, with a directive known as The Free International City Act, Jeju opted to become a self-governing province, free to make its own immigration and investment incentives, and basically free to prosper as it pleases. It has done so with the construction of multiple foreign language academies, international schools and hotels, as well as visa waivers for Chinese travelers. There's even an ambassador to Jeju who deals solely with international relations and attracting foreign investors. Formal motions have also been made to make both Korean and English the official languages of the island.

As much as Jeju might have been an undiscovered haven in the past, it has now overcompensated in some ways and become a blend of secluded island mystery and overdevelopment. It has skipped the in-between.

In a fascinating addendum to such growth, it should be mentioned that engraved commemorations that signify a building's age on Jeju often seem to be boasting the building's newness, not the building's antiquity or historical importance. Near my apartment in Jeju City, there was a brick restaurant that proudly proclaimed in an engraving above the front awning: *Since 2014*.

The most memorable example of Jeju's worldly cultural grab happened for me not while browsing museums or reading about foreign investments, but while on a university campus one day. I had finished teaching an afternoon class and was approached by a Korean student, out of breath and looking frazzled. In his hand, he held copies of the blueprints for a soon-to-be-opened air and space museum on the island. He explained that he was in desperate need of my help. The museum's construction was already under way, and soon all of the signs and billboards for the museum's interior would be ordered. The signs would give directions in Korean, Chinese, Japanese and English. In the haste of the new museum's construction, the student explained, nobody had actually verified the spelling on the English signage. So, the student was wondering if I could spare a few moments and take a look at the blueprints.

I immediately found several mistakes that spoke more to amusing cultural nuance than to misspelling. A room where mothers would be able to nurse their babies in private, for example, was scheduled to be labeled, "Mothers' Milking Room"—essentially a literal translation of the Korean phrase to English, but certainly a designation at which most native English speakers would raise an eyebrow. A gift shop was scheduled to be marked with signage as, "Pleasure Shop," which would have been an unexpected innuendo for patrons to read when searching for a spot to buy museum souvenirs. There was also an oddly titled, "Digestion Room" in one section of the blueprints.

It was fascinating to me that a massive air and space museum was being constructed on a small island without any real landmark aviation history to speak of, but also fascinating that it was done so with such rapidity. This is not meant to be an indictment on the process by any means, but seeing the blueprints and learning that the signs were being printed as soon as I checked off on the spelling taught me a lot about Jeju's ongoing impetus for expansion. If the fire mountain festival was a nod to the lore of the past, it was equipoised with a push into the progressive future. And I couldn't fully know one end without exploring the other.

3. What is it about islands?

In the early 1970s, a twangy singer-songwriter from Mississippi released a three-minute song titled, "A Mile High in Denver," about the rugged beauty of central Colorado. Despite a catchy chorus and heartfelt lyrics that spoke to the wonder of a bucolic place, the tune failed to make much of an impact on the pop charts. But just a few years later, in 1977, the same singer-songwriter released another tune, this time reflecting on another bucolic place—a sun-baked beach—and the anguish of a tropical hangover. That song, "Margaritaville," shot to the top of the United States' charts and established its author, Jimmy Buffett, as the chief troubadour for wanderlusting beach bums everywhere.

As Buffett's career progressed, it became clear that he wasn't just singing pop songs; he was promoting an entire lifestyle. Parallel to this, the idea of tropical and subtropical paradises became more popular than ever in the public consciousness as the end of the 20th century neared. Beaches became vacation destinations and lying around on far-flung islands became a veritable travel objective for Middle America. Aiding all of this was an increasing ease and economic accessibility of world travel, with jets able to cruise to beach resorts on the other side of the world with speed and convenience that travelers nowadays take for granted. 27 years after Buffett's smash hit, a comparable narrative would be conveyed in J. Maarten Troost's 2004 bestseller, *The Sex Lives of Cannibals*, a book about making a home in the South Pacific and finding that paradise is—and is not—everything it's cracked up to be. TV shows at the time like *Temptation Island* and, of course, *Survivor*, also leaned heavily on a parallel foundation of absconding to islands. The notion of dropping everything and fleeing to a beach certainly is not new, but it is more widespread than ever.

This idea of island escapism weighed on my mind for the first several weeks on Jeju as I gazed around the gorgeous belt of pines and palms where the land met the water, observed the camellias in bright red bloom and kicked at shell fragments in the sand. There was a distinct scent to the island, a mingling of ocean bite and floral earth, as if the air was both fresh and ancient in the same breath. Breaking from the coastal breezes and cutting inland one time, the mineral smell of wet stone hit hard. There are a lot of impressive rock formations on Jeju. One of the most famous outcroppings, called *Yongduam*, resembles a dragon's head. Other rocks are remarkably uniform, hexagonal pillars staked deep into the sea or laid

Island Solitaire

across eroding mountain gradients. Being volcanic in origin, Jeju was never part of mainland Korea, nor was it ever attached to any greater land mass; it swelled and erupted from the earth nearly two million years ago. It has always been alone in the ocean, reached at some indeterminate moment in history by travelers of the sea, so its character developed from such isolation.

Wrapping around a row of bushes, the sky high above boldly blue, I came to a meadow punctuated with three holes in the ground. Not far away, a street curved around the meadow's rim and stocky buildings smeared an otherwise exquisite vista. This modest plot of grass represents the crux of Jeju—corporate development all around, ancient legend in the middle. The three holes are the folkloric origin of all life on the island. As the story goes, three spirits by the names of Ko, Yang and Bu emerged from the holes and procreated with the princesses of a wayward sailor to populate the island. In fact, Jeju locals with Ko, Yang and Bu surnames consider themselves to be descendants of the island's original inhabitants.

Pondering this plot of land and the story made me think about mankind's long-time interest in islands. What was the motivation that drove people in history to the sea and to the islands?

It turns out that motives of the seafarers of the past fall into a shortlist of categories. The Spanish Conquistadors around the 1500s, for example, admitted as much, declaring that they sailed on the ocean for the three Gs of God, gold and glory. Long ago, there were individuals who traveled the dangerous ocean waters out of curiosity and a craving for adventure, perhaps the most romantic of motivations, although the reality of a grimy and disease-ridden life at sea tended to conjure up anything but romance. There were also those in search of a commodity, be it treasure, exotic food or additional land. Finally, of course, there were those bands of sailors with imperial interests, either monarchically or divinely inspired.

Once discovered, many islands of the world were developed with additional goals in mind—as bastions of resources such as timber, as residences for criminals, as safe havens for oppressed and persecuted assemblages and as outposts for a host of interests that might include legitimizing land claims or feeding resources such as spices back to a mother country.

Such diversity should not overshadow the sheer risks in all historic journeys to reach islands, especially in the earliest days of sea travel. Pacific islands such as those that make up Polynesia are believed to have been reached by seafarers from the Asia mainland who traveled on the vast ocean in mere outrigger canoes. Propelled by nothing more than manpower and knowledge of the currents and patterns of the wind, early island travelers first populated the land spits peppered nearby their homes, but they gradually ventured farther out on the unknown ocean over time—to Easter Island around 300 C.E., and to New Zealand 600 years after that.

At the same time, other parts of the world were taking to the sea in pursuit of islands as well. In Europe and in the Middle East, shipbuilding was evolving in ways that made ocean travel faster, although taking to the seas was still an extremely grueling endeavor. Nausea, scurvy and starvation were coupled with hazards that offered a more instantaneous demise like drowning or getting shipwrecked on jagged rocks. The Vikings of present-day Norway, famously among the toughest brutes of the sea, traveled as far as the Arab world with their clinkered hulls, long oars and square-shaped sails. In the process, they settled the mammoth island of Iceland around 870 C.E.

The shape of the sails, as minor a detail as it might seem, cannot be overstated, as it became clearer with each extended ocean voyage that the key to long-distance travel for any nation was not the ability to ride the currents or paddle through them, but to harness the wind and utilize it for propulsion on the water. Eventually triangular sails became the standard, although there is uncertainty about their culture of origin. What is certain is that by the early 1400s, the Spanish were using the most up-to-date sailing technology to settle the Canary Islands as stopovers for their lumbering galleons. This was a time of ridiculous flux for the whole world, not only on various islands but also on larger swaths of land. Jeju was no exception, as Genghis Khan and his descendants ruthlessly invaded China, Iran, Ukraine and Korea to accumulate an enormous frame of property for the Mongolian empire in the 13th century. Khan's conquest was the largest land grab in the world, but it would be relatively short-lived by historical standards.

A few important things happened around the world in the 1,000 years following Khan's Asian and European invasions. The long stretch of years, 1400 to 1500, represents one of the more popular chunks of time in social studies classes in the Western World for good reason—North America and South America became major commodities. Columbus famously got caught in the Westerlies while at sea in 1492, stumbled upon the island of Hispaniola in the West Indies and, convinced he was on the outskirts of Asia, managed to get credit for discovering all of North America. The U.S. celebration of Columbus Day every October in the current century is a minor oddity compared to other transgressions in the history of island exploration. For example, around the time of Columbus, the Spanish deported anyone in their country who wasn't Catholic, which laid the groundwork for the country's religious genocide meekly referred to as the Inquisition. While not directly related to island discoveries, the Inquisition holds an important distinction, as it epitomized a mentality of intolerance for other cultures— religious and ethnic—that would come to accompany ensuing island exploration until modern times.

During the Inquisition period, Western ships were starting to venture farther East. In Asia, and particularly in the islands of Asia, it was pepper, cloves and nutmeg that enticed European ships in the years following Mongolia's massive land seizure. Five years after Columbus' historic voyage, in 1497, Vasco da Gama acquired peppery spices in Asia and then sold them in his native Portugal at an astronomical price markup. 22 years later, in arguably the grandest achievement of the era, Ferdinand Magellan (or at least the surviving members of his crew) circumnavigated the globe by sea, reminding the whole world that there really were no longer limits to where ships could travel.

Up to this point, all of the island exploration in world history had been accomplished without thorough knowledge of the continents, let alone concepts such as plate tectonics or continental drift. As Tony Horwitz notes in *Blue Latitudes*, the prevailing belief in Europe at the time was that there must exist a southern mass of continental terra firma comparable to that in the Northern Hemisphere. Couple that with the European trend of the time—evangelizing and converting other cultures of the world to Catholicism and Christianity—and one gets a fairly sound idea of the maritime scene from which a sailor named Captain James Cook emerged in the late 1700s.

Cook proved to be a remarkable student of the sea, despite possessing a modest academic background. He was specifically chosen to sail for King George III of England and stargaze around the world. His main objective, at least initially, was to plot the stars and aid in a more scientific understanding of Earth's place in space. But Cook would ultimately become more famous for the land and the people that he encountered unexpectedly on his ensuing trips rather than any celestial findings. On his ship, *The Endeavour*, crowded with a crew of nearly 100 sailors and stocked with 5,000 gallons of alcohol, Cook traveled to islands as remote as Tahiti and as far south as Australia. In the process, he became the world's most well-known island explorer. In subsequent trips across the world's seas, he hit Easter Island, the Tongan Islands, the Society Islands and New Zealand before being killed in Hawaii.

There is such a long list of famous figures in the storied history of the world's islands that one would need volumes of biographies to adequately present their accomplishments. But turning back to Asia, it is remarkable just how untrammeled the island of Jeju was from cultural outsiders for most of its known history.

Archaeologists have deduced that humans first appeared on Jeju 25,000 years ago as peripatetic, primitive nomads. History also shows that Jeju's inhabitants didn't establish permanent social structures in the form of lasting villages until approximately 2,000 years ago, and those communities produced modern commodities like abalone blades, clay beads and pottery that drew from both the ocean and the inland hills. In the 1200s, Genghis Khan and the Mongols took control of the island, which had gone through several name changes—*Tamna* being among the most established monikers prior to *Jeju*.[1] (The name Jeju came in the early 13th century, derived from a combination of Chinese characters—*je*, which is the phonetic translation of the verb "to cross," and *ju*, which means, "state.") A particularly bloody battle on Jeju in 1273 resulted in the defeat of the Korean military division known as Sambyeolcho; the copious amounts of bloodshed during the fight actually colored a wide band of the

---

[1] Although *Tamna* is not the contemporary name for Jeju, some people on the Korean mainland still refer to Jeju inhabitants as Tamnaian in a joking manner, a nod to the island's long-ago label.

Island Solitaire

soil completely red, and so one of Jeju's small mountains was named *Bulgeun Oreum*—roughly translated as "Red Hill"—in honor of Sambyeolcho's valor.

The Mongol campaigns in Korea ceased by the 1400s, but the effects continued to be felt. In fact, Jeju's population suffered in assorted ways for generations after that. Largely left out of nation-wide politics, Jeju found itself informally divided into comparatively self-sufficient districts after the Mongolian period, and the leaders of those communities demanded a number of levies on everything from citrus grown by families to fish caught on the beaches. Virtually all members of the community below the island's elite were forced to work long hours in the fields or harvest edible fare from the sea. It all amounted to a laborious and poor existence for Jeju's working class. Perhaps worst of all was a ruling in the 1600s that made it illegal for locals to leave the island; this principally imprisoned the workers and made it impossible for anyone to better his lot in life. Not surprisingly, starvation, suicide, protests and general misery became typical in the era.

The Dutch East India Company emerged as the most successful European trading company around Jeju in the 1600s but had no noteworthy commercial interests in the island, and only encountered it by accident in the course of conducting business with other Asian nations. The Japanese, as well, utilized Jeju centuries later during World War II, when all of Korea was under Japanese colonial rule. However, even to peninsular Koreans, Jeju was long considered a blip in the country's geographic scope—first as a reservoir for political exiles from the 14th century to the early 20th century, and after that as a rugged landscape of poor farming communities. Neither reputation made the island an enticing destination in the sun-drenched, paradisiacal sense, despite the fact that it had sunshine and white-sand beaches in excess. In that way, it is imperative to view Jeju in comparison to the rest of the world's islands precisely because it wasn't actively sought by numerous foreign powers on a repeated basis throughout history.

Still, friction was present on Jeju for a long time. Tensions with Japan were ongoing, and Japan's formal colonization of Korea in 1910 brought about far-reaching surveillance and oppression of many islanders. The colonization also resulted in Jeju becoming a tactical base for Japan's other military actions in the region.[2] A cholera epidemic in the 1920s added to the island's woes, and poverty remained extensive.

But the economic complexion of the island began to change in the rough-hewn years following the Korean War. As South Korea rebuilt its identity and infrastructure from the wreckage of combat bit by bit, its government latched onto industries that could bring a lot of money expeditiously to the nation's ravaged economy. It was during this period of reconstruction that South Korea's

---

[2] One major example was Japan's use of Jeju's southern port, Moseulpo, as the rendezvous point for the Japanese military planes that returned from substantial bombing campaigns in Nanjing, China, in the 1930s. The bombings, part of the Second Sino-Japanese War, killed hundreds of thousands of people.

attitude of doing everything *bbali-bbali* (quick-quick) emerged. The industry of tourism, of welcoming foreigners who had plenty of money to spend, fit the bill. Jeju was one of the nearest international destinations for Japanese tourists in the 1960s, and they flocked to the South Korean island in droves. A downside to this Japanese tourism influx was a rise in a sex-work industry on the island that catered to weary travelers, and a particular type of brothel known as the *bangseokjip*—literally "cushion house"—represented this.

One can speculate how seedy things might have become on Jeju had it not been for another demographic of tourists that handpicked the island as the destination of choice around the same time: honeymooners. There were restrictions on foreign travel for Koreans that lasted until the early 1980s, including the government barring young men from taking vacations abroad. Jeju, almost by default, became the viable option for romantic domestic travel; the island had white-sand beaches, it had picturesque, windswept points for photo-ops, it had a burgeoning hotel industry and it had a unique local culture that offered just enough dissimilarity to the rest of South Korea to feel exotic.

In one of the few comprehensive studies on Jeju's honeymoon roots, sociologist Gwisook Gwon notes that it was customary until the 1950s for a married couple in South Korea to travel to the husband's hometown; the idea of taking a vacation honeymoon—separated from the family ties—didn't come to South Korea until later decades. South Korea imported the honeymoon concept from Japan, but for many years such extravagant trips remained luxuries that only upper-class Korean couples could enjoy. However, with the founding of Korean Air Lines in 1962 and the increasing ease of air travel, Jeju honeymoons for mainland Koreans became alluring precisely because they required a plane flight—still considered somewhat of a glamorous indulgence to middle class Koreans, even into the 1970s.

In certain areas, Jeju still possesses a gaudy charm leftover from its honeymoon heyday. Newlywed Koreans now opt often for sunny destinations of a more international profile—Hawaii, Maldives and the Bahamas. But meander down certain roads in Jeju City, and there are lavish honeymoon resorts from the 1960s and 1970s that are abandoned, left adorned with design touches from a previous era. There are also plenty of wedding photo studios still open for business, and tourism packages catering to a whole new clientele of Chinese investors. Mainland Koreans from the cities of Seoul and Busan still frequent Jeju, but usually as backpackers, not honeymooners, taking respites from busy urban life. An entire trend, *sambak-sa-il* ("three nights, four days"), envelops this novel concept of mainlanders traveling to Jeju for a short period of time with the sole intention of getting mentally recharged on the island.

Finished nosing around the plot of greenery with the three holes in the ground, I hopped on a city bus and left the urban bustle for the remainder of the afternoon. I was left with the big phenomenological question burning like an ember in my mind: whether any reality existed in a place—a home or a travel destination—beyond what was sought and seen by the traveler. Realizing suddenly then that one of my good friends on the island had the surname Ko—the same as that of one of Jeju's founding spirits—I felt curious to know what she thought of all the island's lore. I thought that perhaps she could tell me the story of Jeju's initial population with some more local flare, so I promptly reached out to her. She told me regretfully over the phone that she had left Jeju for a few weeks. In fact, she had spent a year saving money and was off vacationing in the United States.

"I wanted to go somewhere exotic," she said, laughing. "Jeju was just getting too comfortable."

4. Mountain lives

The visible onset of fall in the canopies reaffirmed one truism: South Korea loves hiking. In nearly every major town in the entire country, I observed multiple stores selling trekking poles, windbreakers, thick-soled boots and other hiking accouterments. I had even heard a recommendation that hiking should replace taekwondo as South Korea's national sport. Martial arts were taught to most Koreans in elementary school but, unlike mountain trekking, not frequently continued as hobbies into adulthood.

When I first started working on Jeju, a colleague suggested that I keep a pair of hiking boots in my office so that I could hike the nearby mountain during lunch breaks. It wasn't an uncommon suggestion, as a portmanteau word had emerged in recent years in Korea—*walunch*—that combined walking and lunch and implied skipping a meal altogether to hike instead.

Island Solitaire

The mountain that my colleague was referring to was Halla Mountain, known as *Halla-san* to the Koreans, a 6,000-foot tall extinct volcano peak in the center of Jeju that also happened to be the highest mountain in all of South Korea. Hiking Halla Mountain could be a quick, steep affair or an all-day effort, depending on which of its five main trails one accessed. Jeju also boasted 26 shorter hiking trails, known as *olles*, which were established in 2007 by a hiker named Suh Myung-suk and modeled after the Camino de Santiago trails in Spain. Annual walking festivals and trail runs were also popular events on the island. All of this served to draw residents into the outdoors, and onto the mountain paths.

Mountaineering in Korea is as ancient as anywhere on the planet. In the 4th century, the deceased were laid in ornate tombs adorned with paintings and drawings of mountains, mountain animals, shamans and gods. As far back as the Neolithic Age, when hunters and gatherers were still using spears and earthenware to get through the day, various groups used the mountains as important territorial borders.

In Jeju, the importance of mountains to the livelihood and culture of early inhabitants is reflected in the island's creation myth. As it goes, an enormous goddess named *Sulmundae* descended from heaven, landed in the ocean and began piecing together Jeju. In one transcribed version of the legend, *Sulmundae* declared that she would put a large mountain on the island; the peak would play with the depth perception of its pursuers, always near in appearance but geographically quite far away.

John Burgman

With that deception in mind, *Sulmundae* slapped wet sea sand on top of more sand in construction of Halla Mountain, and when she had finished, she stood up and the sand in her lap fell to the ground and formed the smaller volcanic cone mountains—the 368 *oreum* peaks scattered around Jeju. The *Sulmundae* legend likens Jeju, oval-shaped and verdant, to a precious gemstone, and notes that it possessed such natural beauty and tranquility that people couldn't help but be drawn to it from the surrounding lands. And settle they did—in the present, half a million people live on the island, alongside nearly 200 types of birds, 100 species of mammals and 2,000 different types of plants.

In the centuries that followed *Sulmundae's* mythical construction, other popular outdoor activities for enjoying such natural abundance have included rock climbing, wind surfing, mountain biking and kayaking. But hiking remains the most alluring.

The event that really aided in boasting Jeju's mountain stock on an international scale came in the early 2000s, when Halla Mountain and select other geographical features were designated as UNESCO World Heritage sites. Such labels play big globally for tourism and marketing. Other World Heritage sites include the banks of the Seine River in Paris, France, the Acropolis in Athens, Greece and the Taj Mahal in India, which puts Halla Mountain in the company of some of the most sought-after landmarks for travelers.

Hiking is especially popular in the fall for locals because of the chance to view the autumnal changes in the forest. Awakening one Sunday morning at 5:30 to beat the weekend crowds on the mountain, I set out on one of the groomed trails that wound up a spine of Halla Mountain. I was joined by my American friend Dan, who was taking a break from a comprehensive study of Jeju's modern wind power initiative to see the mountain foliage at its colorful peak.[3]

As a long-time island resident, Dan was an authority on Jeju hiking. "I know it seems like there aren't many other people on the trail yet, but just wait," he said.

As our path crossed a shallow river, we encountered a group of women also hiking the trail and posing for photographs on a narrow bridge. Then as if the figurative floodgates had been opened, our trail inclined and we saw behind us a long string of hikers following up the same path. More to the point of hiking being a national pastime in South Korea, it was obvious that the teeming masses bringing up the rear this early in the morning were serious about their hiking. Their metallic trekking poles shimmered in the morning light. They walked at steady, even paces, and their shiny jackets made them look like

---

[3] Several years ago, Jeju's local government unveiled a comprehensive set of plans to make the island entirely dependent on wind power by the year 2030. However, many of the wind farms that were constructed across Jeju's rural landscape—and wind turbines that were yet-to-be constructed offshore—were owned by corporations from the Korean mainland. Some islanders objected to the wind power initiative for this reason. There was also vocal opposition to Jeju's initial proposal because of the unsightly nature of the wind turbines on the scenic grasslands of the island. Needless to say, wind energy remains a big issue on Jeju for multiple reasons. Other islands of the world—Aruba, Hawaii and Jamaica among them—have also flirted increasingly with wind energy pushes.

colorful beetles from a distance. The crowd, equipped and motivated and mountain-savvy, was quickly heading toward us.

"See?" Dan said, nodding at the line. "I told you—they love to hike on Jeju."

Our trek became an attempt to stay ahead of the pack, but by the time we reached a respite point an hour later, all separation had been lost. We ascended farther to a wooden shack selling ramen noodles and hot coffee. Around us, scraggly plants were rustling in a crisp breeze. Sitting on the steps of the shack, we fell asleep briefly despite the crowd, despite the chatter and loud children clomping around on some wooden planks. Upon waking, we continued further on the trail until reaching the top of the mountain forty minutes later. The crater lake known as *Baengnokdam* sparkled in the sun at the mountain's pinnacle. Thin clouds drifted by at eye-level and then disappeared in the distant blue of the sky. It was a breathtaking view.

Reflecting on reaching the summit during his own hike on Halla Mountain years ago, Jeju writer Yang Sang-ick wrote that the top of the mountain allowed him to fully bask in Jeju's natural wonder and brought on a welcomed amnesia, as if one had been temporarily removed from all life's assorted difficulties. The summit was the place where Sang-ick felt he could have a silent dialogue with the earth.

It was impossible not to feel a similar connection with the wilderness and the vast land and elevation at one's feet at the mountain's peak. When Dan and I had soaked in the view for a lazy 30 minutes, we began a sluggish descent. Once again, we were engulfed in the pack of people, but it didn't matter. Being part of the crowd offered a communal aura to movement down the side of the mountain.

At one point we passed tall stone spires rising up from the earth, and Dan explained that they were mythically called the 500 Generals. They represented the sons of the goddess *Sulmundae*. As the myth goes, *Sulmundae* worked tirelessly to cook for all of her sons. One day, the sons returned from hunting and found *Sulmundae's* bones at the bottom of their soup bowls. She had worked so hard to cook for them that she had collapsed into her own vat of soup. The sons were so ashamed that they turned to stone and were deemed "generals" for the manner at which they now watched over the mountainous land.

It was crowded on the mountain and slow going as Dan and I returned to the trailhead and finished our hike through an elongated, shady glade filled with fluttering moths and chattering tour bus drivers.

It was unpleasantly congested, but I suppose it could have been worse—we could have met a different fate and become rocks jutting up from the mountainside, forever guilt-ridden for having eaten our own mothers!

5. The East-West connection

The first historic instance of East meeting West on Jeju—at least, on any interpersonal level—came not through calculated diplomacy or international outreach, but from a violent storm on the high seas and a resulting shipwreck in August of 1653. A ship from the Netherlands, the *Sparrowhawk* (*De Sperwer* in Dutch), traveling for the Dutch East India Company, set sail in January of that year with a long-term itinerary of docking in several well-known Asian ports and gliding listlessly over to Nagasaki, Japan. The merchant ship was carrying a boatload of assorted spices and animal hides for trading that summer. It was a risky trip, not only due to its nautical distance and duration, but also because the weather around Japan grew increasingly unpredictable as the temperature of the air and water warmed. Still, the trip was in keeping with the Dutch ethos of the day, which embraced foreign business ventures and long-distance ocean travel. In fact, the Dutch established New Netherland, an early iteration of present-day New York City, during this same era on the opposite side of the world.

By the time July, 1653, arrived, the 64 men aboard *The Sparrowhawk* had managed to avoid any thrashings from the seasonal monsoons, and began the final leg of their Japan-bound journey with crystalline seas and clear skies.

Shortly after departing from present-day Taiwan on a northbound ocean route toward the Japanese archipelago, *The Sparrowhawk* crew found themselves caught in the clutches of a brewing storm. A journal written after the fact by Hendrick Hamel, a gunner, scribe and member of the ship's crew, describes the ferocity of the ensuing days with bone-chilling detail: winds growing so severe that verbal communication among the crew members became unfeasible, weather conditions steadily worsening to the point where it became impossible to gauge the ship's exact location at sea, waves crashing onto the deck and the ship's architecture springing harmful leaks. Compounding such dismal conditions on the night of August 16th were pitch darkness and an inability to secure the ship's anchor amid the torrent.

Without any stabilization, *The Sparrowhawk* rode helplessly atop the rolling waves of Asia's seas in the black night until slamming into the igneous rocks of Jeju's south shore—200 miles away from the intended destination of Nagasaki.

Many of the crewmembers drowned—some by the crushing force of the waves, others by willfully and hopelessly jumping into the sea as their ship crunched over the jagged rocks. Those who survived the crash, like Hamel, climbed through the shallows in the darkness while nursing various injuries. One can't read Hamel's account without sensing how apocalyptic the scene must have been. He described the small band of survivors as essentially surrounded in the blackness by the moans of dying men still caught in the ship's wreckage.

In the course of sifting through the debris for survivors and salvageable food and materials the following morning, the remaining crew assessed that only 36 men had survived the night's calamity—roughly half of the original group having been killed or otherwise unaccounted for.

At first, the survivors of *The Sparrowhawk* thought Jeju was deserted, so they set up a small camp using remnants of the boat's sails. They used recovered wine to serve as an anesthetic for those men still nursing severe wounds. But as curious locals began to show up, the crew—wrongly guessing that the onlookers were Chinese pirates—took the island to be a haven for bandits. Attempts at verbal communication proved useless. In a rather amusing anecdote in Hamel's notes, Jeju locals approached the injured men with ropes—a gesture that the Dutch sailors took to imply impending execution by hanging; the Jeju locals, in fact, were merely offering their help—and rope—to tow additional salvageable materials from the ship's wreckage.

The next several days were spent swapping cultural subtleties as much as they were spent recuperating and destroying the useless remnants of the demolished ship.

Island Solitaire

The Dutch shared their wine and navigation accessories with the islanders, who in turn fed the wounded men rice and the Korean alcoholic beverage called soju.

Although Hamel and the crew quickly determined their location to be the island of Jeju (known then as *Quelpaert*), they were at a loss to explain their intended route to the line of dignitaries to whom they were eventually brought.

Given the slow pace of news in the 1600s, the tattered crew of *The Sparrowhawk* were forced into a long social holding pattern on Jeju while island officials awaited word from the Korean king on how to best handle the strangely-dressed visitors. They were exposed to shaman healers in the interim, and in a surprising instance of homeland nostalgia, they were brought before another captive Dutch sailor named Jan Janse Weltevree. Years prior, Weltevree had also found himself stranded in Korea, and in rather disheartening honesty, he explained to the surviving crew of *The Sparrowhawk* that there was no hope for escape from the country: the Korean authorities would probably allow the sailors to live a suitable life in Korea, so at least an immediate order of execution by the Korean king was unlikely. But the crew would never be granted freedom to leave Korea.

Hamel and the others, having been declared unlawful trespassers, were eventually taken as captives to the Korean mainland. After forced Korean military servitude and ineffectual protests, eight of the original members of *The Sparrowhawk* did manage to escape from Korea, setting out in a small boat and successfully—finally—

reaching refuge in Japan in 1666. The captivity of Hamel and his shipmates had lasted 13 years.

If Korea's geographic imprisonment of the Dutch crew seems callous and unwarranted, it is somewhat refracted in the cultural intolerance of British naval officer Edward Belcher 200 years later—another instance of Jeju dealing with the West in a union that was less than harmonious. Belcher also landed on Jeju, albeit purposefully, in 1843, and used his gun as a means of controlling the local islanders. Additionally, he cut down sacred trees on the island and renamed well-known features with British epithets. For example, Udo Island off of Jeju's coast became Beaufort Island, although it has since been rechristened Udo.

The historic accounts of Hamel and Belcher make at least two points of significance in Jeju's modern identity. On one hand, the histories exemplify a narrative that is common in the wide fabric of antiquity and exploration—two cultures encountering each other, with the resultant combustion begetting more kinetic aspects such as violence, forced servitude, intolerance and disease.

Equally as interesting to me was the other point. Learning that Hamel—and to a lesser extent, Belcher—are taught to Korean schoolchildren as naturally as Americans are taught about, say, the Founding Fathers, is a bit peculiar. The rub to me was this: while the Founding Fathers and many of the other stalwarts of American history were American in their ideals—however diversified or polarizing any given notion of America might have been—Hamel and the rest of *The*

Island Solitaire

Sparrowhawk crew wanted no part in any sort of Korean ideal. They were prisoners, plain and simple.

In other words, it struck me as a peculiar type of history to teach wide-eyed Korean schoolchildren, highlighting foreigners who had no real interest in adopting the Korean culture and, in the case of *The Sparrowhawk*, didn't even want to be in the country at all. Not surprising, Korean history tends to downplay the fact that the crew members were held against their will. Nearly every pamphlet that I encountered on Jeju related to Hamel's plight cheerily explained that he arrived on Jeju from the Netherlands, stayed in Korea for years, and then left. I had to dig deeper to uncover the truth about his incarceration.

In a coastal bend in southern Jeju, there exists today a monument dedicated to Hamel, erected in a joint effort by South Korea and the Dutch Embassy in 1980. It resides somewhat forgotten atop a windswept hill of daffodils and billowy grass, overshadowed by vendors at the hill's base selling coconut drinks and fresh tangerines. I decided to hike up to the monument one breezy afternoon to see just how Jeju publicly honors the complex history of Hendrick Hamel.

Much like other islands of the world have kept plaques to outsiders like Captain James Cook conspicuously pithy and tepid, a stone plaque in the monument's corner reads:

John Burgman

ON AUGUST 16TH, 1653, THE NETHERLANDS SHIP, *DE SPERWER*, WAS LOST IN A STORM AND LANDED ON THIS COAST WITH HENDRICK HAMEL AND HIS SHIPMATES ABOARD. AFTER STAYING 13 YEARS IN KOREA, HAMEL RETURNED TO THE NETHERLANDS TO WRITE THE FIRST DESCRIPTION OF KOREA EVER PUBLISHED IN THE WEST.

It certainly gave a truncated version of the events, and the phrase "staying 13 years" resounded to me like a public relations spin. But hiking closer to the shore, I was able to get the particulars that the succinct plaque text omitted. Near the site where *The Sparrowhawk* wrecked sat a large-scale replica of the ship, with a walkthrough museum of instructive billboards about the Dutch East India Company and some of the island exploration around the world that preceded Hamel's calamity.

In his journals, Hamel documented everything from Korean marriage customs to the country's houses, all of which were noted inside the museum with small signs. Outside, there was a life-size statue of a tranquil-looking Hamel, although it was hard to imagine the man ever possessing such a calm and unruffled demeanor amid shipwreck, capture and imprisonment.

Amusingly, there was another statue next to Hamel's—of Guus Hiddink, also Dutch, who famously coached the South Korean soccer team to a stellar performance in the 2002 World Cup. The Hiddink statue was meant to entice patrons into a hamburger shack and gift shop near *The Sparrowhawk* replica. I observed no less than a dozen people taking photos in front of this statue in the span of a few minutes, and only one person—a teenager—mugging for a camera in front of Hamel. It is also worth mentioning that the Hiddink hamburger shack had far more patrons than did *The Sparrowhawk* replica. Here was a site where men from the West had been incarcerated in the East—somewhat understandably, if one remembers how terribly foreign explorers often treated the native inhabitants of islands. The hallowed grounds had now been preserved in an attempt to emphasize the positives that resulted from Hamel's detention. Yet, the draw of the whole space for countless tourists was a burger joint.

Perhaps all the complexity was best veiled in total vagueness, giving each individual an opportunity to fill in all of the gaps at will. As one sign proclaimed, simply, Hamel "encountered a storm and drifted to Jeju…After 13 years, he returned to his homeland and wrote, 'Hamel's Journal,' about his experience in Korea."

The Sparrowhawk deserves a place in the annals of Jeju's history because of its lasting effects. Some visitors to the site might not get the enormity of the event, but the presence of the hamburger shack and a gift shop surely epitomize a cross of cultures. Hamel's presence, that is, the presence of the West, is still felt—and, thus, Hamel's story still relevant—in every cultural guffaw made by a foreigner, every idiom or local custom examined by an outsider, every festival explored by a curious bystander like myself and every reminder that in order for East to eventually meet West, they first had to be very far apart.

6. Food in flux

One's diet is a reflection of one's lifestyle, and a quick scan of my apartment a few months into my island life would have revealed an assortment of no-fuss Korean meals and snacks ideally suited for the teaching grind—dishes as simplistic as tuna gimbap, which is a type of seaweed and vegetable rice roll, or as basic as ham and eggs, possibly as pathetic as microwavable ramen in practically innumerable flavors. It was a lot of junk food that could be prepared in a flash. My kitchen cupboards were haphazardly organized with munchies like shrimp-flavored chips, spicy dried rice cakes and green-tea-flavored chocolates.

My refrigerator signified more ambition for complex culinary craftwork. Whole frozen fish stared at me with their dark eyes whenever I swung open my freezer door. I also maintained a stash of pickled garlic cloves, slabs of pork, bags of fermented vegetables, small bowls of chili paste known as *gochujang*, sliced lotus roots,

Island Solitaire

persimmons, anchovies, homemade sesame oil and enough cans of Cass, South Korea's most common beer, to meet the alcohol needs of my entire apartment corridor. It's not that I necessarily drank or ate all that much, but I dreamed of throwing elaborate dinner parties for guests and tossing back drinks amid embellished stories of island reverie. I visualized slaving over my stove to sculpt masterpieces, reaching deep into my spice cabinet that had been left fully stocked by my apartment's previous tenant and utilizing the mysterious offerings that had been forgotten there—cowpeas, Chinese millet, Chinese pepper and mung beans. Despite my penchant for quick meals and easy dishes, I wanted to be a good cook when it came to Korean ingredients.

For most of the globe, the one broad entity that represents Korea is its food. Such exemplification certainly held true for me for a long time. I didn't know much about the geography or culture of the Korean peninsula, nor about the country's complicated history aside from the Korean War, but I knew about the food thanks to an Asian food grocery store within driving distance of my college campus. The place sold Chinese wheat noodles, tofu, fish broth, rice cakes, soybean paste, kimchi and frozen beef ribs. It was eye-opening to me, and just walking down the aisles felt like a *National Geographic* assignment compared to the mundane grocery store trips I was used to. After college, the office where I worked in New York City happened to be two blocks from Korea Town, and such proximity allowed me to explore new Korean dishes on a regular basis during lunch breaks.

John Burgman

Seafood pancakes, peppered broiled pork, barbecued beef, seaweed soup and plump mandu dumplings became the staples that would bifurcate my days. Each night, I would flip through the Korean cookbooks at my kitchen table and dabble in the easier recipes. I learned about Korea largely through exploration of those various dishes.

Korean food is extremely popular around the world, and this is no fluke. During the sushi boom that hit the West in the late 20th century, the entire restaurant industry seemed to realize what the Japanese had known for centuries—that the simplicity and palatability of raw fish on rice was better than the batter-slathered rigor mortis fried variety that had been popular in pirate-themed fast food restaurants in the United States for decades. At the same time, other Eastern food trends began to take off at tables across the West, such as Mongolian barbecue and Thai restaurants. Savvy restaurateurs in the United States were naturally clamoring to discover the next best type of Asian cuisine. Korean food, with a characteristic spiciness comparable to that of Southeast Asian dishes, a penchant for raw seafood like Japan, and distinctive flame-grilled meat seemed to draw the best from all culinary worlds.

Not surprisingly, the South Korean government became aware of this. After all, getting people around the world eating Korean food was one tactic for enticing people to visit and spend money in South Korea. Quick-thinking legislators created the Research and Development Project for Standardization of Korean Cuisine, a type of large-scale effort to globalize Korean

Island Solitaire

food by establishing official ways to write the names of dishes and releasing specialized Korean cookbooks.

The result of such external factors is difficult to determine. Korean food is globally trendy, but still not as ubiquitous in the West as sushi. In fact, it seems like as long as I have had an awareness of Korean food, cooking magazines and TV shows like *Kimchi Chronicles* have been asserting that Korean food will be the collective world palate's next big craze, but it never quite inches over that prognostic hump. Korean food just seems somewhat like the culinary journeyman, always on the cusp and forever in the conversation.

Part of the reason for its stasis is also one of its biggest appeals—Korean food can be eye-wateringly spicy. In ancient times, the food in Korea was spiced with peppers to mask the rot and blandness that were common in meager meals of poor families. But the spiciness caught on with other social classes and is now inseparable from the dishes themselves—indeed, adding spicy ground red pepper to a famous Korean dish like tofu soup, *sundubu*, isn't just a way of garnishing the finished product, it's the dish's main characteristic.

Red-hot foods abound in South Korea, but fiery stews don't suit the preferences of everyone in the rest of the world, nor do pungent, fermented radishes, pickled squid, whole garlic cloves, raw oysters or other common Korean dishes.

In order for Korean food to truly takeover the masses, it must also overcome the challenge of dispelling misconceptions and stereotypes related to the consumption of dog meat. *Kaegogi*, as the delicacy is known, was once a staple in the diet of Koreans; other animals like cows aided in farming tasks and, thus, were not as frequently slaughtered by families and served as food. The meat of the dogs was most commonly cooked in a soup called *boshin-tang* that was believed in the past to have physiological health benefits—*bo* literally meaning "protection," and *shin* meaning "body." Dog meat is still eaten by select old-timers in hard-to-find restaurants and markets in South Korea, but it is a forgotten dish to younger generations. At my apartment in Jeju, for example, I had three go-to Korean cookbooks, and not a single one detailed how to a cook dog. A new superstition has even emerged in South Korea that cautions those who consume *kaegogi*. Dog meat is now said to bring bad luck to anyone who eats it. Old-time perceptions, however, are hard to shake. When I was initially South Korea-bound, one of the last things a New York coworker said to me was, "Please don't eat any dogs while you're in Asia." The stereotype that Koreans eat dogs on a regular basis is still widespread.

 With all this base culinary interest, I traveled to my friend Joohee's apartment one fall morning for a kimjang—the traditional daylong process of making enough kimchi to last a household for much of the winter. Consider that most Korean families have kimchi for every meal, and you have an idea of just how much kimchi must be made in such a process. Being invited to a kimjang as a foreigner, especially one who was not boarding in Joohee's home, was a special honor, a cultural treat akin to

Island Solitaire

becoming a member of the family for a day.

That's not to say that I lollygagged. Upon arrival, I was promptly put to work peeling dozens of cabbages. To get an idea of how much vegetable mass I was working with, consider that many Korean families often purchase kimjang cabbages by the cart. I then joined the women in coating cabbage and radish chunks with a saltwater glaze. Other duties of the day included dicing onions by the crateful and mixing a vat of shrimp and oyster juice in a plastic tub the size of a kid's swimming pool. The apex of the process was combining all of the separate components into a soggy, cold stew until the entire slosh of vegetables had the distinct, translucent-red sheen of baechu kimchi.

By the time we had finished, my arms were stained dark red from pepper paste. My jeans had the odor of garlic tangled within the smallest fabric molecules, and my hands were so tired that I struggled to grip the doorknob. But it had been an honor to help in the preparation of such an important dish.

As a token of thanks, Joohee's mother gave me two backpack-sized bags of kimchi for the road and offered one last caveat. "I worry that you don't have enough kimchi," she said. "You are hungry, I know this. If you need more, please call me anytime for more."

7. Tangerine dreams

By early November, the dense groves lining a curvy road near my apartment had begun to bear fruit. It was officially tangerine season on Jeju. Every evening, the dusk's sunlight caught the orange skins of the fruit and angled off them in glints, and the fall wind gusts swayed the tangerine trees below pillow-like clouds. During a walk along the road one night, I paused to look closely at the edge of the grove and spotted not only hundreds of plump tangerines hanging heavy on the tree limbs, but countless more scattered on the ground in various stages of decay. Soon all the trees would be harvested, lest more good tangerines be lost to bandit birds, scavenging animals and the inevitability of over-ripening.

Continuing my walk, I came to the grove's packaging facility, a warehouse-like building where stacks of plastic bins were ready to be filled with fresh tangerines the following day by a staff of pickers. The place smelled of kerosene. A wooden board was there to guide cardboard boxes of tangerines into a sealing and preparation area. It all looked so streamlined that I could easily envision a systematic progression—the fruit being collected out in the grove, trucked in and sorted indoors by a small staff. Many groves on Jeju are still family-owned and family-operated. It looked pleasantly simple; it was like seeing a cartoon version of what one would imagine a fruit grove's facility to be, yet it was the real thing.

Staring at the machinery through an open garage door, feeling the humming vibrations in the floor from a large fan, I was struck with a curiosity about the grove. Clearly tangerines are big business on Jeju. In fact, Jeju's tangerines—called *gamgyul*—have been big parts of the lives of the island's residents for a long time. While there are questions to this day about the exact origins of the fruit on the island, most researchers trace the existence of the tangerines to Ancient Korea's Koryo Dynasty, a time of substantial cultural and artistic growth.

The Koryo Dynasty began in the year 918 and was a time of elaborate parties if you were a member of the royal inner-circle. It was during one of these parties that the Korean king was supposedly first given tangerines from a foreign visitor. Centuries later, by the Joseon Dynasty, it had become customary to give tangerines to members of the royal family, so dozens of production facilities emerged to accommodate this custom in Korea.

There is also reason to believe that tangerines might have been part of Korea's culture even earlier. According to one account, an early Chinese ruler sent messengers to various mountains in Asia to search for restorative medicines. This was around 200 B.C., and one of the well-searched mountains in the tale, Mount Yungju, is thought to represent Halla Mountain on Jeju. The ruler's intrepid explorers are thought to be, perhaps, the first ones to sprinkle citrus seeds onto the soil of Jeju. Authenticating the legend is nearly impossible, but the timeline would align with Japanese history as well: about 100 years after such searching for all-powerful life serums, a Japanese vagabond named Tajima Mamoru visited Jeju, stocked up on tangerines that were on the island and presented them to Japanese royals upon his return to Japan.

Wherever the reality lies, there are undeniable historical references that associate Jeju tangerines with elaborate treks, royal gifts and magic elixirs in both truth and legend. In the 17th century, a Korean book of medicine specifically cited Jeju tangerines as remedies for scurvy and the common cold.

Despite the long existence of tangerines on the island, for years the fruits were only enjoyed by the monarchs or the families who cultivated the trees in small homegrown plots. That's a stark contrast to today, where Jeju's tangerines comprise more than half of South Korea's entire farming Growth Regional Domestic Product. How the tangerines became such a large-scale island commodity, as opposed to a private garden crop, is noteworthy, as South Korea had a lot of export crops from which to choose. Grains, sweet potatoes, beans, cabbage and cucumbers have all drawn substantial farming hauls over the years. Even raw silk was harvested on a large scale at one time, and in the mid-20th century, there were more than 400,000 families managing silkworm farms across the Korean peninsula.

So why did tangerines become the big winners?

For starters, one of the most common types of tangerine currently grown on the island, the Satsuma mandarin, was quite a hit when it was first introduced to Korea in the early 1900s. A French Catholic priest living on Jeju at the time, Father Emsile, was given Satsuma mandarin seeds from the Japanese. He planted the seeds in a church garden in the Jeju city of Seogwipo, and the fruit's reputation for being particularly tasty started to spread.

That's not to say, however, that Korea developed much of an agricultural industry capable of exporting goods in the ensuing years. The Korean War and the effects that followed it saw the country sink into poverty. Jeju hardly possessed the foundation for an economic boom. Rapid change came, however, spurred in part by aid from the United States. In 1961, President John F. Kennedy appointed W.W. Rostow to South Korea as a national security advisor. Rostow viewed the Asian nation as primed for development. In addition, Park Chung Hee, South Korea's determined president, also encouraged and spurred the improvement of his country's mid-20th century internal economy in an extensive movement labeled, *Saemeul*—"New Town."

Park, as president, wasn't without critics. He was, in fact, a military dictator, and his wide-ranging *Saemeul* program wasn't without faults; many of Jeju's historic shrines, which had served as the spiritual nuclei of villages for generations, were destroyed under the guise of progress during this time. It was definitely a period of change, as other implementations included electricity and sanitary water being provided to Jeju locals, as well as the construction of new roads on the island. *Saemeul* also amped up Jeju's potential to be a travel destination by improving its airport system and building tourist resorts. It was all related to a decade-long plan that Park first fashioned in 1971 to mold Jeju into a fully developed, unabashed vacation site. In line with such progress, the average income for tangerine farming families on the island rose, to the point where Jeju tangerine trees were nicknamed "college trees" because families on the island could presumably garner enough profit from a plot of trees to send their sons or daughters to a university.

Interestingly, in an old book, long forgotten in a dusty corner of the Jeju National University Library, I found an essay from the 1970s by Yang Sang-ick titled "Oranges and Gambling," which coupled Jeju's prosperous tangerine industry with newfound disposable wealth of the time—and all the vices and pitfalls that would come from it: "Two kinds of booms—especially in Seogwipo and its neighboring villages have recently arisen on this island," the essay began. "One is orange cultivation, and the other is gambling. The former is a positive tendency. The latter is a negative one."

My most notable tangerine-related memory came while hiking along one of Jeju's *olle* trails with my friend Dan one afternoon. Slate-colored clouds had unloaded

Island Solitaire

sheets of rain and then slid away to reveal blue sky. Dan and I took the sunny weather as a cue to slow our hiking pace, dry our rain jackets, and take the steeper trails that were more rugged. We clawed through tentacle-like branches of styrax trees and high-stepped over mounds of mud in stretches of the forest that were interspersed with gorgeous tangerine trees. Wild pines and violet berry shrubs filled the periphery.

Rounding a bend in one path, making a half-circle around a patch of firs and pausing to take in the view of the tangerines and the sky, we were startled by a rustling in the leaves. Dan and I glanced at each other and then in the direction of the mysterious noise. Whatever was behind the trees was very large.

Suddenly, two full-grown horses emerged from a wall of leaves and branches with their eyes locked onto us. Horses still roam freely on many rural parts of Jeju, as they have for centuries since their introduction by the Mongols in the year 1276.

Dan and I stood motionless until we heard another sound—more leaves rustling on the other edge of our half-circle. Another horse soon emerged from behind the brush, snorting loudly.

Increasingly nervous, Dan and I took a couple of cautious steps back. The snorting horse took a couple of steps toward us. We took additional steps back, and still it came closer. Then the horse turned its body slightly at an angle and the scenario became abundantly clear: Dan and I had wandered directly in between the stallion and his two favorite females.

John Burgman

I could feel my heart throbbing in my chest. The stallion continued to press forward, even when we stood completely still. Dan and I had to scramble, or else we would have most certainly been trampled—or at least inquisitively prodded—there beside the picturesque tangerine trees.

I darted immediately to the right, and Dan ran to the left. I recall taking several long strides over the grass, sprinting as the trees became a blur in my peripheral vision. I slowed my pace after several seconds to check on Dan. He was running too, and the persistent horse was chasing him.

The horse leaned its long head forward, opened its mouth and nipped at Dan's shoulder. I saw the horse's long, yellow teeth and thick lips close around Dan's plaid shirt.

"Oh, God," Dan yelled, fearing that the horse had chomped down on a meaty lump of scapula muscle.

Luckily, in the bumpy chase on uneven ground, the horse had only managed to get a mouthful of Dan's shirt cloth. Seemingly satisfied at making us retreat like the helpless bipeds we were, the horse turned his attention to the mares.

Dan, on the other hand, continued to sprint. I ran forward too, and we reconvened behind a large cedar tree. We both agreed that we had had enough hiking for the day. We turned so that we could see through a clearing in some gnarly firs. We stared at the vista for a moment and tried hopelessly to calculate our elevation. Distantly visible clouds were striped above treetops far from our vantage point. Close encounters with horses had their empirical place in research, certainly, as did specimen tangerine trees. But what struck me most was how our misadventure had inadvertently led us to such a calm, reflective glade.

Contemplating the sweeping view of the island's landscape then, with my already-injured ribs throbbing from all the running, my thoughts returned to the fire mountain festival, apparently predicated on the potential for one's body and spirit to be reinvigorated—a crossable boundary between a real person and a more mystical essence of a person. Whether or not I believed in such a traversable margin, I wanted to respect it. At the very least, in order to better understand the human aspect of the festival, I felt I needed to find an old myth that actually entailed struggles that were both humanistic and fantastic.

8. The long and winding tale

I had heard the name Samani several times since arriving on Jeju, but I had never managed to piece together who exactly Samani was. At one point, gazing out to sea and hearing a sunscreen-scented elderly couple mention the name, I assumed Samani to be a local celebrity; at another point, upon hearing the name uttered on the steps of an administration office after a conference, I figured Samani must be a political figure.

As it turned out, all my assumptions were laughably wrong. The mysterious Samani wasn't a man from the past or present, but a character in a popular island myth. Samani appears in a local tale that represents a guiding moral principle for islanders. Unlike many Western myths, where narratives follow a steady upward arc, Samani's meandering storyline ebbs and flows with great unpredictability. What initially sounds a little like the Brothers Grimm's *Hansel and Gretel* descends into a macabre existential terror, and eventually ends up feeling weirdly Biblical. It was precisely that erratic and unconventional structure that made the Samani story so fascinating to me.

As a protagonist, Samani fits nicely with the mythic archetype of a callow, male dreamer. According to the legend, he was a destitute orphan who roamed around Jeju long ago, begging, stealing and living on the streets. One day, he met another begging orphan, a young girl with beautiful hair. In order to fill their respective familial voids, Samani and the girl decided to become brother and sister. This union, along with their begging, continued for a few years—until puberty hit, and the brother-sister bond proved stifling for both of them. Samani and the girl decided to change their status to husband and wife, and they consummated the switch in status in a big way: they decided to give birth to a baby once a year for the remainder of their marriage.

Feeling the surmounting costs of popping out offspring like a gumball machine, Samani's wife borrowed money from a village tycoon and asked Samani to head to the market for supplies. But exponential economic prosperity was not to be. Samani didn't get very far with the borrowed money, stopping to buy food for a couple of shivering street boys and also purchasing a warm hotel room and some alcohol for a few down-and-out blind men. When Samani returned home to his wife empty-handed, without new baby clothes or food from the market, his wife actually praised his charitable actions. She then gave Samani a lock of her lustrous hair to pawn at the market.

Yet, again, Samani shirked his shopping duties and traded the valuable sample of his wife's hair for a hunting rifle.

A reader accustomed to Western literature might assume that Samani's narrative will follow an established pattern, with good-natured Samani always losing his wife's money on the way to the market until a climactic incident. However, what's so charming about Samani's tale is that it swerves here and turns out not to be about persistence at all. In fact, the second half of the myth switches themes so unabashedly that one can't help but wonder if the subsequent acts were added long after the myth's initial conception. Whatever the case, get ready for a rather trippy second act.

For starters, Samani's wife surprisingly wasn't upset with Samani for purchasing the hunting rifle. In fact, the hunting rifle turned out to be a smart investment. Samani hunted with it and for a blissful chunk of time, all was well in the Samani household—the children were all fed and the marriage was happy. Then one day while hunting far from home, Samani tripped over a human skull buried in the soil.

For those readers keeping track, this is where the myth takes a dark turn.

The skull began to talk to Samani, claiming to be the former owner of Samani's hunting rifle, and Samani was ordered to dutifully worship the skull. Samani hiked home with the talking dead head, bathed it in liquor, enshrined it on his mantle and worshiped it as he was commanded to do.

For another stretch of time, all was well for Samani and

Island Solitaire

his large family, which now included that talking skull on the mantle. One day three representatives from heaven descended to talk to Samani. It seemed that Samani's time on earth was coming to an end. Rather than resist the representatives and their mandate, Samani made them feel welcome in his home. He served the three men a large dinner, gave them clean clothes and offered them cattle and rice as gifts. So, rather than kill Samani as planned, the three heavenly representatives traveled back to heaven content and overjoyed, and sneaked into heaven's genealogy archives. There, they altered Samani's records and added a couple of extra zeros to his life expectancy. Samani's lifetime was now recorded as 3,000 years, the moral of the winding myth being that a person who works hard and shows compassion for others will live an extremely long, full life.

After learning the full Samani story, I took to the beach in a perplexed but enlightened stupor. The ending of the legend seemed like such a non sequitur—finding a talking skull that used to own a gun was irrelevant to the final scene of heaven's three messengers appearing to take Samani into the afterlife. And none of that related to the early point about Samani selling his wife's hair or to the point about Samani and his wife having first been brother and sister. It was like a storytelling version of splatter painting.

I walked to a crescent-shaped bay that cupped the glassy ocean water on Jeju's northern shore. Hamdeok Beach, one of the most accessible beaches on the island, was lined with tents selling pulled-pork sandwiches and cold Cass beer, beach towels, neon inflatable inner tubes, straw sun hats and juicy mango slices. Three weeks before, I had been to this beach and was surprised at the sheer number of foreigners I saw sunbathing under the blue-white sky—Chinese tourists, a nuzzling European couple, a group of skinny Australians, New Zealand surfers and a trio of Thai girls in bikinis and sheer wraps. Now the busy tent-city was even more overwhelming, accommodating a charity beach volleyball tournament.

Small ocean waves lapped the shore as I moseyed along the beach to watch the volleyball games. I crossed the street that trailed along the beach's edge, bought a can of beer and took a seat next to another American man who had helped set up the volleyball nets in the days preceding the tournament. He was relaxing in the sun and staring at the games as well.

"So why don't many Koreans participate in this tournament?" I asked him.

"Nothing to do with lack of interest," he said. "I think it has to do with the beach itself. Whenever we try to organize teams and invite the local girls, the first question they ask is, 'Do we have to wear bikinis?' Beach culture is conservative on Jeju. A lot of Koreans see beach volleyball on TV in the Olympics, see the athletes in skimpy bathing suits, and assume they'll have to wear something like that here. Of course, we tell them they can wear whatever they want, but I think it has to do with being self-conscious."

I nodded, sipped my beer and then asked for his opinion on how the tournament was progressing this year compared to previous years.

Island Solitaire

"It has a good vibe, but everyone is sluggish and hungover," he said.

"It's 3:00 in the afternoon," I noted.

"There was a big beach party here last night, and everyone had a great time. Still feeling it. It was crazy. One older guy got wasted and ended up taking off his clothes, running around with glowsticks, shouting song lyrics, dancing with all the girls and passing out with his head in the sand. I guess he probably slept all night on the beach."

Glowsticks, disrobing, dancing and a seaside blackout—non sequitur narrative fragments of an entirely different sort.

The sunlight filtered through the volleyball nets and stamped the ground in shadow squares. I had another beer, eventually said goodbye to the few other spectators nearby and traveled home with a buzz of the day's alcohol and mythology, new and old.

9. A multitude of rebirths

A storm arrived from the north. In the early morning, a veil of thunderclouds muted the sunrise and lingered low in the sky, breaking only for the revelation of more imposing cloud masses and wrenching claps of thunder. The rain gushed from this assemblage overhead and splattered on the ground in loud bursts. On the occasion that a gust caught the rainwater, straight lines of precipitation swung to an angle in the rhythm of the wind, nearly horizontal at times. It was the kind of storm that must be observed in awe—merely a yawn from nature but quite a spectacle from a fogged-up apartment window. One easily slips into a veritable hypnosis amid such a downpour, all of it playing out against the gray, meditative backdrop of clouds and mist. It was hard not to get lost in the laziness, but every so often the wind would rattle my windows and accentuate the vulnerability of life surrounded by the sea. One big typhoon, Sara, hit Jeju in

Island Solitaire

1959 and killed 11 people. More recently, in 2012, a storm named Bolaven walloped Jeju and capsized two ships offshore, killing several crewmen. For a segment of islanders, the Bolaven's destruction was still a vivid memory.

I likely would have stayed indoors if not for the minor detail that it was a weekday, and I had an obligation to teach a writing class at the nearby university. On an island where typhoons are fairly common, a morning thunderstorm such as this was not enough to stop the ever-chugging engine of higher education.

I bundled up for the walk to the campus. Still, my preparation was futile, and by the time I arrived to teach the morning course, cold rainwater had managed to drip and wriggle its way to my skin. I was soaked.

The students had a hard time focusing on my lecture, the storm continuing to stir up the atmosphere right outside the classroom window. Rows of trees on the quad's sidewalk were bent so severely by the wind that they had become harshly curved at their trunks. When I thought it wise to direct all the students away from the rattling glass window, we simply watched the storm from a safer distance, nonetheless saving a daily lecture about composing cause/effect essays for a different day.

Seeking a dry, rattleless room at one point in the late morning, I slipped down a back hall during my breaktime and came to a bookshelf of titles as varied as the university's curriculum itself—*The Handbook of Artificial Intelligence* and a Herman Melville dictionary, to name a few atypical academic volumes. There were boxes of outdated textbook catalogs and old grammar reference books on the floor as well—indicators that the entire lot of books had been discarded and left for the trash men. To my surprise, I also came across a volume of Jeju legends and poems. Flipping through the pages, I came across a fitting Jeju tale for a rainy day—about pirates, villagers and a child sacrifice.

The story took place in the southern Jeju village of Soosan-ri, at a time when the quaint, bucolic setting was in danger of being attacked by pirates. The villagers decided that the best protection from the pirates would be to build a massive stone wall around the village. However, when a first attempt at building the wall proved futile, a wise Buddhist monk advised that using a young girl as a keystone in the wall would be a sure-fire way for fortification and security. How, exactly, a young girl would provide such a defense wasn't specified in the volume, but nonetheless, the village found a seven-year-old child and buried her as part of the next construction attempt of the wall. The new wall held off the pirates and allowed the village to flourish. The legend's lesson asserted, obviously, that a single sacrifice could aid the plight of many—if the reader was willing to ignore the miscarriage of ethics that resulted in a village willfully killing a child. The larger takeaway was that one's actions could exist forever in the form of the prosperity of others.

The rain continued outside for a long time. Students came and went. The hues of the day on the other side of the windows changed from morning grays to afternoon blues, and big puddles formed on the campus sidewalks.

Island Solitaire

Then in a sluggish afterward, the rain lessened and the sun emerged. It felt like a morning beyond the already-gone morning, and wet bamboo stalks at the edge of the university building sparkled in the new light.

I decided to take a walk outside and stepped high over fallen tree limbs on my way to a restaurant. Passing by the library, I came upon proof of the storm's ferocity. The large, metallic top of a streetlamp had been wind-whipped off its post, and it now rested with frayed wires and broken bulbs in a nearby patch of grass.

I high-stepped over the fallen streetlamp, grateful that no one had been unluckily enough to stand in the lamp's path when it departed from its post. The lighting apparatus was the size of a large desk fan and could have easily decapitated an unsuspecting passerby.

In an orange-walled café, I bought a bowl of rice and vegetables, and paused in the sunlit moment much like I had paused in the morning to watch the storm. It was easy to understand why so many island myths and stories of gods rode the thematic wave of rejuvenation and its various offshoots—rebirth, restoration and reconstruction. The themes were ingrained in the nature of the weather and the landscape.

With the storm long gone, I ventured into town for a few supplies. I walked on damp streets, past wind-tossed trash and storefront signage. I ducked into a grocery mart, enticed by a water tank filled with the largest live crabs I had ever seen. Browsing the mart's aisles for smaller, more manageable fare, I amassed a nice supply of edible oddities. One of the most enjoyable anecdotes about Korean culture is that there is a food or drink prescribed as a coupling to nearly every activity, mood, or scenario. *Jook*, a type of rice porridge, is almost always eaten when sick and noodles are consumed on wedding anniversaries—the stringy length of the noodles serves as a metaphor for a long marriage. Mustard soup is consumed on birthdays, taffy candy is eaten when studying for a test, eel is eaten by men hoping for sexual fortitude and beans are scattered in one's home to ward off evil spirits. Even something as basic as a rice cake, *tteok*, has a collaborator—it is eaten by students before a big exam, with the thinking that the stickiness of the rice cake will parallel all of the studied material being retained in the mind. (As a converse to this custom, slippery seaweed soup is to be avoided before a big exam, to avoid thoughts and academic gusto sliding away.) Many students in South Korea, open to whatever superstition and divine intervention might beget a superior test score, also cease cutting or washing their hair during exam week; one needn't lose any scrap of valuable academic thought that might be clinging to a dirty hair follicle.

I ambled past the crabs and back to the wet street. By this time, the sun was starting to set and my enclave of retail shops was donning a gray pallor. The dusk and the dampness reminded me of the only time I've ever been mugged in my life—in Seoul, of all places—by a punk teenager who was quite muscular. But now I had to figure out how to get back to the main road. South Korea has one of the fastest construction rates in the world—whole buildings are erected in a matter of weeks sometimes, and this certainly has ripple effects on a quickly developing place like Jeju City. Such development means that a lot of the buildings—high-rises, stores, apartments, villas—end up looking architecturally similar. I must have walked past a dozen white buildings—boxy, matte exterior, glassy windows displaying clothes—trying to find the way home in the dark. Eventually, I found myself looping back to the mart with the crab tank.

Finally reaching my apartment, I clicked on my gas stove and fried up some vegetables in pancake batter. Known as *noek-du-choen* in Korean, the pancake was a fitting choice. Rain had suddenly started to sprinkle again outside, and *noek-du-choen* is meant to be coupled with a rainy day; the reasoning is that the falling raindrops sound similar to the sputters and pops of the pancake frying in the pan. I wondered if there was also a Korean food coupling for getting lost and finding one's way back home just in the nick of time.

10. Ruin and reconciliation

All islands of the world have their atrocities, and if there has ever been a shameful stain on Korea's island paradise, it came in 1948. The Korean War, which pitted the Soviet-backed North Korea against a U.S.-aligned South, was still two years away. However, animosity and frustration with government at all levels, as well as directorial meddling by outside nations, had been lingering on the Korean peninsula since the end of World War II and Korea's subsequent release from Japanese colonial rule. With the Korean peninsula rather arbitrarily split into separate North and South segments in 1945, the Korean population had been left to choose between political poles—democracy and communism—that were diametrically opposed and, as history would prove, volatile if forced to coexist.

In the midst of this flux, clubs, organizations and committees emerged that attempted to solidify specific ideologies and unify like-minded Korean civilians and activists at a local level in the 1940s.

The most significant of these affiliations was the South Korean Labor Party, comprised of pro-communist advocates who feared that their country was becoming a pawn of the United States—a sentiment that is, to this day, often disseminated in North Korean media. In fact, it is believed that the South Korean Labor Party in the late-1940s was receiving funds and encouragement from North Koreans.

The first real sign of trouble specific to Jeju came in the spring of 1948. With the South Korean Labor Party gaining influence, islanders assembled to commemorate and celebrate the anniversary of freedom from Japanese rule. The celebration, however, turned violent and ended with police shooting 10 civilians. In the eyes of some islanders, the incident gave credence to previous assertions that the present government and the civil servants of the entire governmental machine could not be trusted.

In the year that followed, Jeju became a hotbed of anti-government and anti-establishment rhetoric, public demonstrations, election boycotts, and various acts of civil disobedience. Thousands of arrests resulted. This combustible recipe also produced what has since been labeled the April 3 Massacre, when a group of Jeju citizens with communist political leanings gathered to protest both the United Nations elections and, on a more local scale, the squelching of political demonstrations that had been taking place on Jeju. Police facilities were attacked and ransacked as a rebellion spread and gained support. The South Korean government, in response and in conjunction with the U.S. government, acted swiftly and mercilessly—sending military units to Jeju to smother the unrest.

In an extreme act of martial brutality that began then and lasted until the end of the Korean War, 30,000 islanders were slaughtered by the Korean government on Jeju. Many of those people killed had only tangential connections to the pro-communist activities. Most of the islanders were executed inhumanely and without due process. Consider an event that has since been labeled the Darangshi Incident: six men, three women and a child sought refuge in a cave on the eastern end of Jeju. Upon discovering their whereabouts, soldiers threw grenades into the mouth of the cave—killing all the cave's inhabitants either by explosion or suffocation.

Perhaps cruelest of all during so much ongoing mass-murder around the island was that penalties and violence were extended to friends and family members of suspected dissidents, and this resulted in nothing less than an absolute fear-state on Jeju for half a decade. Some estimates now count almost 100 villages as having been utterly annihilated in the period.

In retrospect, equally curious as how callously that staggering amount of killing and destruction could occur on such a serene place is what the massacre led to politically and psychologically for the residents of Jeju.

Sensing that ongoing violence on the island might garner widespread sympathy for Jeju from the general

Island Solitaire

public, and realizing that the whole Korean nation would be particularly vulnerable militarily if its populace grew increasingly splintered, the South Korean government began promoting the idea of anti-communist institutions. These societal organizations and associations were intended to turn left-leaning political and professed communists into law-abiding anti-communists—either by physical force and reprimand or by mental coercion. And since the Korean government considered anyone on Jeju who questioned the status quo to be flat-out left-leaning, the total membership numbers of these institutions swelled into the thousands. Many of them used an ongoing system of checks and balances with cooperating Jeju villagers. With the pervasive threat of imprisonment, the institutions became broad confinement mechanisms, of sorts, for suspected communists. This threat of imprisonment also served as a scare tactic for politically undecided islanders. The choice: profess anti-communist rhetoric or openly side with the leftists and be subjected to the social prison of an institution. Some Jeju locals opted for both, and joined the Korean military as a way to prove total political conversion to their institution supervisors.

The organizations weren't solely for adults, either. The South Korean government realized that one way of having an anti-communist population was to shape the views of young students before those students had the chance and comprehension to make up their own political minds. For example, in 1949, the South Korean government's Ministry of Education started the Student National Corps primarily for middle school students. The corps drilled children—some of whom were as young as the fifth grade—weekly for military service and actively effused anti-communist rhetoric. The young members of the corps were also encouraged and instructed to spy on other students, thus enacting aspects of the social prison seen in other similar community institutions. Although such forceful conditioning of the youth was appalling, many of the former Student National Corps members nowadays reflect positively on the experience, noting that it suitably prepared them for eventual military service during the Korean War.

Other complex social effects of the April 3 Massacre are still deeply woven into the consciousness of Jeju islanders. Considering that the events on the island in the late-1940s and early-1950s are now considered by some scholars to have been a form of civil war, and that many who lived through the extended catastrophe are still active in the Jeju communities, it's easy to understand why the massacre is relevant, despite taking place more than half a century ago. It's also worth noting that throughout the 1970s and 1980s, the Korean government largely prohibited writers and intellectuals from publishing materials or having any public discourse about the April 3 Massacre. One former professor I talked to recounted writing a booklet about Jeju's history years ago, only to have the printing shop delete all references to the April 3 events prior to the booklet's publication—no doubt by order of the government.

It wasn't until the South Korean people gained full

democracy and elected a president without direct military ties in 1993 that complete details of the tragedy really started coming to light.

Today, there are constant reminders. There is an April 3 Massacre memorial museum, a highly acclaimed movie about the events titled, *Jiseul*, a play called *April Rite Flower Seed Sunimi*, and a popular graphic novel. Proposals have been made to make April 3rd a national holiday in South Korea. Still, there are many Koreans who feel that the events are underrepresented on a national level. The phrasing on one plaque I read, next to a blank stone monument in Jeju City, epitomized how much of an emotional open wound still exists for the island, as a whole:

AS THE JEJU INCIDENT STILL DOES NOT
HAVE HISTORICAL DEFINITION,
ITS MONUMENT HAS NO INSCRIPTION.
.

The massacre is simply referred to as *Sa Sam*—"April 3"— to the people of South Korea, the date carrying enough infamy to stand alone. In 2005, the South Korean government formally apologized for the bloodshed and inhumanity. Jeju has since gone on to explicitly promote itself as a "peace island," and construction of an ambitious think tank known as the Peace Institute was completed on Jeju in 2006 as an addendum.

On a practical level, it is difficult to imagine Jeju ever

distancing itself from the April 3 Massacre to a substantial degree, as any question relating to why the place is labeled a "peace island" will likely prompt a requisite narrative of the massacre itself, and rightly so. The gruesome events played a pivotal part in history—not only for the island, but also for Asia—and influenced the trajectory of the Korean War. Compounding this is the fact that the violence was largely imposed on the islanders from outside forces, and that it stemmed from very undemocratic crackdowns on islanders' freedom of speech and assembly. Without intending to do so, Jeju has become a prime example of someplace being justifiably weary of overmilitarization more than a symbol of peace.

In contemporary discourse, this was all evidenced by the *Save Jeju Now* campaign of recent years, which gathered signatures, accepted donations and published blogs to protest the development of a massive naval base in Gangjeong Village, on the south-central coast of the island. The base, which had been presented to the Jeju locals as a strategic defense complex that could be used by both South Korean and American military personnel, had been an ongoing construction project of South Korea's Ministry of Defense since 2007. But protestors had repeatedly pointed out specific criticisms, such as the fact that the United States already had naval bases nearby—in places such as Busan on the Korean mainland and Kadena in Okinawa, Japan. Protesters also noted that carving out enough space for nearly two dozen naval ships on Jeju's coastline was bound to have adverse effects on the seaside's ecosystem. "We don't want a war base on the

Island Solitaire

Island of Peace," the *Save Jeju Now* organization's homepage stated. "Join us to save Jeju Island from destruction." The protests, however, were ultimately ineffective in stopping the base's construction.

I was left to wonder if there was anything positive that could be extracted from Jeju's infamous massacre. Jeju has used the massacre partly as a representation of its resiliency and unity. In the island's official designation as a peace island in 2005, the Korean government noted that the massacre, as a historical event, would be formally elevated to a "higher level with mutual reconciliation, co-existence and shared life." An international peace center was constructed on Jeju, which now acts as a hub for frequent high-level forums and panel discussions on world peace with groups from all over the world. There is no argument saying that Jeju hasn't done its part to market and promote its peace moniker.

One of the most heartwarming and subtle signs of organic unity that I found, rather than the manufactured indicators that are abundant, was a brief anecdote that I read. On September 21st, 1954, the formal end to the infamous institutionalization and brutality came not through organizations, rhetoric, servitude or architecture. The official conclusion was recognized when the island's police lifted recreation bans and finally allowed groups and families to hike up Halla Mountain once again—everyone was free to simply enjoy the trails and drift to any social circle, and nobody was fettered by the outside politics or community surveillance that had nearly destroyed Jeju in previous years.

11. Portrait of the monk as a young man

It was that time of year when I was required to renew my work visa. Rolling out of bed and surprised by the chill in the air early one morning, I gathered my identification documents and sauntered outside. I was to meet a university student named Doguk, who had graciously offered to accompany me to the immigration office downtown and translate the technical visa minutiae. My lethargy stemmed from my expectations for the day. The visa process would likely be an all-day procedure, broken up by a lot of sitting around in a waiting room and an interrogative examination of my work history.

There is nothing statistically special about being a foreign worker in South Korea nowadays. There are more than a million non-Koreans working in the country at any given time. In the past, foreigners brought with them everything from religions like Christianity to diseases, international businesses, transportation services and

Island Solitaire

foreign language schools—all of which have been the focus of scrutiny and investigation by the native Korean population at one time or another.

The profusion of foreigners came as a result of several events. Koreans made a concentrated effort following World War II to regain national singularity and uniformity after years of forced cultural mixing. Chinese people immigrated to Korea following the war, and Peace Corps volunteers from the United States began to enter the country with regularity in the 1960s, but it wasn't until the late 1980s that the immigrant pool started to widen substantially.

By the early 1990s, there were nearly 20,000 foreigners employed in South Korea. Wages for workers in the country increased dramatically as democracy took root, and this attracted hard-working demographics from Southeast Asia, India and elsewhere. Many of the non-Korean workers in this batch toiled under poor labor conditions, and often without legal documentation, but the trend gained enough momentum to continue into the next century. American, Canadian and British college graduates made good money arriving in South Korea to teach English during this influx as well, as South Korea's economy flourished, and the value of English fluency was perceived as a necessity for modern Korean students. Most Korean high school students today hold English with equal parts apathy and incertitude. All Jeju students are required to take English in school from the third grade onward, and while English is probably a beneficial skill for them to learn, the precise importance isn't clear.

John Burgman

Doguk was late picking me up. It was still early in the morning, but he had been awake and studying for a while. I soon learned that his tardiness might have had something to do with the beer that he had guzzled with a throng of friends around midnight. Doguk insisted that he wasn't hungover, but he also said that the morning sun was giving him a headache. When we arrived at the immigration office, I got him a bottle of water for his hangover and spoke in soft tones.

The immigration office wasn't nearly as large as others that I had seen in foreign cities. The dim interior lighting and dark paneling gave the room an old-fashioned aura. A shortage of chairs and an absence of any real lobby added to the tedium. The cramped nature wasn't an architectural fault; one simply got the sense that immigration on Jeju was suddenly booming, and this quaint immigration office hadn't had time to expand, relocate or restructure.[4]

I bellied up to the trough. There is a tendency for many immigration officers to portray a stoic coldness, lest they reveal that they are capable of sympathizing with someone's travel woes, but I was pleasantly surprised to find that the officer in Jeju was exhibiting the clerical rarity of genuine kindness. She was so cheery, in fact, that Doguk and I found ourselves having a regular conversation with her. She loved speaking English because she loved American television programs. She had

---

[4] Since the time of this book's writing, Jeju's immigration facility has, in fact, been updated and relocated. The new building is wonderfully modern (multiple floors, a substantial waiting wing, glorious windows, etc.), but for my money, it lacks the saloon-like charm of the old office.

chosen to do immigration clerical work because it provided an enticing retirement pension and the likelihood of using English on a regular basis. She had never traveled to an English-speaking country, yet she had structured her entire career around an interest in the English language. She rifled through my visa paperwork. To my left, a man in a workman's vest was speaking Vietnamese to his respective immigration officer, and to my right an older couple was conversing in Chinese. For an island that has a well-known reputation for being ethnically homogenous, Jeju possesses immigration offices that reveal a changing future.

Doguk and I left the office grateful that we wouldn't have to waste the rest of the afternoon waiting for paperwork to process. We drove in and out of a drizzle and ate a late lunch at the counter of a convenience store. Over a modest meal of crackers and chocolates, Doguk explained that he was feeling pressure from his parents to find gainful employment.

"What should I do with my English degree?" he asked me. In some ways, his predicament was similar to the plight of many Jeju students and recent college graduates, but Doguk's story had some quirks. His father was a devout Buddhist monk of a unique religious sect that allowed for marriage. As a result, Doguk had been raised in a Buddhist temple. Complicating all of this was that Doguk didn't exactly adhere to Buddhism like his parents had hoped.

"When I was in high school," Doguk said, "I was focused on Buddhism. I was the head of my high school's

Buddhist association, and I learned the proper method for tapping the *moktak*, which is the wooden percussive instrument used in Buddhist temple ceremonies. I planned to be a monk and I meditated twice a week. But Buddhism requires an emptying of the mind, and I think at the time I was too young to empty my mind. I couldn't even understand what that really meant."

I asked Doguk what had brought about the change in his life, his deviation from Buddhism as he grew older.

"A Buddhist must live with strict standards," Doguk said. "My father wakes up at 4:00 every morning, then he meditates, then he has ceremonies, and then he meets other monks at the temple. As I grew older, I didn't want that life. I like eating meat, which a Buddhist is not supposed to do. I like money, which a Buddhist is not supposed to like. I like girls. Buddhism says that a man can overcome the instincts and temptations in his life, and I understand that. But sometimes I think a person only gets one life, so I want to enjoy it."

I noted that such thinking was counter to the Buddhist notions of reincarnation, many lives. Doguk grinned and said, "Yeah, but how much do you remember from any of those previous lives?"

"So, do you consider yourself a Buddhist or not?" I asked.

"Yes and no," Doguk said, laughing. "Buddhism says that everyone is a Buddha, so in that sense, yes. But I also don't think I would be a good monk, so in that sense, no."

Doguk mentioned that many of his happiest memories had come during his mandatory two-year military service,

Island Solitaire

far away from the temple life, shooting guns and talking trash about the North Koreans. ("That's what military service is—learning to hate North Korea.") Some days he considered just giving in, becoming a monk and painting in his spare time. "I also have an idea about starting a coffee shop in my Buddhist temple," he said. "I don't think anything like that has ever been done. People could come to the temple and buy a cup of coffee or a cup of tea, relax and learn calligraphy."

When I told Doguk that such an existence didn't sound so terrible—especially if he would join a sect of Buddhism like his father's that allowed for marriage and raising a family, he disagreed. "Looking at my own family's experience, I don't think a monk should marry or have a family. A monk should live alone," he said, "and that's what bothers me."

Doguk paused and took a sip of a prepackaged cappuccino. "I'm lucky because my father is a good man, and I am amazed that he has no greed in his life," he said. "But sometimes I think it is selfish for a person like that to be a monk because then his whole family must live like monks too. I have talked to my mother about this in the past. She is not a monk. She had dreams—she wanted to be a cartoonist. But she met my father through an arranged marriage, and then her whole life had to become his life, the temple, the ceremonies."

"That's sad," I said.

"Yeah, and it just doesn't seem fair," Doguk said. "I wonder sometimes what my mother's other dreams were."

Doguk explained that despite all of this, he had

immense adulation for both of his parents. He found himself conflicted about what to make of his father's lifestyle choice. "My father's life, the life of a monk, has merits and demerits," Doguk explained. "My father didn't spend much time with me when I was a child because he was so busy with the temple duties. I couldn't even refer to him as 'father.' I had to call him 'monk,' which is the Buddhist custom. But at the same time, he was always unselfish, always kind. I feel like I didn't necessarily grow up with a great father, but I grew up with a great role model."

Doguk also pointed out the obvious: if he were to become a Buddhist monk in Jeju and devote his life to the local temple, much of his college work as an English major, along with his countless hours of studying English and his ambitions to travel to the United States and work at an invigorating business, would be a waste of time. Munching on a rice chip, he stared over the twisting road outside, copper-colored from the mix of rain and sunlight. "For the time being, I'm just continuing to study English without any real goal," he said. "I think that eventually the goal will become clear."

"And once you have a goal, do you think it will include remaining on Jeju?" I asked.

"Yes," he said. "I don't want to leave my friends. All of my friends are on the island. And I don't want to leave my parents. They don't want me to go to another country; they just want me to be a monk. I don't know if my parents are satisfied with their lives—especially my mother. But they're good parents, and I feel a duty to be near them."

Island Solitaire

Doguk dropped me off at my apartment and we said goodbye. Later that night, when I was about to fall asleep, I stumbled across a TV program that seemed apropos to everything. From what I could gather, the show centered on a group of strangers who were stranded on a remote island. Part reality show, part instructional comedy, the program followed the strangers as they learned how to live together on the island without any outside help. Pop-up text would occasionally blink onto the screen to annotate their progress for the viewer, all backed by cartoonish music and sound effects. The show's title translated to *Law of the Jungle*, although there didn't seem to be any cutthroat competitive aspect to the premise. Most of the time was spent showing the characters catching crustaceans and cooking them over a fire.

I stayed awake for an extra 20 minutes—on an island, thinking about life on an island, watching the silly program about life on an island.

I didn't make it to the show's end, so I don't know what the strangers' objectives were. Somehow it felt fitting to leave the premise open-ended in my mind. I recalled one last thing Doguk had told me when we were pulling up to my apartment and I asked him what it was like growing up on an island. He said that it was difficult because it felt too close-knit. The rest of the world supposedly operates with several degrees of separation between people, but on Jeju, in Doguk's words, "There's only one degree of separation." Doguk explained that such closeness made it harder to be unique and individualistic because expectations were never more than one other person away from you.

My response to this was that every place in the world has pros and cons to its social structure, but Doguk quickly refuted this. "I don't think it is pros and cons, good and bad," he said. "It's all up to me. It makes me work harder, but it's my choice. It's not pros and cons, it's more like fried and seasoned."

12. One-day mother

One can't explore perceptions of myth and illusion in South Korea without careening, at some point, into the immense entity of North Korea. Ever since the Korean peninsula was divided into a northern portion and a southern portion in the late 1940s, North Korea has been trudging forward in its own ideological mold, removed from global diplomacy, hostile in its rhetoric, bereft of Western pop culture and resenting internationalism on any substantial scale. By all accounts, there is practically no social media in the country, smartphones are scarce, cell phone usage comes with restrictions, an independent press is absent, Internet usage is limited and American movies are forbidden. Aside from compact apparatuses like the *notels* of recent years, which can be purchased illegally to play pirated television shows and films, North Koreans are shut off from the global technological world. In a measurable way, North Korea is an ultra-private nation that is sustained by the maintenance of its own mythos, most of which exalts its leadership through propaganda—first lauding Kim Il-sung, followed by Kim Jong-il and then Kim Jong-un. North Korea's supreme leaders, as they are designated, are not merely part of a dynasty in the country; they are emblematic gods that are worshipped by a subservient and highly conservative North Korean public. The international media has been fed exaggerations related to everything from Kim Jong-il's divine birth and world-class proficiency in multiple sports to his ability to function without ever having defecated. The people living in North Korea are likely taught more manageable—but still improbable—anecdotes, such as Kim Jong-il's childhood genius when it came to political matters, his ability to author volumes of books and his penchant for creating immaculate operas. His son, Kim Jong-un, was supposedly able to win competitive boat races before he was even a teenager.

For all of Korea's traditionalism, however, the most egregious example of old-time thinking in a contemporary context is North Korea's deification of the aforementioned Kims at the expense of citizens' human rights. The people of North Korea are not free to worship whatever they choose. Rather, they are victims in a one-party dictatorship that, for the most part, does not allow anyone to leave or think freely. This sequestered, self-sustaining attitude has proved problematic in the past, as the country has been bludgeoned with various catastrophes, everything from large-scale famine in the 1990s to treatable-yet-unchecked illnesses like tuberculosis and malnutrition today. Draconian punishment

Island Solitaire

for those North Korean citizens who object to any aspect of the government or try to escape the country can include extensive terms in a gulag or swift execution.

For all intents and purposes, North Korea's routine operations are the epitome of taking legends and twisting them; the myths in the country don't comfort the people, but inadvertently harm them.

A slight percentage of people living among such devastating circumstances in North Korea do break free. The intricate escapes of these defectors often follow a uniform choreography. People who wish to flee from the country must first cross a river into neighboring China under the cover of nighttime darkness—an endeavor that can entail complications like getting lost, succumbing to hypothermia and being shot by North Korean or Chinese border patrol guards. Once in China, the defectors must live in constant secrecy to avoid capture by Chinese officials (which would cause consequent repatriation to North Korea). This ongoing concealment often takes on many layers. For example, defectors might learn the Chinese language, adopt new names and identities or, in more extreme cases, change their appearance and seek reconstructive surgery.

The overarching strain is that most escaped North Koreans find themselves instantly in debt to brokers who aided in their defection. Complicating matters even more, the defectors are usually outliers in their struggles, as the risks and economic costs of escape make it unlikely that an entire family flees North Korea at the same time. Thus, financially broke, lonesome and often poorly-educated, many of the escaped North Koreans—nearly three-fourths of whom are women—either see the sex industry as an avenue for forward progress or get forced into it.

The goal for the North Korean defectors in China, whether they are working as prostitutes, being sold into a marriage, or holding down employment in a disparate field, is to save enough money to travel to a nearby country like Thailand or Mongolia—any nation where they can gain unobstructed access to a South Korean embassy and be assured safe transfer to South Korea. However, scrounging up enough spare travel money for the defection process can take years, and some North Korean escapees never actually leave China. Those who do complete the hard, prolonged journey to South Korea must endure lengthy and intense interrogation from the South Korean government in order to be granted visas. The defectors are detained for months in a high-security facility in South Korea called a *hanawon* and eventually released as new citizens in a largely unfamiliar world.

During my time on Jeju, the island maintained a population of approximately 200 North Korean defectors, roughly eight percent of the total defector population in South Korea, and nearly all of them worked with a lady named Im Soonim. For years, Soonim ran Jeju's Hana Center, a small support institute founded on the island in 2010 that helped the defectors adjust and adapt to diverse challenges. Since everyday tasks like managing personal finances and riding a bus—as well as denser subjects like sex education—could be new to North Koreans, the Jeju Hana Center cast a wide net.

Island Solitaire

"Almost every system is new and strange to North Korean defectors," Soonim said when I reached out to her and asked her to discuss the lives of the defectors on the island. "You can think of it like this: the North Korean defectors need to learn things that children would learn. The Hana Center provides them with basic instructions about South Korean society. As soon as the defectors arrived on Jeju, I took them to a community service center, near their new place to report for move-ins. After that, their new lives began."

The Hana Center was the lowest rung on a national supportive ladder that led up to the more substantial *hanawon* facilities and eventually to South Korea's Ministry of Unification, the governmental tier that dealt with all matters pertaining to North Korea and South Korea relations. Jeju's Hana Center was hardly political, however, tending to focus more on basic education for defectors who often knew nothing about the island. It also provided psychological and therapeutic aid for anyone injured in the grueling journey out of North Korea. "There are so many cases of horrific injuries," Soonim told me. "Some defectors break their legs when they escape from North Korea, some get tinnitus and vertigo. They suffer severe emotional trauma from all that they have been through. If they have been deported to North Korea previously, they have likely been harshly tortured there. Because of such emotional trauma, some of them have insomnia."

That was where Soonim's compassion came in. More so than just running Jeju's Hanna Center managerially, she had dealt personally with various needs of the defectors in timely and effective ways. "Most defectors tend to be physically and psychologically unstable," she said. "So, if they would ever want to change their names, which was very common, I would take them to the court and help them follow the steps for that. If their problems were physical, I would take them to the hospital. If they were mentally unstable, I would counsel them. I was like their mother, making sure they felt comfortable and not segregated from society on the island."

Soonim had been affectionately labeled the one-day mother for her maternal duties, which also included helping North Korean defectors on their wedding days and teaching them about cell phone usage. But aside from matters of personal security and contentment, Soonim was tasked at the Hana Center with elevating defectors to be productive members of South Korea's workforce. Since North Korea's socialist-style economy doesn't leave much room for career mobility, Soonim would have to teach the defectors the basics of creating resumes and conversing during job interviews. "They would need to know how the working system of South Korea functions, and they would need to know that they could get paid for the work they did," Soonim explained to me.

The freedom to choose a college major was also new to many of the defectors under Soonim's tutelage, and they were often intrigued by the concept of university training. "Some of the defectors on Jeju want to go to college," Soonim said, "so I would always tell them how to go to college and what they would need to prepare. Some organizations support the North Korean defector students with scholarships."

From those scholarships to the job opportunities that potentially followed, the defectors tended to struggle greatly with the sudden occupational autonomy and the innumerable choices woven into it all on Jeju. As Soonim explained, "The defectors have many things to adapt to and overcome. They feel desperately confused with capitalism because they have never been taught about it. But they need to clearly understand it—and realize that they have to make money in order to live their own lives."

It's worth noting that this assimilation has to be done while South Korea commerce whizzes all around the defectors in the form of legitimate opportunities, scams, vices and enticements. "I think, on Jeju, South Koreans and North Korean defectors have tried to understand each other," Soonim said. "When the defectors try to merge into the society, the South Koreans embrace them and help them get used to the community, but this also means that South Koreans need to improve awareness about the North Korean defectors. The defectors are just like new neighbors who want to settle down."

Improving awareness is one thing, but getting South Korea to fully embrace the North Korean defectors has proven to be challenging. During Soonim's time at the Hana Center, the South Korean government subsidized the resettlements of defectors—providing everything from spending allowances to housing and school tuition costs. But a vocal percentage of South Koreans have been critical of the administrative handouts across the nation.

Much of the disapproval asserts that government subsidies in South Korea contradicts the moral and ethical goals of resettlement—the subsidies make the defectors reliant on the South Korean government rather than contentedly independent. One undeniable reality is that a great number of North Korean defectors who receive college tuition payments from the government end up dropping out of school before graduating. It is part of a long, South Korea-wide trend that is seen as proof that South Korea's current support system for North Korean defectors is considerably unsound. Additionally, there are nearly 100 organizations in South Korea that are aimed at helping North Korean defectors, which also raises questions about efficacy amid such abundance.

As a capstone to all of this criticism, there have been a number of defectors who have become veritable celebrities because of their chilling life stories. Consistent publicity can be beneficial, but it risks casting defection from North Korea as a spectacle more than a societal reality full of struggle.

Nevertheless, condemnation of the system creates partisan debates that are largely out of the periphery of most defectors from North Korea. Many of those who arrive at the Hana Center on Jeju are burdened by more immediate concerns: "Most of the defectors worry about what they are going to eat," Soonim said. "If they eat something one day, then they are concerned about their next meal. Even though some of the defectors were in high-ranking positions in North Korea, they constantly worry about their next meal like all the other North

Island Solitaire

Korean defectors do. And there have been cases of some of them becoming alcoholics, finding it hard to settle down well."

With those daily struggles and challenges, settling on a place like Jeju could be advantageous, in Soonim's opinion. Removed from the bustle of a metropolis like Seoul on the Korean mainland or Beijing in China, the defectors can easily become part of the close-knit island community, and the island's internationalism can turn the defectors' cross-cultural experiences into assets. "Most of the young defectors—usually in their late twenties or thirties—are good at speaking Chinese, so they choose to come to Jeju," Soonim said. "The defectors know that there are many Chinese tourists on Jeju and think that speaking Chinese will be a great advantage when looking for a job."

The older defectors, however, choose Jeju for more introspective—even animistic—reasons. Soonim explained, "In the case of the older generation, there are various reasons why they choose to live on Jeju. Some of them want to live in nature—with fresh air and quiet circumstances. Others know that their ancestors' hometowns are on Jeju, or like that Jeju is the part of South Korea that is geographically farthest away from North Korea."

It is on Jeju where a new mythology takes over—island life steadily dissolving the indoctrination that had been done by the North Korean government. "The North Korean people that I worked with truly believed the North Korean myths," Soonim told me. "After they escaped and once they realized that all the things they had been taught were lies, they felt deeply panicked. People who live near Pyongyang, in North Korea, or people who live somewhere in the middle of North Korea still believe those myths because they have no connection with other countries. But some people who live near the border of China and North Korea hardly believe them, I think, because they can contact Chinese people."

Winding up my curiosity, I felt a need for clarity and hoped that Soonim could expound on the thin line between mythologizing and lying. "In North Korea, the brainwashing is a tool for rationalizing their system, and I think that goes against humanity," she said, noting how the myths of Kim Il-sung and Kim Jong-il veil reality rather than explaining or illuminating it. "The North Korean government deliberately blinds its people's sight—it doesn't allow them to see the world. The people who live in North Korea believe that people's lives all over the world are the same as theirs. I feel pity because North Koreans live forever with the wrong information. Thinking of the people living in the totally isolated country, I just feel so sorry."

13. Southbound

Christmas came to the island amid a bizarre week of temperamental weather, light snow collecting on the palm fronds one day, melting into shiny streams in the feathery pampas grass the next. For every chunk of daily sunshine, there came nightly winds off the northern ocean and vast blankets of frost fractals collecting on the brush. Outside my home, several dozen pigeons lounged one morning and didn't flee when I approached to observe them. A few Eurasian magpies, streaked with vivid cobalt feathers, also wandered around the grass and plucked their beaks into the frosted earth. It was during a second cup of coffee that I realized I was bearing witness to an avian turf war—neither the pigeons nor the magpies wanted to relinquish the patch of open land that was steadily thawing in the sun.

One wouldn't guess it from those stubborn few, but Jeju plays a pivotal role in the transitory habits of a number of bird species from as far away as Alaska that pit stop on the island during a long southern flight to New Zealand and Australia. There are also birds that annually find Jeju's winter temperatures more tolerable than the frigid Januaries and Februaries of their native Russia, and birds that summer on Jeju but flee when the fall frosts begin. There are so many types of birds on the island, in fact, that *The Jeju Weekly* newspaper once published an article devoted to their migrations. There are regularly birds coming down from China and birds jaunting over from Japan; there are egrets, nuthatches, warblers, sparrows, ducks, wagtails, wrens, Eurasian skylarks, rock doves, occasional peregrine falcons, cormorants, gargantuan crows and seagulls. And since birds of diverse types travel to and from Jeju throughout the year, I could understand how birds vying for real estate might get somewhat competitive.

Later that morning, I filled a daypack with leisure contents—sunflower seeds, a pint of whiskey and a harmonica—and decided it best to light out and spend Christmas farther south too. I knew that on the southern end of the island, where the geography dipped a smidgen nearer to the equator, the temperatures would be warmer and the mood would be slightly more beachy. My friend Dan and I hailed a ride on a bus road that circumvented Halla Mountain. Whatever the route spared on elevation, it made up for with gut-churning twists and turns. We had both bought hot drinks for the 45-minute bus ride, but by the 10-kilometer mark, I was wishing the barista had laced my cup with Dramamine. Understandably, Dan and I didn't converse much at first; I kept my teeth clinched and slowly acclimated to the ride's disequilibrium.

The situation gradually improved. For starters, Dan pulled a box of Christmas donuts from his bag shortly after our bus swooped around a particularly sharp corner. "Breakfast-on-the-go," he said, detaching a powdery pastry from a larger glazed clump.

The view from our seats became increasingly more pleasant as the terrain outside the bus window grew rockier inland. Tall pine branches draped over the meandering pavement. There are many roads on Jeju, but the one on which we were being jostled—516 Road—was the main North-South artery. Its construction had been completed in 1967, after the locals had grown too fed up with having to cruise on the island's perimeter to arrive at coastal Seogwipo, the island's second-largest city. The road's name had been meant to honor the president of South Korea at the time, Park Chung Hee, but it wasn't without controversy. 516 symbolized the month and day (May 16) that Park had orchestrated a coup in 1961—a move that largely led to his control over the whole country. In other words, the road's designation signified one man's military-aided overthrow of the government, which was an action that, out of principle, not everyone on Jeju was quick to praise.

Another one of Park's contributions, and one that is more universally admired, was the organized and efficient spread of palm trees on Jeju. The first palm was planted on the island in 1953, years before Park took office, but it is Park who is credited for the palms' abundance, for he viewed them as a key component of Jeju becoming a tourism hotspot in the 1970s.

As the bus in which we sat crossed into the southern half of the island and the palm trees became more abundant, it was hard to imagine a time when they didn't line the streetscapes or garnish nearly every urban green space. The landscape's entire aesthetic must have been radically different just a couple of decades ago.

I had been to Seogwipo several times, but its warmth in December felt like a great discovery. Halla Mountain tends to trap the fleecy, gray clouds of winter over Jeju City. But Seogwipo, on the other side of the big mountain, seems perpetually clear and shrouded in nothing but the ocean's lore. It wasn't surprising that Jeju's southernmost city had a patina that felt more in line with tropical tourism than seasonal South Korea; head directly south in a boat out of one of Seogwipo's harbors and you'd eventually find yourself in the warm waters off the coast of Okinawa, Japan. Continuing south past that, you'd reach the Philippines.

Seogwipo is particularly notable for being a point that the Japanese held in strategic high regard during World War II, when Korea was under Japanese rule. Such past colonization is connected to broader concepts of lore in present-day Jeju. In conversations with Seogwipo residents, as an illustration, I was told flat-out that the Jeju islanders cling to their myths because foreign cultures had historically worked so hard to extinguish Jeju's identity. Some measures of extinguishment had been academic, such as the Japanese banning Koreans from speaking or

Island Solitaire

learning the Korean language during the colonization, as well as changing Korean surnames to Japanese. Other measures, like forced sexual servitude, were more physically impactful, and obviously just as damaging. But this all extended to myth as well, whether in the execution of Korean shamans by the Japanese or in the introduction of Japanese folklore into Korean society.

It is difficult to gauge how Jeju's culturalism might have progressed if history had taken a different course, but it's also worth noting the reality: Jeju still radiates the effects of Japan's colonization, which lasted from 1910 to 1945. For one thing, Jeju is contemporarily recognized as having an abundance of women, a distinction that has been highlighted both as a historic fact and used as a tourism marketing twinkle. But this notable gender skew owes much to a mass exodus of Jeju men during the era of Japanese colonization. To that point, there's a present-day section of Osaka, Japan, known as Ikuno-ku, which serves as a home for a particular group that still practices Jeju shamanism. The group encompasses descendants of migrants that fled Jeju during Japan's colonization of the island.

As I considered the breeze easing through Seogwipo from the east, Dan and I deboarded a bus near Seogwipo's artists' market. Rows of vendors displayed homemade bracelets and decorated wristwatches, as well as items unique to Jeju—shell necklaces created from Seogwipo beach debris and hand-sewn clothes made of fabric called *galot* that was dyed with island-grown persimmon juice.

For nearly an hour, Dan and I wound through bustling

streets and then passed one of the city's most scenic landmarks, *Cheonjiyeon* waterfall. A vendor in an adjacent parking lot was selling grill-roasted squid on a skewer, and another was selling sweet pastries filled with red bean paste. Beyond the waterfall, the harbor yawned at the ocean of the Korean Strait, where the East Sea and the Yellow Sea merged. Boats were anchored in neat succession, their gunwales squeaking every so often. Continuing towards the water, we soon came to the shore and had to balance on the pointed tops of large boulders that had recently tumbled from higher cliffs.

The eroding shoreline, beige sedimentary rock faces, appeared in a geologic state of instability. A few times Dan and I made it known to one another that we could easily become crushed victims of the ground's ongoing erosion. "Don't talk too loud because it might cause more rocks to fall," Dan uttered at one point. And since he had actually been a certified avalanche rescuer at one point in his worldly past, I thought he might not be offering his advice entirely in jest.

At the base of one especially imposing cliff, we paused to observe a tribe of jet-black mountain goats before we decided to scramble further upward.

The incline of the cliffs grew steeper. Anyone who has never encountered angry goats cannot fully conceive the challenge of having to evade several while also having to move upward on the side of a cliff. I thought Dan and I were on a relatively pedestrian climbing course until my foot slipped and I watched a melon-sized stone role from beneath my boot and explode in a kaleidoscope of gray fragments 75 feet below. Oddly, what crossed my mind then was not fear of falling down the mountain or splashing into the choppy ocean water, but an anecdote I had read about Korean sailors long ago. They considered it unlucky to keep women and dogs aboard their ships; in fact, Korean sailors long ago were encouraged to distance themselves from women altogether even prior to setting sail. Why such peculiar thoughts raced through my mind as I gripped the vertical rock of the steep incline was a mystery—perhaps a subconscious fear of tumbling only to meet a similar fate to that of a keelhauled sailor, chewed and churned among the barnacled rocks. Regardless, I took heed: don't fall.

We paused for photos of a lone tree protruding from the rocky incline; its thick, weathered branches reached out in marvelous, ancient curls. I wondered how many similar trees had come and gone on the edge of the jagged stones in previous decades—some undoubtedly being rooted passengers on the immense chunks of rock that had broken off the larger boulders and tumbled down to the water.

The unexpected end of our climb came in the form of a mysterious concrete staircase cemented to the side of the sheer cliff. Without any rock climbing hardware, Dan and I would have to take the precarious stairs if we wanted to proceed. But the staircase was crumbling and attached to loose rock, and most perplexingly, it ultimately led to nothing but overgrown brush farther up.

"Stairway to...nowhere," Dan said, gazing up the steps.

It occurred to us that the stairs had undoubtedly once

led to *something*, but whatever structure had once stood on this cliff had sloughed away or crumbled long ago.

Standing on the lowest stairs briefly, cautiously, we tested the load-bearing potential of the concrete. The entire staircase seemed to shed bits of its cement underside with our weight. "I don't want to watch us die here," Dan said cryptically.

The stairs' concrete audibly crackled beneath us. "Me neither," I whispered.

More cracking. I pictured the old staircase disintegrating into gravel and dust below the soles of my shoes, and I envisioned me and Dan falling far down, tumbling end over end viciously, to the ocean debris below.

It was tempting to take a chance and gamble on the stairs' sturdiness. I wanted to continue walking gingerly up them. Once past this crumbling staircase, we could reach the upper brush and maybe scramble to an even higher point—perhaps to a remote spot high above that very few other people on the island had reached. We could be among the first!

As if I could see myself then, leaning my weight carefully on the stairs, caught in a moment of hesitation, I realized that there was more than just recreation at the root of my desire to keep going upward. It was about achieving a goal—reaching the top of the cliff—but it was about a release too. The past half year had entailed many bouts of loneliness on the island, and at times, holing up reading books about myths exacerbated my feelings of isolation. This climb, I knew, was a way to briefly forget the frustrations, even if just for a few moments.

"What should we do?" Dan asked.

I looked up the rock, to the empty space that the staircase led to, and wondered if the risk of going dangerously upward was worth the few seconds of enjoyable adrenaline it would bring. I knew I'd still have to grapple with the same lonely feelings eventually upon descending. This crumbling staircase wasn't the solution. So, what was the solution? A traditional fire mountain festival a few months away? I wasn't sure if that was the answer either, but I wanted to at least give the festival a shot. I had been anticipating it for too long now—and I was starting to actually believe in its healing potential.

And just like that, my desire to tempt fate and inch further up the precarious staircase dissipated. We investigated the stairs' load-bearing potential for a few more minutes, but my heart wasn't in it.

Eventually, we decided to leave the precarious spot and start the climb back down the same way we'd come.

As we descended, I thought about how there was something a little existentialistic about climbing halfway up a cliff only to see a random staircase and turn right around. Then, like a perfect intermission to my thinking, the clouds happened to drape a pink glow over the vertical rock as we continued winding carefully down. Had we chosen to continue vigilantly climbing *up* the stairs and the cliff—with our backs constantly facing the ocean and our minds focused on finding suitable handholds and footholds—we likely would have missed the shimmering spectacle of clouds and stone. I love climbing, and I think there is much to be learned by pushing oneself to go higher on a large cliff or great rock peak, but sometimes it's just as meaningful to leisurely come down too.

Closer to sea level, we spotted dark holes at the base of additional cliffs in the distance. They were ammunition tunnels that the Japanese had constructed during World War II and primed for the possibility that the United States would bomb Seogwipo after Hiroshima and Nagasaki. The tunnels were still intact, cosmic black eyes sunken in the precipice and staring out to sea.[5]

By the time we took the long bus ride back to Jeju City, the chilly night winds had returned. In one last act of Christmas cheer, Dan and I split the half-pint of warm whiskey in my daypack and finished the clump of donuts while blasting Grateful Dead tunes through a laptop's tiny speakers. At one point, Dan offered a toast to the eroding cliffs for not crumbling on us, the ocean waves for not pummeling us, and to the angry goats for not trampling us.

"The goats almost got us," I said, sipping from my glass.

"Yeah," Dan replied. "Almost...but here we are."

It seemed a fitting way to herald the remainder of my journey towards the fire mountain festival and whatever was to come. No matter what, *here we are.*

---

[5] When World War II ended, Jeju had massive amounts of Japanese military artillery still scattered across the land. In an attempt at a quick cleanup, American soldiers on the island were told to simply dump the artillery into the ocean. This ultimately resulted in immeasurable amounts of Japanese weapons and ammunitions being discarded on the seafloor around Jeju.

14. Local motion

In a bar in the modestly trendy City Hall district of Jeju City, New Year's Eve ensued in figurative slowmo, a far cry from the hysteria in other parts of the world. The interior of the chosen bar was plastered with a surplus of modern art paraphernalia and painted hand prints, all drummed up amid sundry decorative Western themes. I was pleased to be there, comfortably buzzed, and I was delighted to find that the place was playing host to an open-mic concert that presented a sample of the music predilections of Jeju's youth. A freestyle rapper in a baggy hoodie started the show, stomping around and exhaling his lyrics in mixed Korean and English, followed by a subdued woman in a formal dress belting lovey-dovey ballads over a bossa-nova guitar. Next up was an amusing medley of show tunes from a musical about Jeju—sung solely by the musical's director.

I sipped through beers and let my mood oscillate with

the shift of music genres. It wasn't exactly like watching the ball drop at Times Square in New York, but the concert typified what most people did on the island when it was dark and wintery cold—sit indoors and drink.

Such seasonal repose wasn't unique to Jeju, but the locals took the idea of the winter blues seriously. It was traditionally believed that the chilly weather signified the presence of *Yeongdeung*, a goddess who controlled the wind on the island, and that everyone should enact a social and industrial hibernation. So, people did just that. They hunkered down in their respective homes until *Yeongdeung* left and the warm weather of spring returned. Elaborate ceremonies continue to this day that symbolically welcome the goddess to the island and also bid her farewell. The ceremonies are extensive affairs, involving dozens of participants wearing traditional attire and performing dances for large crowds. Under other circumstances, similar rituals were traditionally performed on the island as exorcisms, called *gut*, which I think aptly sums up most Jeju locals' opinion of the winter and an intense desire to be rid of it.

The island's winter also includes a brief period of time called *Shingugan*, during which all of the gods of Jeju are reassigned to new worldly regions over which to preside. The local custom has long been to move during this period—to a new house and possibly a new town—to evade any evil deities, a game of hide-and-seek with the gods. Whether the locals actually choose to move or just batten down the hatches at home during this period, it is clear that the hope is for winter spirits to get in and get out quickly. Warmer days can't come soon enough to the island.

Wandering into the electric energy and neon glow of the City Hall streets later, I stopped at a street cart for late-night fishcakes. Little more than the seafood version of a hotdog—salty fish innards blended together, pressed and served hot—*odeng*, as the fishcakes are known, is extremely popular as a street snack. At one point, I lost my footing on the corner curb due to so many other people jostling for space at the cart. I attempted to talk with one person and was assured repeatedly by him that this was the best *odeng* on the street corner—the charming logic of a drunk. Deciding to finish my snack in silence, I munched to the sound of reggae music bubbling from a nearby window. The lively crowd swayed along to the easy rhythm.

My taxi ride home offered more nuanced conversation. Prompted by a question of whether Jeju was an enjoyable place for one to grow up, my taxi driver, a 42-year-old from the southern end of the island, explained that he had long felt a burdensome amount of stress in his life. He felt especially crushed by the anxiety now, as a middle-aged bachelor. Driving a taxi had introduced him to many foreigners, and in conversations with businessmen from all over the world, my driver had grown fond of the Western concept of the life-long bachelor. It was quite different from the common Jeju paradigm. The eldest son of a family on Jeju not only has a duty to care for his parents as they age, but also often has an obligation to invite his parents to live in his home and provide them with an independent living space known as the *ahngeori*. Deviating somewhat from other traditional societies slanted toward Confucianism, a man on Jeju historically consulted with his wife in matters of major familial choices. The eldest son of a family also often plays a primary role in planning and performing an extravagant ceremony known as a *chesa*, which honors the family's lineage. In short, being an eldest son on Jeju can come with expectations of stability, responsibility and ancestral focus, which didn't syncopate with what my taxi driver wanted to do in life: "Drive and enjoy women."

All of this is not to imply that marriage on Jeju is any guarantee of harmony. If it was any consolation to my taxi driver, Jeju has repeatedly had the distinction of possessing the highest percentage of divorced couples in all of South Korea. I couldn't find any convincing reason for this in research—some academics cited the historic self-assuredness of women in Jeju's culture, but making such a correlative to divorce felt presumptuous to me. By equally flimsy rationale, one could speculate that Jeju's high divorce rate was influenced by its international tourism push and subsequent interaction with more Western social mores. Long ago, a divorced woman in Korea was deemed a social outcast, but it is worth noting that a vast majority of divorced women on Jeju nowadays eventually remarry, which denotes the absence of any permanent stigma.

Nevertheless, the architecture of the Jeju family as described in my New Year's Eve taxi ride was vacillating in a peculiar space, its long-established parameters being

Island Solitaire

transplanted into a suddenly intercultural arena. As my taxi driver said when we were bidding each other goodbye and exchanging verbal blessings for the New Year, "Lack of marriage in my life now feels more complicated than ever before." He drove away with high hopes of meeting a nice woman who could help him spiritedly ring in the new year.

15. 1,000 previous meetings

Warmer days arrived, and aggressive winds whipped the palms along the main road into town. I decided to take a long walk to the local sauna. Public saunas are a Korean staple, and especially refreshing on the island, where any *jimjilbang* worth its admission price also offers a steam bath and a soak in a tub of tepid seawater.

I hunched forward and tilted into the steady wind gust, encouraged by the anticipation of the sauna's warmth widening my pores and the restorative boiler heat sinking deep to my core. It was easy to still feel lonely on the island at times, with the comfort of isolation occasionally souring to alienation. From time to time, my curiosity about Jeju was met with confusion and consternation from others: I was inquiring about the island's way of life, but a way of life is, by definition, habitual and practiced without need of an explanation. The wind seemed to exasperate this awareness because it had begun to blow at all hours of the day, howling off the ocean or barreling down from

Island Solitaire

the mountain peaks. It was the inescapable reminder of the island's natural solitude.

The sauna, then, was a suitable respite from this gusty morning, and many other locals had the same idea. I took deep breaths to inhale the steam when I reached the sauna's main room. Even with interior stone walls and the propulsive bubbles gurgling in the water hot tubs, the wind could still be heard outside like an ornery creature.

My trip to the sauna was the most recent in a series of leisure fixes while I awaited the start of the new semester of teaching at the university. My ribs had fully healed from the bus accident, so I had spent previous weekends bouldering in the dried-out riverbeds on the island and noodling on my guitar to the tunes of South Korea's folk music idol, Kim Kwang Seok. Kim possesses a massive level of acclaim in the country. His songs were political soundtracks for the youth of a turbulent era—the transitional social period of the late 1980s in South Korea, as students and activists rallied for a fully democratic government. When he committed suicide at age 31 in 1996, it was such a shock to his fans that many Koreans still refuse to believe that there were not more nefarious circumstances at play.

A few days after broken guitar strings had put my musical ambitions on hold, I found myself playing cards with a group of children at one of the local English-language academies to pass the time. The rules of the card game were that all dealings and competitive banter were to be vocalized in clear, full-sentenced English, which inadvertently furnished the Korean children with the vocal swagger of full-fledged gamblers. Consider one exchange, in which I had lost the hand to an articulate 10-year-old named Hanna. Instead of saying to me, "You lose," or some similar brief message, Hanna properly chided, "John, you are not good. You have bad cards. Your playing is terrible. So, you really are a loser." And when the card game was finished, other children found it timely to run around the academy and shoulder-block the furniture, mess up the desk of grammar books, and wreck the neatly organized shelf of board games. I took all of this rambunctiousness to be an explicit protest from the children that their weekends had to be spent indoors, practicing English.

I was considering all of this one night, the filling of one's leisure hours, in a restaurant wedged in between buildings off Jeju City's main drag. With golden light from the ceiling falling across intricately patterned rugs on the floor, the corner felt palatial. A line of books on the wall spoke to a worldly clientele—a Sri Lanka travel guide leaned against a tattered Gore Vidal paperback, along with the normal mass-market dreck of romance novels. The restaurant was subdued, almost hushed from an earlier lunch rush, as I sat picking at a basket of bread with the restaurant's owner. She was tall—or, more accurately, she was made tall by high heels. She wore her long hair split over her shoulders like a shawl. Having operated the restaurant for years, she could now come and go as she pleased, various duties having been delegated to her trusted staff. However, she admitted early in our conversation that she rarely sat in her own restaurant just to eat and converse, adhering to a belief that keeping the business side of her life and the social side separate was best for both tiers.

I enjoyed listening to the restaurant owner talk about the building because I knew it was a popular place for locals and island tourists alike. That wasn't a common mutuality, as most tourist restaurants across the island were too expensive and crowded for the locals' liking—and often encircled by massive hotels—while most local hangouts were thought to be too roughhewn for non-islanders. But somehow this owner had made the coexistence work, and I got the sense that her gregariousness had much to do with the success of her business. She had many questions for me about the United States, so I liked that we could volley our respective curiosities back and forth without feeling too nosy.

The scent of spicy tea swirled from a tray of mugs behind the bar when I mentioned that running a restaurant and catering to customers from all corners of the world must be exhausting. As it turned out, the restaurant owner was hanging on by a thread, in her own words. Her past year had been filled with enough emotional burdens to push anyone to a breaking point. "For starters," she said, "my mother was very sick. She's a strong woman, so she refused to go to the hospital. I had to take care of her." Additional stress of the past year had included a sibling being diagnosed with a severe illness—and choosing to postpone treatment until the mother's medical issues had been addressed. "The English expression—when it rains, it pours, right?" she asked me.

At the front of the restaurant, a sweaty party of people in yoga clothes nudged tables together and ordered bottles of wine, then erupted in laughter at a joke made by someone in the bunch. The group talked loudly, voices piling over other voices, as they passed around a plate of crispy appetizers. What struck me most was the polarity of the moment, the carefree joys of the large group at the front of the restaurant and the gloomy realities being discussed by the owner and me in the back.

After a heavy pause, the restaurant owner sighed and tucked a line of dark hair behind an ear. I noticed that she always fidgeted with a beaded strand of hair when she talked about the terrible aspects of the previous year. "You have to just keep going," she said. "All of those bad things—I just have to hope that this new year will be better."

"Certainly a good outlook," I said. "Easier said than done."

"There's really no other option," she said. "I mean, what else is there to do?"

"Nothing."

"Right. New year, new start," she said.

She nodded as I mentioned the island's myths and history. "Jeju is definitely an island of change," she said, tearing a corner of bread and scooting her chair out of the ceiling light. "This island is so different now compared to when I was born on it, and it was so different then compared to when my mother was born on it. It was different then because of the Korean War and the destruction, and it's different now because there are so many foreigners—American, Canadian, Australian, Chinese..."

"Do you consider the influx of foreigners to be a good thing or a bad thing?" I asked.

"Both," she said. She folded her arms and sat back in her chair. "In the past, I wanted to be friends with as many foreigners on the island as possible. I really wanted to have friends from all over the world. I think there's value in that. But now, especially with how horrible the past year has been to my personal life and my family, I just want peace and quiet. I even bought a small house inland to have more privacy, but I haven't moved into it yet. I don't want to leave my current apartment because that would mean leaving the sight and smell of the ocean."

She explained that there was a therapeutic effect to waking up every day to an ocean view. In a way, it kept everything in her life in perspective. I assured her that I understood.

The scent of the tea in the restaurant was replaced by a stronger waft, more pungent and earthy. A side door was cracked open, and smoke from a hookah drifted into our space.

Have you heard of *in-yeon*?" the restaurant owner asked abruptly.

I shook my head.

"It's kind of a Korean version of karma," she said, and tugged at the beads in her hair. "For example, if something happens, it was meant to happen. With *in-yeon*, if people meet, they were meant to meet."[6]

"Like destiny?" I asked.

"Sort of," she said. "It's like Korean destiny, but it also has to do with the past. If people meet, it means they have already met at least 1,000 times in previous lives. Do you know what that means?"

"It means you already sort of know the person?"

"I suppose," she said. "But it's also another reason why you just have to keep going forward. Maybe you've reached meeting numbers 999 with many people. Or maybe you're just at meeting number one with someone. So, no matter what number you're at, you can't stop. You can never stop."

---

[6] A cautionary note that I offer from experience: travelers and anyone learning the Korean language should be careful not to confuse *in-yeon*, discussed here, with the similar-sounding *i-nyeon*, which is a Korean pejorative for an awful woman.

16. The surrounding waters

One day, I found myself traveling amusingly deep down the rabbit hole of research. On a fog-filled afternoon, an anecdote about Jeju's mountain hunting god, *Harosantto*, led me to a detailed description of a sacrificial ritual, still practiced to this day by some locals, involving the decapitation of a wild pig. I read about various methods for cooking pigs over an open flame. All this somehow routed me to description of another ritual in which a newborn baby's umbilical cord is charred and buried in the island dirt—to be accessed later in life as a medicinal apparatus if the infant contracts an illness; the umbilical cord represents vitality and perfect human wellbeing in the form of a flawless baby.

Fascinating tidbits such as these aside, my curiosity about the fire mountain festival only led to more questions. I had amassed a healthy stack of transcribed folk tales and accounts of shamanic rituals, but on slow, languid days, I feared it all could end up being a lost cause. Perhaps there were no answers to be found, no profound ratiocinations for Jeju locals' adherence to myth, just the uninspiring and inauthentic sallowness of novelty. One of Jeju's most charming physical characteristics, for instance, is the abundance of boxy, stone *dolharubang* statues around the island that represent the mythical founder of the island. The statues were historically placed as guardians of important sites in various regions. But some of their charm is compromised when one sees the same statues being reproduced as marketing tools, peddling everything from green tea to tangerines, televisions to toenail clippers. Scholars are still unsure of the precise origin of the *dolharubang* statues—why they were constructed in the first place, and why they never existed in any other part of Korea. But one can assume that the statues were intended by their ancient creators to be more than mere advertising shills.

My biggest frustrations in researching myths and the fire mountain festival usually came after searching for mythology that was actually *about* fire, of which there happened to be very little. Instead, my inquiries often led in the opposite elemental direction, to water and to Jeju's folklore stories about perilous ocean travel. Chatting with a local professor over baked sweet potatoes one afternoon, I said flat-out, "I want to know more about Jeju's intertwining of myth and modernism—why is mythology still so pervasive on the island and strangely absent from much of the rest of the country?"

The professor just shrugged unenthusiastically. Yet,

Island Solitaire

when I asked where I should go to learn more about how Jeju is unique from other parts of South Korea, the professor put down an orange lump of potato and raised his eyebrows eagerly. "You must go to the sea," he insisted. "That's where all the tradition really is."

As one might expect, the sea around Jeju possesses lore and anecdotes that are both haunting and inspiring. Examples of the former: when an Italian ship, *The Bianca Pertica*, sank in the water around Jeju in 1878, the ocean picked apart the stranded, lifeboat-squatting crew with the callousness and precision of a sniper. High waves capsized the lifeboat and obliterated any rations and supplies that had initially been salvaged from the mother ship. Several crewmembers soon lost their lives. After reacquiring their lifeboat but going progressively mad and starving at sea, the men who were still alive managed to spot land—Jeju—on the horizon. Unfortunately, this sighting was around the same time that their lifeboat was blown way off course and pushed further away from the island.

For more than a day, the sea teased the lifeboat of *The Bianca Pertica* around Jeju—getting the boat close enough for the crew members to make eye contact with the land, but too far away for them to attempt to dock on the shore. In a desperate attempt to harness the harsh wind and angle the lifeboat towards a rocky beach, the men rigged a sail out of pieces of their clothes. Their ingenuity was futile, as the makeshift sail proved ineffective for getting them to the land. Overcome with thirst, one crewmember broke a cardinal rule of ocean survival and gulped seawater—and died shortly after. Other crewmembers met their demise as well, until a lone survivor—Guiseppe Santori—eventually decided to abandon the lifeboat altogether and attempt to swim to Jeju's shore. He ultimately made it to the island, but the ocean had claimed the lives of his 12 shipmates.

Jeju reeled more recently from another ocean tragedy, the sinking of South Korea's ferry, *Sewol*, on April 16, 2014. The Jeju-bound ship, which had been carrying nearly 300 high school students from the Korean mainland, turned too sharply in the Maenggol Channel of the Yellow Sea and capsized. It was later determined that Sewol was greatly overloaded, carrying a total weight of cargo that considerably and disastrously compromised its maneuverability. Many passengers were tossed instantly into the frigid water while others were trapped within the confines of the ship's heavily damaged and quickly sinking hull.

In the aftermath of the *Sewol* disaster, with a death toll of 295 people, criticism was javelined at a number of targets—at the ship's captain for the egregious operational error, at the *Sewol* crew for instructing passengers to stay inside the sinking ship rather than rallying an effective evacuation, at the South Korean government for not enacting a swifter rescue operation, and even at the media itself for not being more forthcoming with the severity of the tragedy. I recall sitting in my apartment in Jeju City on the day of the sinking and hearing a brief radio news sound bite, heartbreakingly erroneous in hindsight: "All passengers rescued."

Island Solitaire

The waters around Jeju have long held a maritime reputation for being dangerous and unforgiving, and the *Sewol* sinking was a weighty reminder of the sea's impenitent nature, of human blunders having catastrophic consequences on the open ocean. There were less-tragic cases in history as well. When a missionary from America, Alexander Pieters, visited Jeju in 1897 as likely the first Westerner to sightsee around the island, he found the shoreline and the culture of Jeju's locals to be awash with beautiful pearls from the ocean and pearl-based rituals. Pieters' trip occurred at a time when Korea was granting Western businesses permission to harvest the pearls from the Korean shore to be sold in Western markets—a significant landmark in East-West commerce. Jeju didn't have the abundance of pearl-bearing clams in its surrounding waters that other parts of Korea possessed, but Jeju did have a firmly-established local economy already centered around the cultivation and harvest of abalone, seaweed and other commodities from the sea—and, as Pieters observed, the economy of Jeju's ocean hauls was run entirely by a close-knit community of hearty women divers.

Pieters was amazed that the women of Jeju played such a significant role in the gruntwork and the retail of the sea's bounties—progressive compared to the limited societal and occupational roles of women in Pieters' more familiar West at the end of the 19th century. Also impressive was that anyone—man or woman—would be able to actively endure diving and swimming in the frigid ocean water in the winter equipped with nothing more than a collection net and a sickle. More than 100 years after Pieters' observations, the *haenyo*,[7] as Jeju's women divers are called, still exist and operate on the island's coastal waters in largely the same way, harvesting oysters, squid and other seafood for profit with the same minimal set of tools. They started wearing wetsuits in 1975, but aside from that, the *haenyo* that one sees nowadays around Jeju look nearly identical to the *haenyo* of centuries past.

Such adherence to tradition has brought the *haenyo* a lot of attention from cultural and preservational perspectives, but it hasn't exactly made the profession a popular pursuit for younger generations. To say that the registered *haenyo* divers, of which there are currently about 4,500, comprise an endangered occupational group in the current century is an understatement; a recent statistic noted that there is not a single, certified *haenyo* on Jeju under the age of 30, and a vast majority of the divers are approaching retirement. Just a few decades ago, the total number of *haenyo* divers was swelling, with more than 20,000 women claiming the occupation.

Part of the reason for the waning interest lies in the obvious hazards of diving a dozen meters without scuba equipment, which the *haenyo* do on a regular basis to collect their various shellfish. Learning the diving trade, which is broadly called *jamsu*, is a long and arduous process that entails years of practice and apprenticeship,

---

[7] It's worth pointing out that some Jeju locals object to this term, *haenyo*, as the word has its origins in the Japanese language. *Jomnyo* is the word for the women divers in Jeju's dialect. However, at the time of this book's writing, *haenyo* is still the more commonly used designation for the divers.

along with physical acclimation to the pulmonary demands of the swimming. To add to these strains of learning the necessary skills, the *haenyo* community operates on a hierarchical system based on experience and ability; a lower-ranked woman, *hagun*, has far less say in matters of business and personal profit than a higher-ranked *sangun*. There is a *haenyo* school on Jeju that is open to all-comers, but even an eager graduate, skilled in diving and harvesting food from the ocean floor, would enter a professional aqua world of hazards. Hypothermia, powerful undercurrents, vulnerability to boat accidents and the dangers of swimming at significant ocean depths all present constant, unavoidable risks, even with formal training.

Another factor contributing to a decline in *haenyo* numbers relates to the organizational structure of the profession. Since hauls are typically pooled and sold communally, being a *haenyo* isn't conducive to significant personal gain. In a country as modernized as South Korea, with enthusiastic 20-somethings on Jeju just a 50-minute plane flight from the city commerce and entrepreneur allure of Seoul, joining the dangerous lifestyle of the sea divers isn't typically an enticing career path.

The Jeju government has been aware of this reality for a couple of decades. While acquiring new active legions of *haenyo* will mean convincing the youth that there is great professional value in the traditionalism of the craft, preserving the distinctive *haenyo* subculture and treating it like a living museum appears to be a more doable task. Efforts to protect the current population of divers and promote their history have included everything from application for UNESCO recognition to the construction of a *haenyo* museum. The Jeju government also subsidizes the divers with medical aid. Academic courses have been taught on the *haenyo* way of life, documentaries have been filmed and books have been written about them. One of the island's aquariums performs a live-action production daily that likens the *haenyo* to mermaids. There is even a popular cartoon *haenyo* character, *Mongni*, who explains the ocean harvesting in a way that is easy for children to understand. I was surprised one day to see a Korean magazine featuring a profile of a man, Hyeong Woo, who handmakes the wetsuits for many of the island divers—the promotion of *haenyo* subculture reaching beyond the subject of *haenyo* and into their cultural periphery.

Whether or not any of these efforts will make a difference—in preserving the *haenyo* lifestyle or acting as advertisements for interested newcomers—is an unanswerable question. But I felt fortunate to be able to take the bus to the shore on a regular basis and watch the *haenyo* bobbing beyond the sandbar, specks in the indigo water, their polished wet-suited heads emerging from the depths like exposed gemstones. For now, they have not yet become novel or extinct. Observing them so dwarfed by the harbor ships and a dock of tourists, their swimming figures foreshortened by a shoreline coffee shop and fishing boats, I couldn't help but wonder how long the living history could possibly continue.

17. Ghost night

Stirred one morning by loud thuds, and with all the *haenyo* ocean hazards still reverberating in my mind, I scrambled from my rest envisioning a colossal storm front. I followed the noise downstairs to the main dumpster of my apartment complex. There, I was surprised to find my neighbor—Hyojun, the medical school student—tossing hefty notebooks into a trash heap. Each notebook clunked into the dumpster's base, and the sound rippled in the enclosed space. Hyojun was at the tail end of a horrible semester at school, and he had just learned that he had failed the annual progress exam. He explained that out of frustration, he was opting to throw away every notebook, workbook, laboratory log, textbook and medical worksheet from the past year. It all amounted to impressive stacks of multi-colored documents, nearly as tall as the dumpster.

Hyojun continued heaving the academic miscellany as

he verbalized to me precisely how his exam score would wreck his class rank and his career prospects. As he aptly put it: what hospital on Jeju would ever possibly want to hire a doctor who was ranked near the bottom of his class?

I was surprised by the whole morning scene because I had witnessed over the recent months how dedicated Hyojun had become to his studies. He had pulled all-nighters at the library, dismissed any sort of social life and buckled down diligently to squeeze in extra studying during the holidays. He had come a long way in his commitment to the school's program.

He had also managed to keep his parents in the dark about his steady academic slippage, apparently, and he was now at a crossroads. He admitted that he was more concerned with telling his parents about his exam failure than about the failure itself. In the meantime, while he worked up the courage to break the news to them, he was content to discard anything that reminded him of the curriculum.

I didn't have much wisdom to impart to Hyojun at the moment, but I didn't want this thrashing of notebooks to be the beginning of a mid-life crisis for him—before he'd even reached mid-life. He quickly refocused all of his attention back to tearing up loose-leaf papers, and I told him that we should meet later to talk more about the dilemma.

I was still feeling bad for Hyojun a week later when I signed up to work at a camp for middle school students on the island. I hadn't been able to get in touch with Hyojun in the interim, but my life quickly slipped into the frenetic

Island Solitaire

tempo that emerges when 100 teenagers—boys and girls—are corralled under a single roof. Such a collective causes particular wildness for most Korean students, who are accustomed to school classes that are not co-educational. Mornings at the camp were spent teaching English-language reading, speaking and writing to the campers. The main challenge for the small staff came during the interlude between the structured programs—keeping campers' energy and enthusiasm elevated while also refereeing all the inherent teenage mischief. A sampling of the madness, as jotted down in my notebook over the course of a single day:

- Campers' cell phones were collected, to be held by the staff until camp's end. The campers seemed devastated by this—several actually cried.

- One camper thought it would be impressive to stuff as many tomatoes in her mouth as possible at mealtime. She stopped somewhere between three and four, at which point a crowd of onlookers had gathered to watch her attempt to swallow the mushy wad. Extremely messy and ultimately unsuccessful.

- One camper was caught chugging a carton of whipping cream during cooking class. Not surprisingly, a bad stomachache took her out of commission for the rest of the day's activities.

- Two campers were caught stealing tangerines from the cafeteria. When confronted, they told me, "Teacher, don't be angry. Tangerines are healthy." Nice logic.

- Several campers enjoyed Korean wrestling, *ssireum*, which might best be referenced to Americans as a hybrid of judo and sumo. Fun, but not good in the crowded classroom.

The camp was, despite minor disciplinary hiccups, a pleasure to be a part of, as another point of the programs was to introduce campers to Jeju's heritage. Included in this objective one day was a field trip to *Seongsan Ilchulbon*, a 5,000-year-old volcanic crater on the island's east coast, followed by a meal of sliced pork wrapped in lettuce.

From a marketing perspective, Jeju's pork industry is a marvel. The meat is one of the island's most famous commodities, and photographs of Jeju's unique black-furred pigs are slapped all over restaurant banners, menus and brochures. However, a survey of Jeju's livestock history reveals that pigs on the island used to have the distinct job of being families' waste-disposal units. Prior to running water and indoor plumbing, which weren't prevalent on many parts of the island until the 1960s, the pigs were fed a steady diet of human feces in an open-toilet system known as *deong-doe-ji*. Imagine an outhouse atop a pigpen, and you have a fairly accurate representation of how the arrangement worked. The pigs provided valuable fertilizer at a time when Jeju was mostly agricultural. Really disconcerting is the prevailing island rumor that the pigs' dark fur is attributable to their fecal diet, much like flamingo feathers pinking from a steady regimen of pink-pigmented crustaceans. As I said, however, Jeju has managed to evade any modern disapprobation of this history and hearsay, and position *heuk-doe-ji*—black pigs—as a symbol of the island's prosperity and culinary eminence. They might not be as awe-inspiring or photogenic as the tiger, South Korea's principal animal symbol, but the black pigs were even designated as natural monuments on Jeju.

None of the campers cared where the meat came from, and they all were content to jam-pack their lettuce wraps with slices of pork and garlic cloves and spicy pepper paste. Meals became social frenzies. Dinner conversations whirled above the tables before everyone collapsed in sleep back at the camp's residential headquarters.

As the days progressed, the staff became better acquainted as well. It was an eclectic crew—a professor fresh off a plane from a wedding in South Africa, a Korean camp director who had lived in Arizona for years, a good-natured teacher who ran a non-profit in Namibia in his spare time, as well as a number of college-aged locals who were working towards their teaching certifications. The would-be teachers told me that high school teaching jobs on the island were highly coveted. The gig brought a good salary, job stability and great community standing. I couldn't help but think of the diametric: my friends who were teachers in the United States, slogging through their careers in frequent frustration, with unjustifiably low salaries, overcrowded classrooms and overmedicated students.

Outside the cafeteria at camp one night, I noticed that the campers were particularly jittery. They circled each other and made howling noises. When I asked them what it was that had them so riled up, they pointed to snow-capped Halla Mountain in the distance and said, "Ghosts."

"Tonight is a ghost night," one of the campers said, running around in a fury.

The camp staff had spent days teaching the campers assorted facts about Jeju, showing them photos of blue-water beaches, traditional folk villages and tranquil hiking paths. Yet, it was the perceived spirits, emerging from the riddles of trees when the weather was crisp and clear, that captivated the imaginations of the campers deep into the night.

"Do you really think there are ghosts around here?" I asked the group.

The young campers stood dumbfounded for a moment before one of them said bluntly, "Teacher, don't say that! The ghosts might hear you."

By the end of the week, the campers did express a newfound appreciation for all the history that Jeju had to offer, but the dichotomy was that the campers expressed this while typing rapidly on their smartphones. As the staff waved goodbye to the campers on the final day, I wondered what the teenagers would retain from the experience, whether they would end up settling on Jeju years later or spread throughout the Korean peninsula as their ambitions and adulthood took shape.

At night, with a glowing moon starting to peek out of a white furrow of clouds, the camp's director said it was interesting how each seasonal roster of campers possessed its own unique personality. Just as groups of assorted travelers, or in this case camp staff members, coalesce around some common destination, the campers unified around daily examination of Jeju nuance.

The director nodded and sipped a cup of *makgeolli*. "The island, man," he said in a thick Korean accent, acutely ambiguous. "This island."

And that was all.

18. A receding tide

In terms of getting to know the island, Jeju offers residents and tourists everything from ATV rentals to scuba diving packages, yet a car road trip felt as suitable to me as any mode of examination could be. No doubt my decision to take an island-wide drive was influenced by a week of forecasted diamond-bright sunshine and yellow wildflowers blooming in the meadows. I had been steadily relaying my various island fascinations to my adventure companion, Zooey, ever since my bus accident on the icy road. She proposed a more interactive methodology to my inquiries; within a week, she had arrived for a visit to Jeju with an annotated map and a sightseeing itinerary in her hand. We ordered pizza at night and planned a driving route that would stretch around Jeju's coastal perimeter.

Zooey was a teacher by trade, and she had worked hard to allow for this vacation. Prior to joining me on the island, she had been pulling double shifts, tutoring and teaching extra nights at an academy in Seoul. These were the only

Island Solitaire

vacation days she'd be granted all year. I was most appreciative. She was the perfect partner for a road trip. She wasn't too fond of bugs, but that was her only caveat to the travel. She would prove to be open-minded when it came to nearly every other iteration of roughing it, from traipsing through wet sand in her dress boots to getting lost in a grubby cactus field and slipping on wet rocks as we both angled a little too determinedly for views of the ocean sunset at roadside vistas.

My desire for a trip had emerged after some surprising news from back in the United States, which felt as distant as the sunset itself. One of my former roommates was now the proud father of a newborn boy; his wife had given birth and promptly blasted out a photo-announcement over e-mail. Essentially this all affirmed that during my time on the faraway island, life had indeed continued elsewhere— a fundamental truth that had been surprisingly easy for me to ignore around the emptiness and seeming perpetuity of the ocean. I had spent many weeks comfortably removed from the norm—perhaps even purposefully bucking against it. Several other good friends in the United States had also decided to marry and start families. It was enough to make me a little reflective. I felt as if I was witnessing the combustion of a firework: everything that had once been packed so closely together suddenly diverging.

To Zooey's credit, she knew the best remedy when feeling somehow out of place was to simply find another place. In that spirit, there were to be no computers as we circled the island, lest we forget that the plan was to connect with the Jeju landscape rather than connect with the proceeding lives of friends. The best part of it all was that Zooey had been spot-on in the approach. We left my apartment after a lazy breakfast of leftover pizza, and within 20 minutes, I had once again forgotten about life beyond the island and disregarded the nonsense that existence supposedly has a norm.

The sun was high in the sky by the time Zooey and I stopped to snack on blueberry cheese bread one morning. A chill had already dissolved from the air. Zooey somehow managed to disrobe from her long underwear while keeping her outerwear fully donned by the car, and we continued past Jeju's five-day outdoor market, west along the shore. Flanking the highway were cabbage fields and scrubby ferns. In a different context, on a different side of the planet, the view could have been of California's Highway 1, but blips of Asia blurred past every so often—slate-roofed Buddhist temples and Hangul billboards. The ocean beyond the cabbage fields lightened as we drove farther away from home.

"The seawater doesn't look real," Zooey said, scooting to the edge of her seat to be as close to the beach as possible from the confines of our car.

There was a still-life effect to the view, even as we arrived at Hyeopjae Beach, one of the island's premiere seascapes. We got out of the car and crunched on triangular shell fragments, lucky enough to briefly be the only ones in sight on the knuckled bay. A seagull glided to ground level from high above and paused on the sand, perched like a toy in front of us. It pecked at lapping water, trotted through the foamy suds in a little dance and then flapped away, leaving Zooey and me alone again. "This is probably the most exotic scene in all of Korea," Zooey said, gazing at the sea, blinking from the flickers of sunlight on the tips of the waves. "So different from the mainland. It doesn't even feel like we're in Korea anymore."

Zooey told me an old Jeju saying, about the southern ocean crying when rain is coming; the western ocean, on the contrary, cries when the ensuing day will be sunny. "Breathe in deep. You can smell all the pieces of the ocean," she said, closing her eyes.

We hiked upshore and briefly wound through a grove of thick palm trees. We had to sidestep a snuggling couple that had converted a flat patch of beach sand into a campsite. The outside of their tent was littered with empty *makgeolli* bottles.

"I envy them," Zooey said with a smile. We made an impromptu pact to return to Hyeopjae Beach at some indeterminate time—a year, a decade—to sleep under the stars and amass our own collection of empty alcohol bottles. I wondered which elements of my life would be diverging and scattering then, and how I would feel about the further flux of old friends in time.

In unison with such lingering thoughts, we left the palm grove and came upon small stones stacked in an ancient act of prayer further down the beach. Observing them, I felt as if I had rudely intruded on people's private dialogues with God. Zooey assured me that the stone towers had been purposefully displayed so prominently and publicly, residing as they were on the very edge of the land and sea. "People here pray to the mountains when they are in the mountains, and the people pray to the water gods when they are near the ocean," Zooey said. The stone towers then, at constant risk of being demolished by crashing waves, represented the threshold between those godly realms, but more importantly, they epitomized the solely human belief that an expression of prayer mattered. "Right or wrong, good or bad, anyone can go to the ocean and pray, right?" Zooey said.

"Yeah, or go to the mountains," I said.

"That's the best part about Jeju—this island has both."

Almost without thinking, I snapped a photo of the towers. I instantly felt regret for doing so, in part wanting a memory to be my only recollection of the stones. I also felt that taking a photo devalued the people's prayers somehow. I deleted the photo and stood with Zooey as a big wave crashed between huge basalt fingers and sprinkled the stone towers with white sea suds.

"I wonder what all the people who stacked the stones were praying for," I said.

Zooey squinted into the sun and held a hand to block the splashing mist from another wave. "I guess it doesn't really matter with a prayer," she said.

"Doesn't matter?"

"I mean...people pray for anything and everything," she said. "Always have, and they always will. Every prayer must have been a subject by itself."

Back on the road, we spent the next few days crisscrossing island towns, sustaining ourselves with mackerel lunches. While hiking a grid of partial streets and cactus gardens once, we sauntered through an abandoned seashore house, high stepping over broken windows and crumbled brick interior, through thin splinters of shingled roof that had collapsed into the house's back room. Strewn across the floor of the house were artifacts of a family such as a toilet oddly discarded in an entryway, broken coffee mugs and torn shreds of blanket fabric.

"The saddest thing is that there must have once been happy people living here," Zooey said.

Less than 100 yards from the front lawn, which was now just a thorny wall of overgrown frizz, the ocean was the brightest shade of green, and it met the blue sky in a fine horizon line. There were no clouds overhead and no boats on the water, just the expansive green jutting against the equally expansive blue.

I had been delighted by Zooey's inherent curiosity about all sites passed on the trip—an abandoned house on the beach simply couldn't go unexplored, nor could the tide recede without our recreation. We left the rickety house and ran down to the sand, where the ocean water was pulling steadily out of the bay.

Zooey and I walked far out on sand that moments ago had been completely underwater. Soon we found ourselves standing in the middle of an immense oval of sand surrounded by the ocean. The ground sank around us to reveal intricate tafoni patterns at our feet. Jeju, at once exotic in comparison to mainland Korea, now felt exponentially removed from all familiarity. Zooey and I trailed along the honeycomb sand for a long distance, but

John Burgman

we might as well have been traversing another world.

On another early evening in the week, we made a point to visit *Sanbang*, a sacred cave on the island. At the top of a long series of S-curves in stone stairs, we hunched at the base of a mountain slab. This rock was also covered with distinct honeycomb designs, and within the stone pockets were smaller stones—placed in public acts of prayer not dissimilar from the construction of the stone towers on the beach. Higher in elevation than even these worship stones was the mouth of the cave and a makeshift Buddhist altar. *Sanbang* trickles constantly with water that is mythically said to be the tears of a mountain goddess who longs for her missing husband. From a collection trough, the water can be sipped for good luck by hikers.

A monk sat at the entrance of the cave, serenely monitoring the small concrete platform at the base of the altar. It was quiet, with an audible trickle of the goddess crying and an offshore breeze rising up the slope of the mountain and rustling the tree leaves. Zooey said that being at the top of the cave would bring good luck to us.

We drove home later beneath a clear sky, the coast's blue and white waves darkening and catching glimmers from highway headlights. In the downtime on the trip, I had finished two paperbacks about mankind's connection with the earth—one about mountaineering and another about Buddhism. When the spiritual text got a little too heavy for a carefree road trip, I turned to fiction. Author Andrew Foster Altschul, himself having been anthologized in Buddhist-themed collections, said that a writer is free to

Island Solitaire

try anything on the page as long as the ending succeeds, and perhaps that was the most applicable sentiment for the whole week: break conventions and stray from the path, but always remember where the path is.

19. A day at the races

On an average Friday on Jeju, one will likely observe some degree of construction or destruction taking place, workers building a new structure or tearing down an older one. It would not be surprising for one to also see, within close proximity to such transformation, a Buddhist monk strolling along the sidewalks adjacent to his ornate temple and a middle-aged woman, *ajjuma*, browsing the bright assortment of fruit and fish of an outdoor market. At any of the coffee shops around the island, on the same given Friday, one might also notice recent graduates studying for a civil service exam and hikers preparing to trek up a mountain. Somewhere in this patron parade, one could also spot locals gearing up to watch some horse racing.

Easing into the morning on one such Friday, I assessed my options and decided to spend some time at the nearby horseracing track. My neighbor Hyojun was still conspicuously absent from the apartment complex, having

Island Solitaire

absconded in an impulsive fit of self-disappointment—but absconded to where? Nevertheless, I figured that throwing down a little money on horses was an appropriate way to pass a day as the fire mountain festival loomed on the calendar.

I arrived at the racetrack early, intent on taking in the rhythms of the place and hopefully learning about Jeju's unique breed of horses. As it turned out, the Jeju racecourse was designed precisely with such inexperience in mind—even the greenest of gamblers were welcome to visit and lose their hard-earned cash. The track was built in 1990, and still maintained a garish 1990s charm; admission only cost 2,000 won, roughly equal to $1.75 USD. Passing through the entryway of the park, I felt cast into a bizarre dream, otherwise disparate visuals coexisting at every turn. The park's entryway, for starters, was modeled in the architectural scheme of a Buddhist temple, with tall columns supporting a large, tiered roof, yet the columns were flared with pastel polka dots. Taking a few steps further and swept into the entering crowd, I was on the main grounds, where I found myself staring at a group of cartoon character statues garnishing a woodland square.

I slipped through the betting area so that I could see the horses for the day's first race warming up on the paddock. The first thing that I noticed was just how small some of the horses were, much more diminutive than the hulking thoroughbreds of the derbies in the United States. This was by design, as Jeju's horses are known for being stockier and shorter to the withers than most breeds.

John Burgman

Horse racing has its ethical opponents who see the sport as a way of exploiting the animals, sometimes cruelly, for entertainment. However, there were good intentions behind the origins of Jeju's horseracing craze. Jeju's native horses, known locally as ponies or, technically *jejuma*, had long been a meat staple in the locals' diet. The pony also held mythological significance; one Korean folk tale tells of a woodcutter who was given a horse by spirits to ride in pursuit of a deity wife. The symbolism was clear: horses were the vehicles of the gods.

Jeju's ponies had also suited utilitarian needs in the days before automobiles. By the mid-20th century, however, changing attitudes of horsemeat as food, and a decrease in the horses' carrier services, rendered them out of demand on Jeju. The Korea Racing Association had the idea to bring horseracing to the island to give ponies a new purpose. The first documented instance of animal racing on the Korean peninsula had been an organized donkey race in the 1890s, but betting on horses in Korea had been on a steady popularity incline ever since it was first introduced as a public activity the 1920s. Jeju's native horses were bred with non-native types to create a hybrid racing breed known as a "Halla horse," named after Jeju's most famous mountain. Now, nearly 70 years since the first betting system was implemented in Korea, Jeju horse races were firmly in the locals' consciousness as a way of acquiring or losing money swiftly. The fact that betting on the races kept money steadily pumping into Jeju's economy sweetened the whole operation.

I picked a sturdy, dark-colored horse for my bet.

Island Solitaire

Something about the animal's slow trot around the paddock, with such a casual and unruffled demeanor, conveyed confidence. At least I thought it did, and then I headed to the grandstand for the race and promptly watched the horse lose—no place, no show, just a hapless deceleration from the front of the pack at the start of the race to the pathetic rear 900 meters later. A middle-aged bettor in a beige vest of pocketed programs standing beside me at the rail didn't win any money either, and he took the loss particularly hard. A noise that began as a snarling curse from him steadily worsened into an aggressive cough. He hung his head and spit. The potential complexity of wagers at a horse race is astounding. Anguish and defeat, however, always maintain their unmistakable simplicity, and to that point, the man in the vest coughed once more and receded into the dimness of the smoking area to suck on a cigarette in despair.

Once the day's races had begun at the track, they continued at regular intervals. I had a little time to explore, so I headed indoors to watch the next race on the monitors. An otherwise subdued room erupted in screams for the last few seconds of each race, and then the whole interior settled into a studious calm once again. In that way, the racecourse was comparable to a casino anywhere in the world, sustained by brief and wild fragments of enthusiasm. As one would expect, there were multiple ATM machines around the betting area, but there were also uniquely Korean touches. There were multiple instant coffee vending machines, a South Korean staple since the concept was borrowed from Japan in the 1970s, and a *jajangmyun* restaurant selling thick-sauced noodle lunches. There were ushers in abundance that could speak Korean, English and Chinese, but there were no security guards in sight. There was also an area for checking blood pressure—not a bad idea given the swells of emotion in each horse race. Nobody was drinking alcohol, however, which was surprising given the commonality of alcoholic drinks at virtually all other Korean social functions.

Stepping out the side door of the main betting plaza, it became clearer why alcohol was not allowed. The place had fashioned itself as a family destination, not solely a racing or gambling operation. In fact, a playground section on the grounds took up nearly as much space as the racetrack and betting area. Among the offerings geared toward children were pony rides, extravagant horse-themed jungle gyms, a performance bandstand and a soccer field. The playground was adorned with *dolharubang* figures and palm trees. One often hears that a compound of this magnitude is fun for the whole family; the reality is that such a place is usually a zone for one demographic to sit bored while the other demographic enjoys a kind of artificial freedom at an observable distance. A gambling establishment was an especially anomalous choice for attempting to forge family togetherness. Although I did see children of varying ages scampering through the greenery and galloping across quaint river bridges, their parents weren't usually anywhere in sight.

I made it back to the betting plaza just in time for a

Island Solitaire

three o'clock race. It didn't prove to be any more profitable—for me or the gentleman in the vest, who let the curses fly again: *Shi-bal*, one of the stronger Korean expletives.

I'd had my fill of horse races and defeat for one day, but I wasn't quite ready to leave the grounds. The most noteworthy tidbit I'd ever heard about the racecourse had nothing to do with the horses or the park itself. According to island gossip, the wooded hills and valleys surrounding the racetrack were havens for suicides. Gamblers who had scraped everything but the lint out of their wallets, dejected from compounding losses, chose the nearby cliffs as the most immediate means of ending everything. "Suicide Ridge" was a label sometimes given to a number of the surrounding tree-covered inclines. The entire concept seemed to be a patchwork of various realities—many gamblers on Jeju had committed suicide upon abhorrent losses, and in fact, two accomplished Korean jockeys had committed suicide in relatively close succession—Lee Myoung Hwa in 2005 and Park Jin Hee in 2010. As for Jeju's racecourse, it was difficult to verify various claims. South Korea has infamously held the title as the developed country with the highest suicide rate, which translates to as many as several dozen Koreans killing themselves each day.

Still, where the truth ended and where the gossip began provided enough curiosity for me to stroll beyond the edge of the racetrack grounds and hop over a line of orange construction cones. Slinking through a partition of prickly brush, orbiting the outskirts of the grounds as best I could,

John Burgman

I stepped onto a makeshift road on a bluff. Spindly, leafless tree trunks shot up through thick, mixed grasses.

With the horse races briefly forgotten, lost somewhere beyond the wall of brush, I continued on the small road and listened to distant highway traffic. I heard the slick swish of cars speeding to their respective wherevers and thought about the old road that I was following through the peaceful boscage, an ancient space on an evolving island. How long would it be until the shrubs and the road were swallowed up by larger roads and highways, or perhaps more probably, racetrack expansions? Recently, the Korean government had unveiled major plans to grow the country's horseracing industry in a big way, and since 90 percent of the nation's horse population was raised on Jeju, this had big implications for the island. The details of the plans were ambitious to say the least, calling for...well, everything: increased breeding of horses all over the Korean peninsula, an increased use of horse byproducts in cosmetics over a five-year period, 200 new racetracks, and schools/training facilities for horseback riders. Jeju's racecourse had carved an ostentatious facility—an entire family-aimed experience, in fact—out of the earth, and it clearly wouldn't be the last to do so.

The extent to which the trees around me blocked out the world beyond the immediate space conjured, though, an eerie sense of concealment. Even the canopy became progressively restrictive, with nutmeg branches intertwining overhead and blocking out the sunlight.

I don't know what I expected to find as I continued on the dwindling road—at best a splendid vista from the

Island Solitaire

forest, at worst a suicide corpse. The island gossip also chattered about the police pulling dead bodies from the woods on a weekly basis, so I scanned the weeds along the road's edge in morbid curiosity for an unnerving arm, a decaying leg. It came as a surprise when the road opened up to a patch of flattened grass. Sun pierced the clouds and fell over old concrete on the ground. The space wasn't exactly a parking lot, but there were three cars lodged in a shady corner. Like the shoddy road that must have led them there, the cars were in various stages of disarray. One was decaying at the tires.

It was impossible to gauge how long the cars had been abandoned—a week? A year? Without context, and without warning of such an encounter, my mind wandered about the remnants and their rightful owners. I didn't discover any dead bodies, if it needs to be said, but the old cars conveyed their own mystery and melancholia. Beyond the open space were a drop of hills, tree cover and steep heights. At some point, people had left these cars and ventured somewhere into the thick.

I thought about all of this as I began to head back. I eschewed the road and chose to cut through some more brush, which called for snagging through wiry vines and hopping a rock wall. I would have continued mulling over the gambling and the suicide topics except the vines and the shrubs parted and I was face to face with a statue of a cartoon character. Its permanent smile and pearly, plastic dermis meant that I had found my way back to the grounds, back to the gambling civilization of the racetrack.

John Burgman

What does one take away from a day at the races on Jeju, with all of its juxtapositions? I wasn't entirely sure, even as I hunched over a dinner of spicy soup at a horse-themed restaurant, and even as I arrived back home, discarded my race day program and a couple of unused betting tickets and slid my feet into my house slippers. The racecourse had certainly delivered on its intentions and provided an enjoyable experience heavy on eclecticism. I wondered if there was any honest way to separate the mystery of a place from its possibilities. It was a good rumination for a traveler or a horse industry primed for expansion on an island that gambles on races, eats pony meat and offers amusement for people of all ages. That seemed like the ultimate win for Jeju's horseracing industry, the fact that I was still thinking about the track long after I had left its polka dot-painted front gate. Admittedly, I wanted to go back, catch another race or two, actually win some money and play another day.

20. Day and night

The days leading up to the fire mountain festival were filled with uncertainty. Persistent rain turned the whole island's surface into a brown slosh. As a result, everyone seemed stuck in a perpetual state of gloominess. I used the string of gray mornings and afternoons to hole up and gather informative bits and pieces about the festival's longstanding importance to the Jeju community.

In fact, the fire mountain festival, in its contemporary iteration, didn't begin until 1997. However, for generations prior to that, farmers had purposefully ignited the mountains and the fields of the island on an annual basis in order to expunge the dead grasses in the winter. Festivals historically followed such great burnings and served as celebratory punctuation marks 15 days after the start of the Lunar New Year. In the present century, though, powerful winds off the ocean often cast unpredictable breezes up the mountainsides and rendered exact dates for the festivities each year unreliable. So, apparently it was quite common for island residents like myself to wait in anticipation for the lousy weather to clear.

On this particular year, word had spread on the island that the multi-day celebration would actually be cancelled altogether. This news only added to the gloom. Then gossip trickled through the city that the fire mountain festival might continue, but on an unspecified day at some point in the near future. There was a degree of pertinence to all of the uncertainty, as it fit with the poetic flexibility of all the island's stories—plots, descriptions and mythic messages conveyed in great variance, depending on the storyteller and the audience. Still, I was greatly disappointed to learn that the festival might be called off, and I forced myself to embrace the real possibility that I would be left to wonder about the festival's mysterious specifics after such a long chase.

Luckily, the festival did eventually take place, on a day when the winds were calm to the point of eeriness, and a net of clouds obscured the sun's brightness. The rain held off too, allowing the ground to harden. I took a crowded shuttle bus to the base of a mountain, which had been practically transformed into a small city of vendors and performance stages by the time I arrived. Slipping abruptly into a mob of people at a tent labeled "Personal Wish Corner," I observed a family transcribing their wishes for the future onto thin pieces of paper, then hanging them alongside hundreds of other paper wishes. Rounding a corner beyond the wishes, I found myself

Island Solitaire

delightfully enveloped by a crowd of gambling middle-aged men tossing dice in the corner of a different tent.

The aim of the whole tent city, which was comprised of hundreds of vendors in total, was to keep the masses spending money until the real highlight came after dark—when the grassy face of the 300,000-square-foot mountain would be lit on fire as the thousands of onlookers stood wide-eyed at its base. There was fluidity to the intervening food and entertainment options, everything from churros and draught beer to group dances and tug-of-war competitions. It was a unique environment that a Westerner like myself might describe, however futilely, as a sort of Burning Man festival blending with an open-air heritage museum. There were chants performed on a stage by a group of Jeju *haenyo* and there were frequent K-pop sing-a-longs over a loud speaker. The previous day, a pig had been sacrificed in a ritual similar to one that would have been performed on the island generations ago.

I elbowed closer to the mountain's necessary tinder and came upon a line of massive teepees of hay and twigs ready to take a flame and erupt in a blaze. I took a seat by the towering kindling and watched more of the commotion. Couples walked through a makeshift aisle of bells and wind chimes, and a lone man levitated above the tents on a motorized parachute contraption. Near the center of the crowd, a rainbow-colored banner read: HOPE, HAPPINESS AND ABUNDANCE, and a brochure in my hand read, "The hopeful rejuvenation of fire spreads throughout the world."

The hay teepees weren't necessarily primed for

reflection, but I couldn't help but stay there and think about the uncertainty that I was facing in the coming season. I would likely be leaving Jeju and pursuing a writing job back in the United States. Zooey had left Jeju and returned to her teaching duties in Seoul. My neighbor Hyojun was nowhere to be found. My friend Dan had made arrangements to enter a Ph.D. program back in the United States. Other friends of mine had rushed off to Thailand to do some rock climbing before the summer humidity gripped Southeast Asia. I remembered what the lady at the coffee shop had told me about the fire mountain festival months ago, about my wishes for *newness* coming true. For the first time in quite some time, though, I wasn't craving newness; I just wanted to enjoy the friends I had already made and the experiences I had already found.

Being alone but feeling very much part of the festival crowd, I made a mental note to remember the scene's organized chaos down the line, when Jeju and all of Asia would feel like a distant dream to me.

Groups of people began to migrate from the vending tents to the mountain's edge as the daylight grew dim. Soon the sun was setting in a blister of orange, and an MC's voice was notifying everyone through a speaker system that the giant fire would be lit shortly. Everyone turned their eyes to the main stage by the mountain, where a dance troupe gyrated through a musical composition of ancient Korean instruments backed by techno beats—perhaps the most overt example anywhere on the island of elements of the past being mixed with pop culture. Kids in the crowd danced and cheered beneath floodlights on the lawn while their parents swayed from side to side.

Despite the collective energy from the concert, I found myself still feeling sullen. I was supposed to be refreshed by the vibrant scene, so why was I feeling low? Then I realized exactly what it was. The festival's impending finale also signified a possible end to my own time on the island. While I hadn't spent my time on Jeju necessarily checking off specific goals on a tourism checklist, I had attempted to develop a more numinous understanding of the place and its people, to embrace the fictions that envelop the intriguing realities. Simply, I had grown close to Jeju—it was a land that I was studying, but it was also my home. It was that mix, more so than the old-new or the rural-urban pairings, that had stuck with me the most. And I didn't want to say goodbye to it.

On the main stage in front of the mountain, torches were lit and passed to some high-ranking city workers. The workers posed momentarily for a few photographs and then passed their lit torches to bystanders in the crowd. Part of the appeal in observing this spectacle for a foreigner like me was that this type of thing would be unlikely to happen in any other country. For one thing, the liability of a fire festival would make most event promoters disinclined to endorse such an event in the first place. On top of that, having a hundred lit torches passed throughout a crowd of adults and children could potentially lead to chaos, burns and lawsuits before the torches ever reached the kindling teepees.

John Burgman

Eventually an arc of people toting the small, flaming torches encircled the base of the mountain. The powerful floodlights on the lawn were turned off for the full effect of profound darkness. Only the flickering torches and illuminated cell phone screens were visible as glints of light at the mountain's base. By the time the mountain was lit on fire by the torchbearers, the crowd was clapping and cheering with excitement. Fireworks sparkled and popped to add to the spectacle, and the mountainside became steadily wrapped in the yellow braids of flames. In the intense glow, it seemed no coincidence that Jeju's mythic god of fire also acted as the god of art and creativity.

A flaming mountain would have been a thing to behold by itself, but the scene was made all the more spectacular and eccentric by the cadres of costumed people twirling about in revelry on the grass—clowns, monks, drunks, parents in traditional dress frolicking with giddy children. Everyone, it seemed, was caught up in the celebratory momentum, and a fair percentage were like me—enjoying the pageantry more so inwardly while being outwardly awestruck, mouth probably foolishly agape.

The flames flattened into wide smudges after a great initial blaze. Smoke twirled from the smoldering grass on the mountain and the night began to smell like scorched earth. The air was noticeably warmer now too.

Families vied for positions on the grass. Groups of friends spread out blankets and reclined with cushions to take in the display. Some people danced, others trotted around the perimeter of the mountain, following the path of the flames at a safe distance. I followed lines of smoke with my eyes as it trailed from the mountain and disappeared high in the sky.

There was no formal chronology to the rest of the festivities—once the *Saebyol oreum* had been lit on fire, people were free to watch, lounge and leave the grounds as they pleased. Even as groups began filing out and the surrounding lawn beside the parking fields became a makeshift traffic jam, I watched some of the flames continue to pop and drift over the mountain curve.

I wasn't the only person who stayed. Plenty of other people stuck around until the blaze relaxed into embers. We stood there for a long time, quietly staring at the great orange light.

When we finally left, it was to wedge into the last shuttle bus past the parking fields on an empty strip of highway. I kept my eyes on the mountain's primeval glow until it was completely out of sight.

I tried to sleep on the bus ride home, but my mind wouldn't rest. Instead, I watched Jeju City pass by outside the window in neon blurs, all the glowing signage and bright billboards in the night trailing off like severed arteries. The year's fire mountain festival had come and gone, and I knew that meant—whether true or imagined—that peculiar *newness* was now upon me.

21. In a fog

Packing up some of my belongings the following weekend, I opened the screens of my apartment to let in a mellow breeze. It felt like summer. The air smelled like clover. Cherry blossom buds, not yet blooming, were visible on tree branches poking through fog. Soon Jeju would be awash with the icing pink of the cherry blossoms, fallen petals clumped in streets, puddles and streams forming the island's natural confetti. Despite years of academic investigation, nobody knows from where the cherry blossom trees on Jeju originated; some dendrologists believe the trees to be native to the island, others attribute them to China. Adding another angle to the debate, Japan has its own variety of cherry blossoms, which generates speculation that Jeju's trees were actually Japanese in derivation. The uncertainty has spurred near-constant debate between the nations, bringing a tint of contention to an otherwise serene natural symbol.

Island Solitaire

I brushed away a windowsill ant, the first bug I had seen in many months. Somewhere beyond my screens, a dog bellowed four times—a rhythmic bark that made me think the animal must be chasing something, hot on the trail and quick through a grove. Aside from these snippets of wildlife, there was human commotion as well, in the form of my new upstairs neighbor pounding on a piano. The neighbor had recently moved into the apartment building, and I was now provided with partial melodies through my ceiling on a daily basis.

Carrying some cardboard boxes out to the recycling bin later, when the peripheral noises had subsided and only the breeze was making noise, I decided to take a walk through the fog. Visibility was barely an arm's length and the murky air distorted shapes into soft casts. The edge of a wooden bench and cherry blossom branches were only fully recognizable when I was directly upon each of them. I could see why Jeju's creation myth began with depictions of duality and confusion: two suns and two moons, humans and ghosts interacting freely on a landscape that had no order and no stability. On my own ghost walk then, in earnest, I padded slowly through the fog and tried to high-step across a brook. I slipped on the mud and glided in a long streak on the embankment. I was a clumsy fog walker in the ghost air, but it felt enlivening to be exploring the familiar forest near my home with such clumsiness and sightlessness. In the same creation myth, it is explained that the world could not continue to exist with two suns and two moons, so a Jeju spirit shot the extra celestial bodies out of the sky.

John Burgman

I ambled through a grove of ivy and found my way back to my apartment's recycling bin. I returned to the work at hand and crushed a few cardboard boxes. When I was almost finished and ready to clomp away in my mud-caked shoes, I heard my name being called from somewhere in the white fog. I looked around and saw my long-lost neighbor Hyojun walking under the recycling bin's canopy. He had his jacket hood cinched tightly around his head, and his face looked gaunt. Even in full sunshine clarity, I never would have recognized him. I was shocked to see him, and I explained how I had been searching for him since the last time we spoke.

Hyojun set into a detailed explanation about hitting rock bottom and being overcome with shame and self-doubt after failing his medical school exam. "I couldn't sleep, it was hard to eat," he said. "I was going mad, so I had to leave the island for a while."

Hyojun explained to me how he had fled to the Korean mainland but found existence there to be even more challenging. "Nobody consoled me, nobody comforted me—my parents didn't sweet-talk me, and I guess I'm kind of infamous now to my friends."

"Infamous just because you had one rough school year?" I asked.

"No," Hyojun said. "Infamous because I actually decided to come back to Jeju and come back to school. I'm going to redo the whole year of academic work. I have a new goal: I want to go to America for my medical residency."

It was a grand ambition. Rather than tone down his

expectations for his medical future, Hyojun had reemerged on the island with amped up objectives. He knew it would take a lot of hard work, not to mention that he was now an oddity in a school social scene that revolved heavily around academic achievement. However, he explained, he didn't have much of a choice in the matter. His parents would not accept his failure of medical school under any circumstances.

While Hyojun stood in the middle of the concrete recycling space and admired the thickness of the fog, I told him that he shouldn't continue pursuing a medical degree just because it was a future that his parents envisioned for him. I imagined that type of servitude would eventually make him a bad doctor, not to mention fill his head with ample regret once he reached his 30s and 40s. But Hyojun assured me he had made up his mind. His parents wanted him to be a doctor, so that was the dream he would continue to chase.

"Anyway," I said, "it's great to see you back on the island."

"Yeah, this is where I should be right now," he said, gazing at the fog, jutting his chin back and forth in thought.

Not long after that unexpected meeting with Hyojun, I found myself riding with a group of other university professors along a sloping curve that approached green tea fields. The fog was absent in the lower elevation. We happened to be trailing behind a truck that was hauling a big mound of garlic.

I was sitting in the car's backseat. I caught big whiffs of

garlic and tea plants, along with occasional snags of truck exhaust. When we passed by a particularly long and untouched line of brush on the side of the road, one of the professors noted that a Chinese company with specific plans to construct a lavish resort had recently bought the plot of land. The purchase had been met with extensive protests by Jeju's locals, but the development ultimately could not be stopped; the resort would be built, blocks of hotels would rise up in front of the beach, and the ocean view would soon be available only to paying customers. I thought about this news, which wasn't exactly uplifting, and I thought about Hyojun's adherence to an ideal other than his own.

I glanced out the car window at the world of green tones, leaves of ovular shapes and various sizes. Even green tea, now a well-accepted industry on Jeju, had been steeped in publicity at one time, when the wealthy owner of a cosmetics empire brought the plant to the island in 1979 with grand ambitions of production and commerce.

A few minutes after our car had left the soon-to-be resort, I posed a broad question to the other people in the car. What did they all think of Jeju after living on the island for decades and witnessing all of its development?

"Jeju is such a sad island," one of the professors said, and the others immediately nodded in agreement.

It wasn't the answer that I had expected.

The professor glanced outside. Trees sloped up the side of a small mountain *oreum*. "There is a lot of sad history—the April 3 Massacre, for example, and the destruction of all the nature to make hotels. And island life, in general, is

Island Solitaire

hard," she said.

We drove past a famous beach town called *Sagaeri*, where a dinosaur footprint was fossilized in fenced-off rock, a geologic snapshot of the island prior to the calamities of people, prior to the marketing of paradise or the unending corporate development. We went to dinner in an old stone restaurant and then walked together under a canopy of cherry blossoms. I could understand the logic of Jeju being considered a sad island—poverty, war, unforgiving weather and the perilous sea. I appreciated the professor's honest answer. Such lack of romanticism and unique dysphoria presented the island as a complete place to me, more compound and more intricate. Perhaps that was why I didn't want to leave, even after spending so much time on Jeju and living as part of its community. I felt as if I hadn't even fully found the island yet, but I also knew that I likely never would.

I kicked at a coagulated bunch of damp, fallen cherry blossom petals. The mess smeared across the pavement. This street was quiet, unlike the row of cherry blossom trees near my apartment that was frequented by photographers and sightseers from the university. The sun was sinking in the sky, the outside around the trees slipping into an amber translucence. It wasn't paradise because, of course, paradise doesn't exist. Nor do myths. In the vacancy of each, however, I had been free to fill the space with whatever realities I chose—sad or not, fleeting or twirling in permanence, as big as the island or as small as all the pink flower petals of indiscriminate origin.

22. The newness

In 1970, shortly after the first Apollo moon landing, Joseph Campbell explained that times and technology might change, but the universal nature of myths allows a person to forge personalized meaning from existence in an increasingly industrial world. My desire to chase the truths and the novelty behind the fire mountain festival, along with curiosity about the history and parables veining through such a chase, was predicated on an initial interest in the island lore of the world. Beyond that, my pursuit was perpetuated by circumstance; I found myself in a place and time that allowed for inquisitive roaming around an island on a limited budget, following research leads at will and giving in to travel whims as I pleased. I could write off entire days chatting with grizzled locals at beach bars and cafes. I could hit up the kitschiest tourist traps like a chocolate museum or a popular brewery without shame because they all felt relevant, as if they were pulling me closer to some sort of grander understanding. In a way, everything I did was bringing the island's intricacies steadily into focus.

Of course, the chase was never exclusively about the fire

mountain festival. I just felt lucky to have opportunities to explore a place that had, perhaps, not quite let its myths evaporate in the manner that some academics and scholars feared. More often than not, I felt like I was experiencing authentic scenes from the past while still existing in the present on the island. As an example, I once visited an old Buddhist temple that was wedged in between a dive bar and a Samsung electronics store; furthermore, the Buddhist temple was only a block from a city administration building—the central hub for Jeju's modern development and contemporary commerce.

The intriguing fire mountain festival certainly provided architecture for my entire quest, but it was ultimately the complexities and dichotomies all over the small island that kept me motivated in my extended exploration.

Somewhere along the way, and certainly by the conclusion of my research, I realized that I felt better than I had in a long time. Physically better. Emotionally better. I found that I went through my days with a certain lightness that I hadn't possessed before. When I thought back to the lonely days in my apartment, back to the nights when I was hobbling around with injured ribs and frequently missing the familiarity of the United States, the memories felt increasingly distant and disengaged from who I had since become. The kindhearted woman that I had first met in the coffee shop might have linked such general improvement to the rejuvenating power of fire mountain festival, others might have just said it was in line with the natural ups and downs of life. I can't be sure, but I like to think now that there were multiple components helping me get my act together, nudging me forward.

One factor that I cannot overlook is the purpose and initiative that the mythic aspects of Jeju sparked in me. Engaged in the research, I quickly let myself become more inquisitive than I had ever been, curious about every segment of the day, every unfamiliar custom, and every reference by islanders. I still had occasional periods of loneliness and frustration, of course—it would be nearly impossible to live on the other side of the planet and not feel misplaced from time to time. But in the constant, outward study of life on an island, I somehow pulled myself out of a veritable funk too. Or maybe the island did the grunt work. Who knows? It's more fun to believe than to not believe.

I didn't go into this endeavor naively expecting everything on an island to be stuck in a time capsule or entirely swathed in mythology. South Korea is, after all, one of the most digitally advanced countries in the world. The nation is forced to cope militarily with North Korea constantly breathing down its neck and regularly threatening nuclear annihilation. Jeju, more specifically, will be forced to modernize exponentially if it chooses to continue with its aspirations of being a global tourism hotspot. Digital, Wi-Fi, High-Def, high-speed, eco-friendly: this nomenclature represents the modernity and innovation that popular island destinations must embrace in the current century, for better or worse. But I felt that my time spent examining Jeju as both a residential local and also unavoidably as a cultural outsider was an enriching experience precisely because of those abundant contrasts. I had witnessed the many myths not necessarily in a narrative vacuum, but present at times in the lives of everyday citizens. Jeju is a special place where villagers still wander to the local shrines to honor their ancestors. It is an island where exorcisms are still performed on a regular basis by some families, fortune-tellers are still sought out by persons in times of crisis and gods have traditionally reigned over everything from the bathroom toilet to the family's finances, from the food being cooked in the kitchen to the rice being grown in the fields. Only recently has the concept of thrift stores taken off on the island, as it was long believed that a person's spirit dwelled in his worldly belongings even after death.

However, Jeju is also the antithesis of itself, a self-governing complexity of foreign businesses and foreign investors, golf courses, pop music festivals, swanky museums and a booming hotel industry. Korean celebrities frequently choose to vacation on the island, as do famous Korean athletes. Jeju's local government even sponsors free classes about the island's history and culture for new island residents. It's all part of a 21st century Back-to-the-Land movement that has been 30 years in the making: In the mid-1980s, Jeju made a conscious effort to fashion its growth and prosperity in the romantic, palm-fringed model set by Hawaii—drawing loads of tourists from around the world but also maintaining and promoting local uniqueness. The goal was to constantly balance tourism with local quality of life.

During my time living on Jeju, more than two decades after the Hawaiian framework had been decided upon, the island hosted a seashell festival, a barley festival, a *gosari* fern festival and an event that celebrated ancient cave engravings, but it also hosted an international symposium on polymer processing, a conference devoted entirely to magnesium, a conference dedicated to mercury pollution and an electric vehicle expo to coincide with a vow that all cars on the island would be electric by the year 2030. In the past, Jeju locals created thousands of myths; in the future, investors from Hong Kong and Singapore will spend the equivalent of nearly 2 billion USD to construct a Myths and History Theme Park boasting thousands of hotel rooms.

In one of the most pertinent examples of Jeju's duality, mountain land is annually lit on fire to honor the many island gods, but mountain land is also surveyed and bulldozed in order to build new apartment complexes, new highways and new schools. In 1840, a 55-year-old artist and government worker named Chusa Kim Jeong Hui was famously exiled to Jeju after being convicted of conspiring against the Korean king, yet now artists come to the island from around the world precisely to gain inspiration from the island's wilderness and solitude.

Jeju is proudly a global destination, and with that, it is caught in global torque. It is fair to conclude that, while the locals obviously don't believe the island's ancient myths and old tales, they undoubtedly believe *in* them. Put another way, as the entire landscape continues to modernize and digitize in myriad ways, the myths and the mystique are resolutely kept as part of the island's contemporary identity.

Island Solitaire

Perhaps it is appropriate to say that a new mythology is emerging on Jeju too, with morals garnered from such modernizing, with business transactions carrying weight alongside the ancient parables, heroes and anti-heroes making real decisions and investments that create their own storylines. Who knows how the narratives of the present will evolve and be interpreted by future generations on the island?

One of my favorite pastimes on Jeju was killing time around a small wharf as the moderate-sized ships coasted in from the sea and funneled through the bay. With the day's sunlight weakening, the shipmen would tie up to the docks and concrete platforms to unload their daily hauls of squid. Usually the ships' hulls were stained with grime, and the decks were strewn with tangled ribbons of lanterns and frayed lines. The captains of the ships were usually weathered too, as if true life was lived out at sea and the rest—like a trip to the shore—was just inconvenience.

I would pace around the azalea-lined periphery of the wharf like a stray dog, not wanting to get in anyone's way but staying close enough to catch the radiating elements of the action—enjoy the stiff scent of the squid, hear bits of conversation being volleyed back and forth between the shipmen, feel the faint engine rumbles in the air before the ships' motors clicked off.

Amid all of these sensations, the commerce of the wharf materialized. Barefoot locals padded to the concrete platforms to examine the ships' cargo, poke the fish in the baskets and assess the opaque squid that was already draped to dry over the decks. Some people made offers to the shipmen for the seafood, other times the captains and the shipmen gave away small samples of the fish free of charge. There was a friendly quality to all of the wrangling, but the objectives and the give-and-take were clear. The bounty of the sea was being bought and sold, and everyone in the equation held equal importance. In this model, with the buyers being as vital as the shipmen merchants, a principle of the island's myths could be drawn as well: the listeners are as necessary as the storytellers. By diving into the various island tales, visiting the shrines and basking in the lore, one becomes part of the very mythos being researched. There is no possibility of fractionation, and the distinction between the story being told and the moment being lived becomes less definable. If one says that the myths from a faraway past are disappearing, then one must also note that these myths will remain as long as there is an audience. That was what I observed while living on the island.

Early one afternoon, I happened into a bookstore in Jeju City with a friend of mine named Jiseon. Jiseon's mother was Im Soonim—the defacto matriarch of Jeju's Hana Center. Although Jiseon often helped out with the social education of North Korean defectors at her mother's office, she had no work obligations on this particular day—and, like most of Jeju's youth, wanted to spend her free time shopping downtown.

Together, Jiseon and I browsed a wall of Korean magazines and flicked through a rack of discount CDs at the front of the bookstore. Eventually we found ourselves hunched in a back curve of the room where many English-language novels resided. While flipping through one of the books, Jiseon turned to me and asked, "How do you feel about America's Declaration of Independence?"

I was befuddled—not because it was a bad question, but precisely because it was such a good question, such a fundamentally basic question for any American citizen to be asked. Yet, I was ashamed to realize that I had never before thought about the Declaration of Independence in such frank terms.

"How do I feel about it?" I replied, stumbling over my words. I finally came up with an utterly inglorious response: "I think it's good. The Declaration of Independence is a fine thing."

I explained that the very question had caught me off guard. I admitted to Jiseon that the Declaration of Independence was such a foundation of the United States that I had somehow managed to get through school without ever having dwelled on it. The document was, to many Americans, inexplicably beyond the realm of personal opinion. I tried to elaborate and said that unlike America's Constitution or state laws, the Declaration of Independence wasn't in flux or constant evolution—perhaps that was why I hadn't formed much of an opinion about it. Or perhaps I had just taken it for granted, regrettably.

I was still thinking about our brief exchange later in the day as I pulled a chair out to my apartment deck and waited for some laundry to dry on a rack. A yellow dusk was just beginning to seep into the clouds above the hills. A traveler, especially one who intends to explore a culture other than his own over an extended period of time, inevitably wrestles with the ethics of any ensuing reportage. Seeking out the otherness of a place, even if the traveler lives in that place, and continuing to compartmentalize that location as *other*, can mutate into a resistance to assimilation. Long-term observation always carries with it a risk of exploitation, and it is up to the observer to justify the pursuit on the whole and give the components meaning. However, such quandaries are tempered by moments like my Declaration of Independence dialogue with Jiseon at the bookstore, occurrences where an overarching curiosity about otherness unexpectedly leads to an assessment of my own ignorance, faults and fixed habits—and ultimately leads to learning about oneself and the space at large.

Even a chase after myths is largely a chase inward as much as outward. Whether or not that justifies spending more than a year hunting down stories that are thousands of years removed from the present is a matter of opinion, and whether or not the lore and the wildness of a place—in my case, Jeju—can be effectively captured at all beyond the split second that they are seen, heard or lived is a dilemma as old as narrative itself. I suppose these issues compose the mental residue of trips, both long-term and short-term. But luckily there are surefooted first steps for coming to terms with all of this: just go there—wherever *there* might be—take a seat and listen.

Sources

When working on a book such as this—about an age-old subject, in a foreign country and surrounded by a foreign language—a writer is undoubtedly dealing with sources that possess varying degrees of reliability. It's worth noting here that by nature oral tales and legends evolve and change over time; talk to three different people, and you might get three different versions of the same myth.

During my research of Jeju, I did my best to verify any claims or anecdotes about the island's mythology with professional-grade texts. That being said, sometimes the only texts that could be found on a given subject were authorless manuals, old pamphlets or poorly translated materials. What follows are the texts that aided in my research or provided clarity about Jeju's history and culture. One will notice a number of articles from *The Jeju Weekly* listed here. In my opinion, that newspaper is the best English-language resource for specifics about Jeju's history, and I am grateful for the frequent correspondence

I had with the former editor-in-chief there, Darren Southcott. Additionally, Fred Dustin supplied me with a wealth of information and a number of fascinating anecdotes. I would also like to formally acknowledge Jenie Hahn of Jeju National University—another friend and colleague who provided valuable research materials and conversation on virtually all matters of Jeju's folklore.

Breen, Michael. The Koreans: Who They Are, What They Want, Where Their Future Lies (2nd Ed.). New York: St. Martin's Griffin, 2004.

Campbell, Joseph. Myths To Live By. New York: Bantam Books, 1972.

Erwin, Nicole. "Jeju is heaven for birds and birdwatchers." The Jeju Weekly. 27 November 2010. http://www.jejuweekly.com/news/articleView.html?idxno=1088.

Exploring Jeju's History, Culture and Nature. Jeju Tourism Promotion Division, 2003.

"The fiery genesis of Jeju's inner core," The Jeju Weekly, 22 August 2014. http://www.jejuweekly.com/news/articleView.html?idxno=4337.

Harris, Matt. "The Jeju Fire Festival sparks into life." The Jeju Weekly. 17 February 2014. http://www.jejuweekly.com/news/articleView.html?idxno=3860.

Horwitz, Tony. Blue Latitudes: Boldly Going Where Captain Cook Has Gone Before. New York: Picador, 2003.

Island Solitaire

"Jeju a haven for Fairy Pitta," The Jeju Weekly, 29 August 2014.
http://www.jejuweekly.com/news/articleView.html?idxno=4345.
Jeju Island. Cheju National University (Educational Science Research Institute), 2006.

Jeju Island [Guidebook]. Jeju Tourism Organization

"Jeju Land of Goddesses."
http://english.jeju.go.kr/index.php/contents/culture-nature/samda/women/goddess/intro (accessed 4 September 2014).

"Jeju Olle friends and family," The Jeju Weekly, 21 January 2015.
http://www.jejuweekly.com/news/articleView.html?idxno=4567.

Kernow, Petroc. "Korean culture shock: Lessons from history." The Jeju Weekly. 9 January 2014.
http://www.jejuweekly.com/news/articleView.html?idxno=3812.

The Korea Foundation. Jeju Island Reaching to the Core of Beauty. Seoul: Seoul Selection, 2011.

Lang, Tamara. "Lessons from Nanjing for Jeju Island." The Jeju Weekly. 19 December 2014.
http://www.jejuweekly.com/news/articleView.html?idxno=4532.

Lankov, Andrei. The Dawn of Modern Korea. Seoul: EunHaeng NaMu, 2007.

"Mega park billed a Jeju 'game changer,'" The Jeju Weekly, 27 February 2015.
http://www.jejuweekly.com/news/articleView.html?idxno=4599.

Min, Jean K. "Open to Chinese wealth." The Jeju Weekly. 5 February 2011,
http://www.jejuweekly.com/news/articleView.html?idxno=1223.

Myths of Jeju Island. Jeju Cultural Center, 2012.

Neff, Robert. "Part 1 The Wreck of the Barracouta." The Jeju Weekly. 30 May 2011,
http://www.jejuweekly.com/news/articleView.html?idxno=1617.

Neff, Robert. "Part 2 The Wreck of the Barracouta." The Jeju Weekly. 11 June 2011,
http://www.jejuweekly.com/news/articleView.html?idxno=1666.

Neff, Robert. "Part 3 Turn of the century Jeju, A to Z." The Jeju Weekly, 2 January 2011,
http://www.jejuweekly.com/news/articleView.html?idxno=1167.

Neff, Robert. "The Samarang's misadventures in Jeju." The Jeju Weekly. 14 August 2011,
http://www.jejuweekly.com/news/articleView.html?idxno=1849.

Neff, Robert. "Superstitions of the Sea." The Jeju Weekly. 10 April 2011,
http://www.jejuweekly.com/news/articleView.html?idxno=1443.

"Opening the inner path of exile," The Jeju Weekly, 10 March 2014. http://www.jejuweekly.com/news/articleView.html?idxno=3906.

Pearson, James. "Insight – The $50 device that symbolizes a shift in North Korea." Reuters. 27 March 2015, http://uk.reuters.com/article/2015/03/27/uk-northkorea-change-insight-idUKKBN0MM2UW20150327?feedType=RSS&feedName=everything&virtualBrandChannel=11708.

"Play of Jeju Massacre tells victims' stories," The Jeju Weekly, 21 April 2015. http://www.jejuweekly.com/news/articleView.html?idxno=4710.

Reid, T.R. Confucius Lives Next Door. New York: Vintage Books, 1999.

"Save Jeju Now." http://savejejunow.org/ (accessed 25 August 2014).

Southcott, Darren. "The lost families of Goneul." The Jeju Weekly 8 May 2015. http://www.jejuweekly.com/news/articleView.html?idxno=4567.

Stories of Jeju. World Conservation Congress (Jeju Development Institute), 2012.

Yang, Sang-ick, Echoes of Mt. Halla. Jeju: Cheju National University, 1977.

Acknowledgments

This book owes a significant debt to The Fulbright Association—and specifically the Korean-American Educational Commission—for first providing me with an opportunity to explore South Korea so many years ago. Thank you to all my friends and colleagues during that period.

I would like to formally acknowledge several dear friends for their kindness, conversation and hospitality in South Korea over the years: Doug and Sook-Ja Hansen, Tony Kim, Wookyung Kim, Soohang Lee, Yuni Zung, Youngji Han, Hansem Jang, Joohee Kim and family, Dogook Lim, Jaewon Kwon, Seongmin Lim, Hyoju Kang, Sunny Bae, Sungji Jung, Jane Kim, Lauren Chung and family, Youngji Kim, Jungeun Han, and Yenny Choi. Thank you also to Will, Vicki, and Bill Burgman for the constant encouragement during the researching and writing and revising processes. Thanks as well to Sooyeon Seong, Chloe Wang, Matthew Davis, Sue Song, Damon Morelli and family, Becky Toney, Christine Gallagher, Jeremy Polio, Kendra Pugh, Dave Duffy, Eric Fileta, Eric Hevesy, Jake and Candace Barr, Brooke Morton, Rolf Potts, and Jaegyun Kim. I am also grateful for the friendship of Jaemin Lee and Mimi Lee at Selfish Table—in my admittedly biased opinion, the best little coffee shop on Jeju.

Many of my colleagues at Jeju National University were generous and helpful as I navigated my way through the island's complex past and fascinating present—there are too many to name, but a tip of the hat is due to all.

Dan Kojetin deserves a special nod for sharing in many of my earliest travels around Jeju. Finally, I want to thank Zooey Ahn—for her spirit of adventure, insight and support, I am forever grateful.

About the author

John Burgman is the author of *Why We Climb: A Dirtbag's Quest for Vertical Reason*. He is a former editor at *Outdoor Life* and a former Fulbright grant recipient, with which he documented the lives of North Korean defectors living in Asia. He has taught at New York University and Jeju National University, and has given seminars about the history of Jeju tourism. His fiction and non-fiction have appeared online and in print at *Esquire.com, Portland Review, Boundary Waters Journal, Climbing Business Journal*, and other outlets. An avid rock climber, he writes a monthly opinion column for *Climbing.com*.

www.ingramcontent.com/pod-product-compliance
Lightning Source LLC
Chambersburg PA
CBHW020650220526
45464CB00001B/368